LORD SANDWICH AND THE PANTS MAN

**Eamon Evans** is the author of *The Godfather Was a Girl … And Blanche DuBois Was a Guy: Real people who inspired famous and infamous characters* and *Smalltalk: Tailor-made trivia for every social occasion*. He's also aiming to produce a website at www.eamonevans.com.au before too long, and perhaps one day grow a beard.

# LORD SANDWICH
## AND THE PANTS MAN*

## EAMON EVANS

**hardie grant** books
MELBOURNE · LONDON

*An **EPONYMS** and **TOPONYMS** Companion

Published in 2012 by Hardie Grant Books

Hardie Grant Books (Australia)
Ground Floor, Building 1
658 Church Street
Richmond, Victoria 3121
www.hardiegrant.com.au

Hardie Grant Books (UK)
Dudley House, North
Suite 34–35 Southampton Street
London WC2E 7HF
www.hardiegrant.co.uk

Cataloguing-in-Publication data is available from the National Library of Australia.

Lord Sandwich and the Pants Man

ISBN 9781742702599

Cover and text design by Josh Durham, Design by Committee
Typeset by Cannon Typesetting in Electra 10/13 pt
Image reproduction by Splitting Image Colour Studio
Printed and bound in China by 1010 Printing International Ltd

*To Jenny, Henry and Eliza*

# CONTENTS

## Society

Clichéd words..................2
Wordy words..................11
Homely words..................18
Legal words..................25
Political words..................30
Financial words..................35
Timely words..................42

## Sex & violence

Romantic words..................48
Adventurous words..................53
Tawdry words..................58
Intolerant words..................63
Warlike words..................68
Fighting words..................78

## People

Shady words..................86
Stout-hearted words..................91
Intelligent words..................94
Small-minded words..................100
Mad words..................106
Subservient words..................111

## Food & clothing

Thirst-quenching words....120
Nutritious words..................128

Less nutritious words...........133
Stylish words..................142
Less stylish words..................149

## Recreation

Fun words..................160
Theatrical words..................166
Musical words..................171
Sporting words..................177
Travel words..................185

## Science & nature

Unhygienic words..................194
Scientific words..................199
Colourful words..................206
Animal words..................210
Anatomical words..................218

## Geography

Astronomical words...........228
European words..................234
American words..................238
Australian words..................243
Landmark words..................248

Index..................256
Acknowledgements..................262

# INTRODUCTION

'*Words are illusions. They're no different from
things that appear in your dreams at night.*'
BODHIDHARMA, 5TH CENTURY ZEN MASTER

'*Wrong, O Great Sage Bodhidharma.
You can really be a bit of a chump sometimes.*'
EAMON EVANS

Lasting fame is pretty hard to achieve in this world (just ask what's-his-name from *Big Brother*) and it's even harder once you've left it. For every ancient warrior whose deeds live on in legend and song, there are ten armies we've completely forgot. For every ye olde writer who's still celebrated after centuries, I give you a thousand whose books rest in peace. And for every Roman city that was expected to last out eternity, we have a small ruin and some broken pots. Life is a thin slit of light in between two vast slabs of eternal darkness. All cities crumble and all achievements fade.

Many words, however, live on. For true immortality, don't worry about the history books—try and get into a dictionary instead. We don't talk about Queen Margherita because she was a queen, but because at one time she ate some pizza. Earl Grey may have been a PM, but his name is remembered because he liked his tea. Samuel Maverick was a maverick and Jean Martinet a martinet.

What we're saying here, Mr Zen Master, is that words aren't always illusions. Some of them are based on real people, who truly did live and breathe. And others come from the names of places, where real people walked and talked. A man called Charles Boycott underwent the first boycott, while a Lord Cardigan took an interest in knitwear. The Vandals were a destructive tribe, the Zealots an intolerant sect. The first 'slaves' were Slavs and the first 'philistines' came from Palestine. Women call men 'guys' because of Guy Fawkes, and expect them to be 'romantic' because of Rome.

Language is the archives of history, as Ralph Waldo Emerson once put it. Like flies captured for centuries in amber, people and places from the past live on in our tongues. *Lord Sandwich and the Pants Man* is your guide to this hidden history: a treasure trove of fairly plausible theories enriched with some improbable truths. Enjoy it while you can.

# SOCIETY

## CLICHÉD WORDS

*Buckley's chance,*
*Name was mud,*
*In like Flynn,*
*Beyond the pale,*
*Czar, Kaiser,*
*Cross the Rubicon,*
*Great Scott,*
*Colonel Blimp,*
*Sad Sack,*
*Keeping up with the*
*Joneses, Blind Freddy,*
*The back of beyond,*
*The devil to pay,*
*What the dickens!,*
*Speak of the devil,*
*Devil's advocate,*
*Doubting Thomas,*
*Good Samaritan,*
*Even Stevens,*
*Pleased as punch,*
*The real McCoy,*
*Put up your dukes,*
*Happy as Larry,*
*The life of Riley*

---

## WORDY WORDS

*Babble, Mumbo jumbo,*
*Gibberish, Solecism,*
*Spoonerism,*
*Malapropism, Cant,*
*Bible, Parchment,*
*Manila folder,*
*Pamphlet,*
*Yellow journalism,*
*Blurb, Hack, Frankness,*
*Morse code, Biro*

## HOMELY WORDS

*Palace, Xanadu,*
*Labyrinth, Byzantine,*
*Baroque, Frieze,*
*Attic, Bungalow,*
*Jerry-built, Lounge,*
*Chesterfield, Ottoman,*
*Venetian blind, Hoover,*
*Blanket, Doily, China,*
*Wedgewood*

---

## LEGAL WORDS

*Guillotine, Draconian,*
*Nemesis, Lynch mob,*
*Forensic, Forum,*
*Miranda rights,*
*The thin blue line,*
*Bobby, The Bill, Fink*

---

## POLITICAL WORDS

*Lobbyist, Hansard,*
*Dorothy Dixer, Bunkum,*
*Gerrymandering,*
*Bob's your uncle,*
*Tory, Whig,*
*Downing Street,*
*Capital,*
*Banana republic,*
*Young Turk*

## FINANCIAL WORDS

*Money,*
*As rich as Croesus,*
*Hallmark, Dollar,*
*Guinea, El Dorado,*
*Midas touch, Silhouette,*
*Tariff, Beggar, Cheap,*
*Shambles, Lumber,*
*Shopping mall*

---

## TIMELY WORDS

*Month, March,*
*April, May, June,*
*Julian calendar, July,*
*Caesarean section,*
*August, February,*
*January, Janitor,*
*Watch, Saturday,*
*Sunday, Monday,*
*Tuesday, Wednesday,*
*Thursday, Friday*

# CLICHÉD WORDS

**WILLIAM BUCKLEY'S CHANCE**

'Avoid clichés like the plague,' advised William Safire, but the average writer has **Buckley's chance**.
This time-honoured Australian cliché doesn't refer to singer Jeff Buckley's chances of swimming across the Mississippi, but to the various misfortunes of one William Buckley (1780–1856). For a start, he was born in 18th-century Cheshire: good news if you like disease and poverty, but otherwise not ideal. And things took a turn for the even-worse when he was arrested for receiving stolen goods and transported to Australia for life.

Then the convict finally got a break. Or rather, he **made** a break. Having somehow managed to his escape his captors, Buckley didn't slowly perish in the harsh, unforgiving outback, as the etiquette of the time required, but instead became chummy with an Aboriginal tribe. For thirty-two years he lived a happy life among the Indigenous people, before finally stumbling across a few white folk and finding that all was forgiven.

A good story. But the phrase 'Buckley's chance' probably has more to do with a bog-standard Melbourne department store that went by the name 'Buckley's and Nunn'.

**SAMUEL'S NAME WAS MUD**

Being convicted of a crime, of course, wasn't all that great for your social prestige. There are very few haughty convicts in the novels of Jane Austen.
Want another example? Then look at Dr Samuel Mudd (1833–1883). Until 14 April 1865, a respectable physician and prosperous slave-owner, much respected by his (white) neighbours. But after 14 April 1865, a social pariah. A man whose **name was mud**.

What happened? Well, the US President Abraham Lincoln got shot by a crazy actor named John Wilkes Booth. Booth himself got hurt in the process, breaking his leg as he fled. But luckily the good Dr Mudd was on hand to fix said leg and put him up at his house for a day. Mudd later insisted he hadn't known what Wilkes had just done, but the law didn't believe him at first. He spent three years in jail before finally being pardoned, but his social standing was never the same.

Samuel, whose name was Mudd

### WHEN ERROL WAS IN LIKE FLYNN

Errol Flynn (1909–1959) also had a few run-ins with the law. Famous for bonking everyone in sight, be they animal, vegetable or mineral, this swashbuckling star of the silver screen once found himself on trial for statutory rape. He admitted to having had sex with two underage girls, but maintained he hadn't known their age.

A sad story, with no winners. Except for the media, obviously. The feverish coverage of the trial (which—entirely incidentally—found Flynn not guilty) made the actor widely known as a 'wild man of the mattress'. 'The slogan *In like Flynn* rose like smoke from the trial and ran laughingly around the globe', as one biographer put it.

### WHY IRELAND IS BEYOND THE PALE

Such behaviour might seem a bit *beyond the pale*. But technically this would only be true if Errol was in Ireland.

Named for a 'palus', the Latin word for fence, The Pale was the part of medieval Ireland that was under English control. The area beyond the fortified rampart that encircled Kildare, Dublin and Meath was, for the English, where civilisation ceased.

**THE CZAR WHO CROSSED THE RUBICON**

In 49 BC, when he was just a general, Julius Caesar (100–44 BC) did something beyond the pale. In order to become head of state (a position Russians and Germans would later call *czar* and *kaiser*), he had to breach one of his city's strictest and most ancient laws. March troops into the vicinity of Rome. An act of civil war.

To do this, Caesar's troops had to **cross the Rubicon**, a little river to Rome's north. Legally speaking, once they'd done this, there was no going back. Which is what that phrase means today.

**GREAT SCOTT, IT'S WINFIELD!**

It seems a pity that General Winfield Scott (1786–1866) wasn't around when Caesar did this. He too loved a needless war.

Known to his troops as 'Old Fuss and Feathers', and to the wider world as 'The Great Scott', this 140-kilogram soldier was the longest-serving general in US history. But while

he fought in the Black Hawk War and the Second Seminole War, it's important to note that Scott didn't just shoot Native Americans. No, at one time his troops just 'rounded up the Cherokee and held them in rat-infested stockades with little food' until they died.

Described by the Duke of Wellington as 'the greatest living general' (and by colleagues as 'too fat to ride a horse'), Scott may have inspired the exclamation **Great Scott**.

The great(ly fat) Scott

Or not.

Not all military men are well served by the English language, however. Take the case of **Colonel Blimp**.

**COLONEL BLIMP AND THE SAD SACK**

A jingoistic 'half-pay colonel with a bull neck and diminutive brain', Blimp was a pompous 1930s cartoon character designed to mock the English establishment. 'The epitome of pudding-headed diehardness', he was created after the cartoonist overheard a retired military officer insist that cavalry officers who'd been put in tanks (and thus taken off horses) should be allowed to keep wearing their spurs.

Ten years later, when WWII broke out, another cartoon character was less enthused. 'The Sad Sack' was created in response to the US army's over-the-top recruitment ads, in which 'soldiers always looked bright and cheerful, bedecked in tailored uniforms that were immaculately pressed and shined'. **Sad Sack**, in contrast, looked 'looked resigned, tired, helpless and beaten'.

So-called as a nod to the military slang 'a sad sack of shit', this lowly, otherwise-unnamed private helped readers appreciate some of the downsides of military life. It's not all about slaughtering the enemy. Mostly you just clean the latrines.

**THE MAN WHO COULDN'T KEEP UP WITH THE JONESES**

Of course, to the spiritually inclined, many of us Westerners are sad. Contentment, they would say, comes from being at peace with your place in the world — not from endless grasping and earning and striving.

Arthur Momand (1887–1987) learned this lesson a little too late. In 1910, that cartoonist moved with his wife to Cedarhurst, one of Long Island's most affluent towns. There, he later recalled, they 'lived far beyond [their] means in an endeavour to keep up with the well-to-do class'. Three years later, a poorer but wiser Momand returned to New York and started to write a cartoon strip about his experiences. It featured an ordinary couple who were locked in endless competition with their neighbours, an affluent family who always had more. The strip's name was **Keeping up with the Joneses**.

**BLIND FREDDY, HUMAN BLOOD- HOUND**

Sir Frederick Pottinger (1831–1865) tried to keep up with bushrangers, but they were always a few steps ahead. An Eton-educated aristocrat, Pottinger fled England for Australia after blowing his inheritance at the races, and somehow ended up as a policeman.

But it turned out that losing money was the only thing Freddy could really do well. He just couldn't seem to catch a break, and catching an actual bushranger proved completely beyond him. **Blind Freddy** was finally forced to resign in 1865, after he attended a day of racing at the Wowingragong Racetrack unaware that the bushrangers he was chasing were right beside him, enjoying a day off too. He then accidentally shot himself, bringing a glorious career to a close.

**SIR GILBERT GRIZZLE- CLEUCH AND THE BACK OF BEYOND**

Of course, Freddy can't be held entirely to blame. Australia is a wide brown land, with many a place to hide.

Don't go calling it **the back of beyond** though. That's actually just outside Arbroath, a remote Scottish town that was renamed 'Fairport' by the author Sir Walter Scott. Written in an utterly unintelligible Scots dialect, The Antiquary tells us that 'The Laird o' Tamlowrie and Sir Gilbert Grizzlecleuch, and Auld Rossballoh, and the Bailie, were just setting [into Fairport] to make an afternoon o't, and Monkbarns, wi' some o' his auld-warld stories, that the mind o' man canna resist, whirl'd them to the back o' beyont to look at the auld Roman camp'.

That all clear now? Good.

Perhaps it's a good thing that Sir Frederick was so incompetent. If those poor bushrangers had been caught, there would have been *the devil to pay*.

I speak metaphorically, of course. To actually pay the devil, they would have needed to go to a pub. Located near the Civil Courts, The Devil was a 17th-century drinking hole much patronised by London's lawyers. Since getting in trouble with the law meant handing over money to a lawyer, it in effect meant paying the pub.

As it happens, we also speak of the devil when we say **What the dickens!** (Not that anyone actually does.) 'Dickens' is a polite euphemism for 'devil', just like 'Blimey' means 'God blind me' and 'Goodbye' means 'God be with you'.

Come to think of it, we also speak of the devil when we say **Speak of the devil**. This is a modern abbreviation of the proverb 'Speak of the devil and he doth appear'—a medieval superstition used to discourage the peasantry from thinking about the nature of good and evil (or, indeed, thinking much at all).

A devil's advocate, while we're on the subject of the dark lord, is properly known as a 'Promoter of the Faith'. He's a canon lawyer appointed by the Catholic Church when it's considering whether or not to make someone a saint. The advocate's job is to 'take the devil's side' by arguing against the would-be saint's canonisation (by questioning one of their alleged 'miracles', say, or uncovering a character flaw). Just like the **devil's advocates** of everyday life, he won't necessarily believe what he's saying, but will charge ahead anyway for the sake of argument.

We don't know who argued against Thomas the Apostle becoming a saint, but he would have had a pretty good case. St T, you see, was a sceptic. Rather than relying on faith, he liked to use his brain.

Bad, very bad. You may as well grope a nun. Thomas's blasphemy is on display in the New Testament, just after Jesus comes back from the dead. 'I will not believe,' declares that apostle. 'Unless I see in his hands the print of the nails, and place my fingers in the mark of the nails, and place my hand in his side, I will not believe.'

Fast-forward to a week later, and Thomas is feeling a little sheepish. Turns out Jesus is back after all. 'Do not be faithless but believing,' JC reproaches him. 'Blessed are those who have not seen and yet believe.' In other, slightly snappier words, don't be a **Doubting Thomas**.

**WHY GOOD SAMARITANS DON'T GO EVEN STEVENS**

You should, however, be a **Good Samaritan**. Love thy neighbour, commands Jesus (though he never says that we have to talk to them). The Lamb of God elaborates on this idea with a story about a Jewish traveller who gets attacked and left for dead on the road. A priest and a Levite wander by … and then wander on without trying to help. But then a man from Samaria turns up and, as luck would have it, he's good. 'Moved with compassion, he brought him to an inn, and took care of him.'

There aren't any Good Samaritans in Jonathan Swift's *A Journal to Stella* (1713), and one character is particularly bad. Steven is the sort of person who'd think 'Loving thy neighbour' was some kind of communist plot. More of an 'eye for an eye and a tooth for a tooth' man (provided he could also hack off a leg), that character's idea of 'proportional retribution' rather brings to mind the Israeli government. '"Now we are even," quoth Steven, when he gave his wife six blows to one.' And gave us the phrase **Even Stevens**.

**A PUPPET AS PLEASED AS PUNCH**

Punchinello was also fully prepared to hit a woman. Which was one reason why his name was shortened to 'Punch'. Along with Judy, his stick-wielding wife, this puppet has been a highlight of low-rent theatre since the 16th century, when he was created for Italy's *commedia dell'arte*. And from there it was just a hop, skip and a thump to the British seaside, where his wife-beating, serial-killing antics made Victorian kiddies smile and laugh.

Punch would laugh too, we should add. His main shtick was being as *pleased as punch* whenever a victim hit the ground.

### NORMAN, THE REAL McCOY

Norman Selby (1872–1940) would have just got up again—and then feinted and weaved and ducked for a bit, before landing a punch of his own. A welterweight who fought under the ring name

'Kid McCoy', Selby could also get pretty violent outside of the ring. Married ten times to eight different women, he also had time for lovers— and was convicted of manslaughter after one of them died. He committed suicide after nine years in jail.

But back to his heyday. The story goes that Selby once got into an argument in a pub. Some drunk didn't believe he was the all-conquering 'Kid', and so challenged him to 'put up his dukes'. Selby duly did so—and,

The real McCoy

sure enough, the drunk went down. Rubbing his swollen chin on the floor, he supposedly mumbled something like 'Yeah … that's *the real McCoy* all right'.

### THE DUKE THAT PUT UP HIS DUKES

But why did McCoy *put up his dukes*? Does that cliché even begin to make sense?

Well, sort of, if you know your peerage. Some say it's a reference to Frederick, Duke of York, (1763–1827), a successful military commander. When he wasn't shooting people, that peer apparently liked to hit them; he had a very well-known passion for boxing.

The cliché probably makes more sense if you know your rhyming slang, however. Those charming Cockney urchin-types ('Shine yer shoes, guvna?', etc.) would never use a prosaic word like 'hand' when they could say something more lateral, like 'fork'. And what does a fork (with its five finger-like prongs) rhyme with? Correct: The Duke of York.

The happy Larry Foley

### HOW TO BE AS HAPPY AS LARRY FOLEY

*Happy as Larry* now? No? Well, what if I told you that that phrase was also inspired by a boxer, a bare-knuckle Australian heavyweight named Larry Foley (1847–1917)? After spending his teenage years as a gang leader in Sydney, Foley was discovered while bashing someone's face in and trained to do so with more polish and style. He retired after one ridiculously lucrative prize fight and used the money to buy a hotel.

### THE LIFE OF (JAMES) RILEY

James Whitcomb Riley (1849–1916) would have bought a bigger bed. Though this American poet did manage to crank out some world-famous works in his time (mostly about barefooted boys doing not very much in the summertime), he was equally well known for not working, and being a bit of a dreamy drunk. It would have been nice to live *the life of Riley*.

# WORDY WORDS

**THE TOWER OF BABBLE**

The benefit of learning a foreign language is that it helps you to chat with more people. This is also the problem with learning a foreign language—understand nothing, and you get left in peace.

Once upon a time, people didn't have this dilemma: the Bible tells us that all of God's children originally spoke one language. But then the people of Babel, just south of Baghdad, decided to build an enormous tower—something grandiose that reached right into the heavens and so symbolised their lofty place in the world.

'Not so fast,' said the Almighty One, and swiftly punished them for their hubris. He 'confounded the tongues of the people that they might not understand one another's speech'. The Tower of Babel is the reason why we *babble* in different languages and why very few Mandigo tribespeople will buy this book.

The tower of Babel

**MUMBO JUMBO AND A HEALTHY MARRIAGE**

Which is not to say that we understand *their* language either. In 1795, an English explorer named Mungo Park (1771–1806) took a trip into the heart of Africa, and misunderstood more or less everything he saw. *Travels in the Interior of Africa*, his widely read book, told readers all about Maamajomboo, a god worshipped by Mandigo villagers. It said that they liked to honour him by making nonsensical noises and dancing about in strange masks.

In fact, maamajomboo—or ***mumbo jumbo***, as it came to be pronounced—wasn't a god at all. It was just a technique for resolving domestic disputes. If a husband was dissatisfied with his wife in some way, he might tie her to a tree and make a racket for a bit, so as to shame her or give her a fright.

**GEBER THE GIBBERER**

But don't sweat it, Mungo Park. Even when people talk in your own language, it's not always easy to know what they mean. Take the case of Geber ibn Hayyan (ca 721–815), a well-known Arab alchemist. Now this was a smart guy, there's no denying it. Chemistry, astronomy, geology, philosophy: all were strings to his brainy bow.

But communication was less of a strength. Jam-packed with jargon and formulas and anagrams and equations, Geber's books were so incomprehensible that his name became a synonym for nonsense. If your writing is Geber-ish, it's just plain ***gibberish***.

**IS IT A SOLECISM TO SAY SOLECISM?**

Not that Geber was the only poor communicator in the ancient world. The citizens of Soloi, for example, spoke what was considered by Athenians to be a truly dreadful form of Greek. Probably this was just a case of their language evolving in another direction, just as Americans sound a little different from Brits. A Greek colony in what's now Turkey, Soloi was sufficiently isolated to develop its own rules of grammar and its own ways of pronouncing words.

But to the other Greeks, they were just plain wrong. 'Soloikos' in that language came to mean 'speaking incorrectly'. In English, we now say *solecism*.

**DR SPOONER- ISM AND HIS PISASTER- DRONE TONGUE**

A longtime lecturer at Oxford, Reverend William Spooner (1844–1930), was a past master when it came to solecisms. Though he would probably say 'mast paster'. On Spooner's slippery tongue, a toast to 'our dear old Queen' would end up being a toast to 'our queer old dean'. 'Sons of toil' would become 'tons of soil' and a 'half-formed wish' would turn into a 'half-warmed fish'. When he was finally forced into retirement, it came as 'a blushing crow'.

We now know that the good reverend was probably suffering from metathesis, a mild form of verbal dyslexia in which letters and syllables get transposed. But that's not a very fun word. Generations of unsympathetic Oxford students called his mishaps *spoonerisms* instead.

**MRS MALAPROP AND THE REVEREND CANT**

Mrs Malaprop could also mangle her meaning. A comic character in Richard Sheridan's 1775 play, *The Rivals,* her schtick was to say words that were almost, but not quite, right. So instead of saying 'the pinnacle of politeness', she would say 'the *pineapple* of politeness'. Instead of 'an alligator on the banks of the Nile', she'd say 'an *allegory* on the banks of the Nile'. Cue laughter, thigh-slapping and tumultuous applause. Some audience members then had to be rushed to hospital because their sides had split. Anyway, it's because of Mrs Malaprop that pretentious English students get to say *malapropism*.

Of course, some of us *deliberately* talk nonsense. The term for this sort of thing is **cant**, and in all likelihood it springs from 'cantare', a Latin word for singing or chanting. (The idea being that those who mouth pious platitudes generally do so in a singsong voice.)

It just may be, however, that the word comes from Andrew Cant (1590–1663), a less-than-silver-tongued Scottish preacher. Said to deliver sermons in a way that was 'understood by none but his own congregation, and not by all of them', Cant was a staunch supporter of the king during the English Civil War, and was generally regarded as a bit of a bigot.

### THE CITY OF BIBLE

Cant got a lot of his bigotry from the **Bible**: there's a little bit of evil in 'the good book'. So perhaps we should just call it 'the book'. After all, that's what 'biblios' means.

'So *why* were all books call "biblios"?' you ask. 'Because of Lebanon,' I swiftly reply. Byblos is an ancient port city near Beirut. Once upon a time, however, it was the place from which the Greeks got most of their papyrus, the material from which books were made.

### PARCHMENT AND THE GREEN-EYED PHARAOH

Not everyone could get their hands on papyrus, however. In around 200 BC, a slightly childish Egyptian pharaoh decided to make sure that his library in Alexandria was the best in the world. So he enforced a trade embargo on Pergamon, an ancient city in modern-day Turkey, that had a great library of its own.

So no papyrus for Pergamon. But that city didn't just have readers and thinkers, it had practical types as well. Later named after the French 'parchemin' ('of Pergamon'), they put their heads together and invented **parchment**: dead animal skins, scraped and stretched, with a bit of powdered chalk rubbed on.

**PAMPHLET, THE HORNY OLD BAWD**

In the Philippines, people write on plants. *Manila folders* are named after a type of paper first made in Manila. They used the flattened fibres of the abaca plant. Which come in a shade of yellow you might find familiar.

Yellow paper wouldn't suit a *pamphlet*, though. No, they need something a bit glossier—a vibrant colour to catch people's eyes but not engage their brain. 'Pamphlets' didn't start out as polemics, however: the word once just meant 'small book'. It originated, appropriately enough, *from* a small book: a three-page love poem called *Pamphilus* that took 13th-century Europe by storm. (The plot involves an 'old bawd' called Pamphilus pining after someone called Galathee, while people called Aurelius and Doreigen get up to various hijinks. Authorities seem to disagree as to whether it was comic or erotic. Chances are it was neither.)

Anyway, the poem proved so popular in those pre–printing press days that eventually any kind of short publication became known as a 'pamphilus'.

**YELLOW JOURNALISM AND THE KID**

If you want to laugh at people's love lives these days, you must buy a tabloid newspaper. Censured by all right-thinking people, who at the same time secretly enjoy it, *yellow journalism* started life in America. Joseph Pulitzer's *New York World* and William Randolph Hearst's *New York Journal* began a race to the bottom in around 1890, and both ran extremely fast.

Along with the ever-scarier headlines, ever-bigger pictures and ever-more sensationalist stories, both papers introduced ever-crappier comic strips. Pulitzer and Hearst fought continually—and, some thought, symbolically—for the right to publish the most popular of those strips. Called 'The Yellow Kid', it was about a bald, snaggle-toothed urchin in yellow pyjamas, who ended up giving the new journalism its name.

## THE BUXOM BELINDA BLURB

*Blurbs*, by the by, are also named after a cartoon character, though this one was a little more sexy. In 1907, the Booksellers Association of America got together for its annual conference. Publishers tended to hand out their most popular books at these events, but this time one decided to do things differently. He printed out 500 'limited edition' copies of his company's most popular book (Gelett Burgess's *Are You a Bromide?*), so that each

Miss Belinda
the blurb

one had a special jacket. *Bromide*'s back cover now featured 'Miss Belinda Blurb', a buxom bombshell praising the book to the skies.

His idea had been to mock the extent to which publishers like to applaud their own books. But instead they applauded a new word.

## THE HARD-WORKING HACKS OF LONDON

We don't hear much about Gelett Burgess these days. Perhaps he was a bit of a *hack*. There's no shame in this (I write, rather defensively). Ever since the days of Grub Street, writers have been dutifully cranking out copy in exchange for scraps of cash. Art may feed the soul, but it's drudge-work that fills the tum.

Grub Street itself is not far from Hackney, a largish borough in London's north. Once upon a time, it was a self-contained village — one surrounded by plenty of paddocks. If you were travelling to the north of England, and so needed a cheap horse, Hackney was the place to get one. By the 12th century a 'hack' was any kind of plodding, mediocre nag loaned out for hire and 'hackneyed' work meant uninspired toil.

**THE FRANK
TRUTH
ABOUT
FRANCE**

But at least hacks get to write with a certain *frankness*. When digging for dirt on behalf of some sleazy rag, they can at least call a spade a spade.

The Franks could also write with frankness (though unfortunately most of them couldn't read). This Germanic tribe charged, stabbed and slashed their way into Gaul during the 5th century, then decided to stick around and make cheese. They're still there, having renamed the country France (but are now quite a bit less warlike, if we go by World War I and II).

For quite a few centuries there, however, the Franks were pretty damn powerful. Their privileges in their new country were so extravagant that they more or less became Gaul's only free men. Which is why to speak freely is to speak 'frankly'.

**SAMUEL
MORSE'S
CODE**

Stranded ships, however, do not speak with frankness. It's all 'dash' this and 'dot' that. Totally incomprehensible.

Blame Samuel Morse (1791–1872). The inventor of *Morse code* could easily have won fame as an artist—he was

an exceptional talent who exhibited at the Royal Academy—but I think it's more fun to remember him as a racist. Slavery, Morse liked to argue, was 'a divine institution'. 'It is a social condition ordained from the beginning of the world', and any attempt to abolish it was 'a sacrilegious and sinful endeavour'. The head of two influential pro-slavery organisations, Morse denounced Abraham Lincoln as a devil and considered democracy to be 'poisonous'.

**Samuel Morse**

**LÁSZLÓ
BÍRÓ,
PEN-MAKER**

Ok then, good to know. But returning to those dashed ships for a moment, it seems clear that what they need is a pen. Enter László Bíró (1899–1985). Yes, that's László *Biro*. At some point in the 1920s, this Hungarian journalist noticed that the ultra-thick ink used in newspapers dried much faster (and so smudged much less) than the sort of ink everyone wrote with at home. The problem was that it wouldn't work in fountain pens, being far too thick to flow.

So Bíró invented the ***biro***: a pen tip made of a small steel ball that he somehow managed to make turn in a socket. Smart guy. Sort of. Bíró was so busy being a genius that he forgot to purchase a patent.

# HOMELY WORDS

**THE FIRST
PALACE**

Home is where the house is, unless you're a Roman emperor. For those people, home was where the *palace* was. When Rome became an empire, the likes of Augustus and Caligula all needed a place to live, and where better than where it all began? The Palentine Hill, according to age-old mythology, was where a she-wolf suckled two babies who grew up to found a city called Rome.

Whether or not that's true, 'Palatium' was clearly very desirable real estate, located as it was just next to the Forum. As successive emperors took over ever more of it, so as to build ever more lavish mansions, 'Palatium' ceased to be the name of a suburb and became a word meaning 'magnificent house'.

**THE XANADU OF KUBLAI KHAN**

Mongolia's emperors also liked a big house. *Xanadu*, the summer residence of Kublai Kahn (1215–1294), was described by Marco Polo as 'a very fine marble palace, the rooms of which are all gilt and painted with figures of men and beasts and birds, and with a variety of trees and flowers, all executed with such exquisite art that you regard them with delight'.

Samuel Taylor Coleridge (1772–1834) tended to regard opium with delight. In 1797, that poet was reading a history book about the Mongolians and then drifted off into a drug-induced sleep. He duly dreamed about an earthly paradise and, upon waking, quickly dashed off a poem. It made Kublai Khan's 'stately pleasure dome' a byword for opulence.

**A CRETE WAY TO CONTROL YOUR MINOTAUR**

Not all old buildings get such a good rap, however. Consider the **Labyrinth** of Crete. The history of said building began when Minos, the king of said island, managed to upset one of the ancient gods. (He had planned to sacrifice a white bull during a religious ceremony, then changed his mind, being rather cheap.) The god got his own back by making Minos's wife fall madly in love with the bull in question, and not in a platonic way. The result of their romantic entanglement was a minotaur, a half-man with the head of a bull, who liked to snack on boys and girls.

Now a Minotaur, you might think, is also one of God's creatures and, as such, deserved to be loved. Stuff that, said the king. He instead got one of his lackeys to design a massive, maze-like prison to trap the dreadful beast and called it a 'labyrinth'.

**THE BYZANTINE BUREAU-CRACY OF BYZANTIUM**

If a pompous person was ever feeling especially pompous, they might describe such a maze as *byzantine*. And as tempting as it would be to denounce them, they would kind of have a point. That word, you see, also comes from Crete—or, at least, from the huge, sprawling empire that swallowed up that island for the best part of a thousand years. Stretching from Eastern Europe to Iraq, the Byzantine Empire emerged after the Roman Empire collapsed, and essentially comprised its eastern half.

Land was about all the two empires had in common, however. Named after its capital of Byzantium (which is now called Istanbul), the Byzantine Empire encouraged good government in the same way that an armchair encourages fish. It had all the irritations of a slow, sprawling bureaucracy and none of the stability: all the top government officials seemed to do was assassinate one another, while everyone below them shuffled paper.

'Of that Byzantine empire, the universal verdict of history is that it constitutes, without a single exception, the most thoroughly base and despicable form that civilisation has yet assumed,' wrote one 19th-century historian, who didn't believe in mincing his words. 'There has been no other enduring civilisation so absolutely destitute of all forms and elements of greatness.' So now, whenever something is needlessly elaborate, we have the perfect word to describe it.

**THE GAY COLOURS OF FREDDY BAROQUE**

By the 15th century, the Byzantine empire had done its dash, and Byzantine architecture quickly went with it. Round arches, low domes and geometric frescoes all gave way to the *baroque*. The architectural equivalent of Lady Gaga, baroque essentially meant making a building as big and showy and ornate as possible, then adding garish decorations for the next hundred years.

So what's with the name? One theory is that baroque was named for Federico Barocci (1526–1612), a flamboyant Renaissance painter famous for his 'gay colours' and dramatic style.

**THE EMBLEMATIC ATTICS OF ATTICA**

Of course, not everything we associate with fancy architecture comes from the Italians. Take *friezes*, for example—those thin decorative strips that sometimes lie over columns. (I could use terms like 'entablature' and 'architrave' here, but they would just confuse us both.) Friezes, I'm told, are named after Phrygia, a region of ancient Greece where people wore clothes with embroidered gold bands.

Another region of Greece is Attica, a peninsula by the Aegean Sea. Best known for its capital, Athens, Attica also had plenty of decorative columns back in the day—in fact, probably more than any city in the world. This is because when Attican architects designed a house, they tended to shove a shortish, squarish column immediately under the roof—an unusual feature which became known as an *attic*. Eventually, that term came to mean the room that was effectively created by such columns, i.e. the top of a house.

**BENGALESE BUNGALOWS AND A JERRYBUILT TOWN**

*Bungalows*, alas, don't have an attic. Should you live in one of these small, single-storey houses, all your old junk must live in a cupboard. Derived from 'banglà', the Hindi word for 'Bengali', 'bungalows' originally referred to the sort of tiny, thatched hovels that were once common in the Indian province of Bengal. One of the world's most densely populated regions, Bengal has about a thousand people in every square kilometre. And presumably a lot of junk.

Sometimes a house itself can be junk. With their sloping floors, cracking walls and crumbling roofs, *jerry-built* homes may be better than thatched hovels but not by all that much.

So who was this Jerry and how can we sue him? Well, one theory is that 'he' is actually an 'it'. Open your well-thumbed, ever-present Bible to the bit about Jericho, that walled city beside the Jordan River that stood between the Israelites and the promised land. We read that God's chosen people duly did battle with it, but they didn't face much of a fight. Like so many people who have bought a house off the plan, all they had to do was march about blowing trumpets for a bit, and Jericho's walls came tumbling down.

The jerry-built walls of Jericho

### THE SOLDIER WHO LIKED TO LOUNGE

That's far from the only violent bit in biblical history, of course. Take the story of Longinus. This Roman-soldier-turned-Christian-saint had a less-than-Christian moment in his soldiering days: one day, while guarding Jesus on the cross, he jabbed a spear in his side.

Bad. Anyway, Longinus-guarding-the-cross was a staple of many medieval plays and—aside from that one brief action scene—we have to assume that he wasn't much of a part. What else was there for the actor to do, after all, except sit just there? Or perhaps just stand there, leaning on his spear?

Maybe, though, this was doing quite a lot. The verb *to lounge* comes from the Old French word 'longis'. Which might just come from Longinus himself.

**LORD CHESTER-FIELD AND THE OTTOMAN**

If you're going to lounge, do it in a *chesterfield*. A bit of port and cheese here, some dusty bookshelves there, a roaring fireplace and a well-lit cigar: there's really nothing cosier.

But why do we call them 'chesterfields'? Etymologists generally point to the 4th Earl of Chesterfield (1694–1773). Not because he had anything to do with furniture, but because around the time chesterfields became popular, his name was synonymous with style.

While he was a reasonably well-known diplomat and politician, Chesterfield's main claim to fame was a book he wrote, called *Letters to His Son*. Cynical and slightly tongue-in-cheek, it was all about how to get ahead in high society by being sort of urbane and droll. Dr Samuel Johnson was not a fan, declaring that the book taught 'the morals of a whore and the manners of a dancing master … [I had thought Chesterfield] a lord among wits', he wrote, but he was really just 'a wit among lords'.

Should you ever fall out of a chesterfield, we hope that you land on an *ottoman*. God's gift to the calf muscles, these deliciously squishy footstools are named after someone who probably thought he was God. Othman I (1258–1326) was an all-conquering warrior and all-powerful sultan, and the founding father of the Ottoman Empire.

It seems wrong that a man who created a throne should be best known in the West for a footstool, but such are the ways of trade.

The exotic splendours of the East were all the rage in 19th-century Europe. The word 'Persian' had already been taken by a carpet, however, and 'Turkish' was the name of a sweet.

**THE FIRST MAN TO HOLD A HOOVER**

*Venetian blinds* came from the Ottoman Empire too. So why were they named after Venice? Here again we have an accident of commerce: Venetian traders were the first to import these slatted blinds from Persia, and the rest of Europe bought the product from them.

We can tell much the same tale about WH Hoover (1849–1932). 'Ah, the inventor of the vacuum cleaner,' you say—but no Sir, you say wrong. WH Hoover was just a leather goods salesman (and quite possibly not even a good one). The first 'electric suction sweeper' was actually invented by one J Murray Spangler, an elderly janitor at a department store who wanted to solve the asthma problem he got sweeping up dust.

Luckily, his invention worked. Less luckily, it didn't earn him much cash. Spangler sold Hoover the patent—which is why we *hoover* today—then set about planning his first-ever trip overseas. Then died the day he was due to set sail.

**THOMAS BLANKET AND MR DOILEY**

Still, at least Spangler had actually managed to exist up until that point. Can the same be said for Thomas Blanket?

As unlikely as it sounds, there may just have been a *blanket* weaver of that name in 14th-century Bristol. Rather dismayingly for that theory, 'blankette' was already a French word for cloth at the time but it's not entirely out of the question that young Thomas made it more used in England.

A few centuries later, another British draper came onto the scene--but he would never make anything so coarse as a blanket. According to a 1712 edition of *The Spectator*, a Mr Doiley of

The Strand had 'raised a Fortune by finding out Materials for such Stuffs as might at once be cheap and genteel … [and so sell] a frugal means of gratifying our pride'.

So if a petticoat was delicately embroidered and easily torn, chances were it came from Doiley's. The word *doily* probably came from there too.

**SOME CHINA AND TWO COUSINS** The sort of people who invest in doilies will generally own *china* as well. Somewhat unsurprisingly, so do lots of people in China. Europeans have been importing porcelain from that country for well over 500 years.

Another type of porcelain is made in England. Not much of interest can be said about Josiah Wedgewood (1730–1795), the one-legged founder of **Wedgewood**. Except this: he was the grandfather of Charles Darwin. And, err, of Emma Wedgewood, Darwin's cousin and wife.

# LEGAL WORDS

**DR GUIL-LOTINE, DO-GOODER** Over 15,000 people lost their heads during the French Revolution and the feeling was that they should be grateful. Not because they had been spared the trouble and expense of haircuts, but because in former times most wrongdoers had been hanged by the neck. Beheading was once a privilege of the aristocracy, but in the new France all were equal.

Dr Guillotin

So, yes, hooray for the *guillotine*—but is it right that it was given that name? Dr Joseph-Ignace Guillotin (1738–1814) didn't think so.

This well-meaning politician didn't actually invent the device that bears his name, he just happened to be an early advocate of it. In a parliamentary debate about execution, the good doc proposed six reforms. Five advocated better treatment for the deceased's family (non-confiscation of property, etc.) and the sixth was also meant to be humane. Severing heads with a machine would be a kindness, Guillotin felt—a punishment that was painless and swift.

The National Assembly took this final recommendation seriously. A satirical journal did not. *Les Actes des Apôtres* published a song mocking Guillotin's concept of kindness, and a new word quickly followed.

## DRACO THE DRACONIAN

Draco wouldn't have found this anything to laugh about. That 7th-century Greek legislator would have considered Dr Guillotin's concern for criminals to be a case of political correctness gone mad. An example of the sort of tree-hugging, latte-sipping fuzzy-mindedness that currently prevents us from torturing hippies.

Nemesis, your nemesis

Stern but fair, Draco was invited to codify Athens's unwritten laws in 621 BC, and took a fairly straightforward approach: one strike and you were out. Murder and treason merited the death penalty, he felt, and so too did stealing a cabbage. 'Written in blood', the **Draconian** Code recommended execution for pretty much any wrongdoing, including blasphemy, petty theft and idleness. A wise ruler repealed it thirty years later. But by then there were fewer people to rule.

Such tends to be the fate of bad legislation (unless you're a Republican Congressman, in which case you just make more).

One reason, perhaps, why Draco's code was finally judged to be excessive was the fact that ancient Greek evildoers were always assured of divine justice, whatever their punishment might be on earth. For soaring through the skies with her wings, sword and apple branch was **Nemesis**, the goddess of retribution. Appointed by Zeus to maintain a balance between good and evil, this remorseless deity dealt out just desserts.

**GUILTY UNTIL PROVEN GUILTY: THE FIRST LYNCH MOB**

Charles Lynch (1736–1796) didn't need Zeus's approval to deal out rough justice. He just appointed himself.

This Virginian planter and justice of the peace was a nemesis of 'traitors' during the American War of Independence. At the time, any Virginians thought to be in league with England were supposed to go on trial at the colonial court in Williamsburg. But Williamsburg was far away from where Lynch lived—a difficult and dangerous journey of around 320 kilometres. Due process is all very well, but there's no need get carried away.

His solution was the very first **lynch mob**. With two neighbours, Lynch set up a self-constituted court that was 'proper in all respects but its jurisdiction' and started handing out guilty verdicts. We could just as easily talk of a 'Callaway mob' or an 'Adams mob', but for some reason they never took off.

**FORENSICS IN THE FORUM**

Nowadays, we're happy to say, the wheels of justice turn a little more smoothly. For one thing, people generally need to be guilty before we punish them. This exciting new phenomenon is largely due to *forensics*—that Sherlock Holmes–like science that allows us to deduce a person's movements, sexual preferences and favoured sports teams from the tiniest shred of their DNA.

But though mitochondrial DNA analysis is new, the word 'forensic' is actually quite old. Meaning anything 'used in or appropriate for courts of law', it began life in the *Forum*, the central plaza of ancient Rome. Though mostly used as a market, it was also the venue for most of Rome's trials.

---

**MIRANDA AND HIS RIGHTS**

Of course, cutting-edge science isn't always required to establish guilt: some crimes are pretty straightforward. But even if a man was to stab his wife in front of a video camera, then write a press release saying 'I killed the bitch', he is still entitled to the presumption of innocence. And an innocent person has rights. Specifically, they have *Miranda rights* — 'the right to remain silent' (because 'anything you say can and will be used against you in a court of law'), 'the right to an attorney', and so on.

This well-known staple of cop shows (and good friend to every bad scriptwriter) was named after Ernesto Arturo Miranda (1941–1976), a poor, uneducated Arizona labourer who was accused of kidnapping, raping and robbing several women in the 1960s. He finally broke down and confessed under questioning — unaware that, under the Fifth Amendment, he was not under any obligation to incriminate himself.

Miranda's conviction was eventually overturned by the Supreme Court, the judges ruling that it was wrong for the police to assume that every American was aware of his rights. Ever since then, police have been equipped with 'Miranda cards', listing the rights they're required to read out.

After he got out of jail, Miranda made money signing them.

---

**THE MULTI-COLOURED THIN BLUE LINE**

Annoying, no doubt, for police officers — but such is life on *the thin blue line*. Though that should perhaps read the thin *red* line. This expression for those who patrol the border between order and chaos once came in a different colour, and dates back to an incident in the Crimean War.

During the Crimean War in 1854, a tiny group of red-coated Scotsmen found themselves stranded on a remote road. Face-to-face with a thousand Russians. Their leader, Sir Colin Campbell, believed in the power of positive thinking, so he said, 'There is no retreat from here, men. You must die where you stand.' Heartened by this pep talk, his soldiers formed a 'thin red line' two men deep (conventional lines were at least four men deep) and prepared to meet their doom.

But it never came: having such a strangely thin line of infantry ended up being their salvation. When the Russian commander saw it, he concluded that the British must have set a trap. They simply had to have more soldiers hiding somewhere, so he ordered his troops to turn back.

Imagination captured, a poetic journalist later wrote about the 'thin red streak' of Scotsmen, 'tipped with a line of steel'. A police-specific version of the phrase soon followed.

### BOBBY'S BOBBIES AND THE BILL

The British aren't always so poetic when naming policemen, however. There's nothing very lyrical about *bobby*. That term for the boys in blue probably comes from the man who fathered them: the British Home Secretary Sir Robert Peel (1788–1850), who established the world's first police force in London in 1829. Based in Scotland Yard, 'Bobby's boys' proved so successful that they could be found in every English city within six years.

So that's Bob, but who's Bill? Why is it that (when they're not being called 'pigs' or 'cuntstables') British policemen are known as *the Bill*? Nobody really knows, but one possible answer is 'Kaiser Bill'—the goose-steppingly militaristic Prussian emperor, Wilhelm I (1797–1888).

**Bobby Peel**

Forever strutting about in a helmet and tunic, he was in England at the time when the police uniform of a top hat and tail coat was being replaced. With, yes, a helmet and tunic.

A more plausible explanation, however, involves the London City Council. In the 1920s, it required all police, fire and ambulance licence places to begin with the letters 'BYL'.

**WHY PRIVATE EYES ARE FINKS**

On the other side of the Atlantic was America, the home of the brave and the land of the free. There, detectives could drive around in whatever they liked, dammit. They could also work for whoever they liked. And most of them worked for Pinkertons.

Founded by Allan Pinkerton (1819–1884), Pinkertons was the world's largest detective agency for decades. It actually had more agents than there were soldiers in the US army. Responsible for the term 'private eye' (its logo was an open eye alongside the motto 'We never sleep'), the agency protected presidents and hunted outlaws, but its main business was breaking strikes. Undercover Pinkerton agents would often infiltrate workplaces to root out troublemakers— or kick a few heads if trouble had already started.

Unsurprisingly this made them unpopular. Workers hated the pinks. Or, as they became known: the *finks*.

# POLITICAL WORDS

**WHERE TO LOBBY IN LONDON**

'The best argument against democracy,' said Winston Churchill, 'is a five-minute conversation with the average voter.'

Fortunately, politicians rarely have to endure this; they're too busy talking to *lobbyists*. No MP can move an inch in the 21st century without consulting at least five special-interest groups and then having a pollster gauge the public mood. And if they *do* move an inch, they'd better go on public transport or at least drive a locally made car.

'Twas not always thus. Back in the good old days, ordinary citizens could be lobbyists too. All they had to do was go to an actual lobby and collar their local MP. Often described as 'the political centre of the British Empire', the large Central Lobby in the Palace of Westminster sits in between the House of Lords and the House of Commons. It's a great place for a cosy chat.

### THOMAS HANSARD AND DOROTHY DIX

Whenever English and Australian politicians talk, we can all read their words in **Hansard**. This not-very-interesting book was first compiled by a not-very-interesting man. In 1809, a printer named Thomas Hansard (1776–1833) was employed by William Cobbett, a well-known radical journalist, to publish *Parliamentary Debates* as a supplement to Cobbett's *Political Register*. Publicising Parliamentary debates had long been illegal, but by 1800 it only ever led to an occasional fine.

Decades later, in the grand tradition of radicals, Cobbett found himself facing bankruptcy. So he sold the *Parliamentary Debates* part of the business to Hansard, who promptly renamed it … 'Hansard'. The Parliament itself took over the business in 1909, but 'Hansard' it has stoutly remained.

So why is **Hansard** so uninteresting? Ok, not every speech is going to sway the fate of nations, but surely some should be of interest to *somebody*. The problem (in Australia, at least) lies in the **Dorothy Dixer**. This is the name given to questions asked by backbenchers on the government side … to ministers in the government. Pre-arranged and tightly scripted, they're basically just an invitation to make a self-congratulatory speech. 'Why are you so amazing?' the hard-hitting backbencher might inquire. 'Have you *always* been this great?'

Dorothy Dix, on the other hand, really was amazing. One of the most widely syndicated journalists in US history, Dix was the prototypical agony aunt. Her pioneering advice column spoke to the hearts of American housewives, carefully avoiding their minds. But tall poppies often get cut down. Some unworthy souls liked to say that Dorothy didn't just answer her reader's questions, she actually wrote them too.

**THE FIRST MAN TO SPEAK BUNKUM**

The US Congress also offers its share of tedium. The only thing worse than a Democrat droning on about liberty's sacred flame and America's special destiny is a Republican saying anything at all.

Every now and then, however, even a Congressman can crap on too much. In 1820, this happened to Felix Walker, the member for Buncombe County, North Carolina. The House had come to the end of a month-long debate and was finally ready to vote. When Walker spontaneously rose to speak, therefore, his fellow Congressmen were in no mood for more fatuous blatherings, and in one voice shouted him down. 'But gentlemen, I must speak for Buncombe!' Walker cried—and was met with a mighty laugh. 'Speaking **bunkum**' from that day forth meant speaking total crap.

**GERRY'S GERRY- MANDER**

But given the amount of *gerrymandering* that once went on in America, it's not surprising that its politicians were second-rate. That technique, if you don't know, involves redrawing electoral boundaries so that they favour your political party. Gerrymandered electorates tend to come in pretty strange shapes and sizes, and it was the misfortune of one Elbridge Gerry (1744–1814)—a dodgy-but-no-more-than-most governor of Massachusetts—that one of the new electorates he drew up happened to look like a salamander. Amused, a cartoonist drew a picture of it—renaming the shape a 'gerrymander'.

Elbridge Gerry's gerrymander

**THE MAN WHO HAD BOB AS AN UNCLE**

The British have traditionally looked down on this kind of corruption. Its politicians have never gerrymandered. They use nepotism to get jobs instead.

In 1887, for example, the Prime Minister Robert Cecil (1830–1903) appointed Arthur Balfour (1848–1930) his Chief Secretary for Ireland. Balfour's qualifications weren't immediately obvious. 'The country saw with something like stupefaction the appointment of the young dilettante to what was at that moment perhaps the most important, and certainly the most anxious, office of the administration.'

But his bloodlines were top-notch. Robert 'Bob' Cecil was his uncle. This may well be where we get the phrase *Bob's your uncle*—meaning, 'don't worry, you have a guarantee of success'.

**WHY TORIES BELONG IN JAIL**

Just like England's current prime minister, David Cameron, Bob Cecil was a *Tory*. In medieval Ireland, this would never have been allowed. Back then, 'tóraí' was an Irish word for 'brigands'—the robbers and rebels who lived outside of the law and died on the end of a rope.

The term acquired its current meaning in 1678. England's Charles II had just died and the Parliament was divided on whether to let his Catholic brother succeed to what had become a staunchly Protestant throne. The politicians who said he should were derisively called Tories (the implication being that they were Catholic rebels). And the politicians who said 'no' were in turn labelled Whigs—a 'wiggamor' being a lowly, plodding cattle-driver in that bastion of Protestantism, Scotland.

**DOWNING'S STREET AND A CAPITAL HILL**

Should you wish to take justice into your own hands and arrest David Cameron, the place to do it is *Downing Street*. Perhaps appropriately, this age-old residence of British prime ministers got its name from a 'perfidious rogue'.

One of Harvard's first-ever graduates, George Downing (1623–1684) was 'marked by all the mean vices: treachery, avarice, servility and ingratitude' and made a career out of switching sides. He somehow managed to be both an MP under Oliver Cromwell and a senior diplomat under Cromwell's arch-enemy, Charles II. (The new king gave him a small block of land that later became Downing Street, after he ratted out three former colleagues.)

You need more than perfidy to make an ambassador, however. It's been said that Downing's 'diplomatic intransigence' was the direct cause of the second Dutch War.

Downing Street is, of course, in London, England's ancient, storied *capital*. For a truly ancient capital, however, we must go back to the source of the word. One of the seven hills of Rome,

Capitoline Hill, was home to the Temple of Jupiter, the Roman Empire's most important god.

**A BANANA REPUBLIC AND SOME YOUNG TURKS**

Here's an interesting fiscal fact: Rome's economy around 80 BC was roughly on a par with that of early 20th-century Honduras. That Central American country was the original *banana republic*. Not content with buying up huge tracts of forest and forcing the landless peasantry to become cheap labour, some giant American fruit companies decided that it would make good business sense to sponsor a coup d'état. In 1910, the government of Honduras was effectively run by the Cuyamel Fruit Company.

Modernisation came in 1954, however. Government was taken over by the CIA.

What Honduras needed were some *young Turks* — a group of brave, democratically minded politicians ready to take the country by the scruff of its neck and give it a bit of a shake. That wasn't possible, however; they were all in Turkey. Headed up by the likes of Yusuf Akçura (1876–1935) and Ahmed Bey (1873–1912), the Young Turks were an underground group of university students. They managed to restore parliamentary government during the dying days of the Ottoman Empire, despite fierce resistance from the sultan.

# FINANCIAL WORDS

**IN GEESE WE TRUST: THE STORY OF MONEY**

Prepare yourself for a goose anecdote. In 390 BC, assorted barbarians were marauding their way through Italy, so Rome's soldiers were on high alert. And, sure enough, one pitch-black night, a few thousand tribesmen tried to sneak into town.

But was it some keen-eyed legionary who raised the alarm, and so saved Rome's citizens from being slain in their sleep? No. It was a bunch of geese. Sacred birds that lived at the Temple of Juno (the goddess who gave us 'June'), the geese started honking madly at 3 am, alerting the nightwatchmen and saving the day. Their reward was presumably more grain, but Juno herself got an additional name. That goddess became 'Juno Moneta', a name meaning 'the one who warns'.

Relevance? Well, a few decades later, the spirit of commerce had become more powerful than any religion, so the Temple of Juno Moneta started to double up as a shrine to capitalism. It was turned into Rome's first mint. Gold, silver and copper coins all came from that one building—and so too did an often-used word. **Money**.

**CROESUS, A MAN AS RICH AS CROESUS**

The Romans certainly weren't the first people to mint coins, however. That honour probably goes to King Croesus (595–547 BC), a ruler of Lydia in what's now Turkey. His realm encompassed the Pactolus River, an area rich in electrum, a pale-yellow alloy that includes silver and gold.

Croesus made a mint from his mint, becoming far and away the world's richest man. A legend in his own lifetime, he subsequently became 'a figure of myth, who stood outside the conventional restraints of chronology'. The phrase *as rich as Croesus* has been bandied around for thousands of years.

**WHERE TO GET A HALLMARK AND MAKE A DOLLAR**

In London, however, Croesus wouldn't have been that rich. Goldsmith Hall doesn't think much of electrum. Before they can be put up for sale, all gold and silver products manufactured in England's capital must be examined at the home of the Goldsmith's guild. If they're good enough, they get a mark of quality.

Which, yes, is called a **hallmark**.

Money's been minted in all sorts of places over the years and the most famous is Joachimstal. Now home to a uranium mine, this Czech 'thal' (or 'valley') was once stuffed full of silver. The local landowners, the counts von Schlick, took full advantage of this situation in the 16th century, not only digging up all the silver but cannily using it to make their own coins. 'Joachimstalers' soon became one of Europe's most popular currencies.

But in the pacy world of business, who's got time to say four syllables? The coins began to be called 'thalers' by the Czech, 'dahlers' by the Germans, and 'dalers' by the Danish and Dutch. It may not altogether surprise to learn that, in England, they became known as **dollars**.

(If the von Schlicks had been really slick, they would have built a mint in West Africa. Gold, after all, is worth more than silver—and the British found plenty of it on the Guinea Coast. Then used it to make lots of **guineas**.)

**EL DORADO, THE MAN** An even better place to mine would have been *El Dorado*, South America's fabled city of gold. But despite several centuries of searching, no fortune-hunter has ever managed to find it.

This is largely because it doesn't exist. El Dorado was never a local legend; it only started after Spanish conquistadors made their way to the New World. In 1638, one of those conquistadors wrote a 'long, rambling chronicle' about the Muiscas, a tribe based in what's now Colombia. The Muiscas, he claimed, liked to celebrate religious festivals by covering their chief in lots of gold dust. A metal so gloriously abundant that the chief would later dive into a lake in order to wash it off.

'Ay caramba!' said Spaniards reading this back home, adding an 'Adios!' to their family and friends. The legend grew as the centuries passed, and more and more people set off to find some streets paved with gold. It's curious that none of them seemed to take much notice of what the words 'El Dorado' actually mean. Directly translated, they don't refer to a city, but simply mean 'the gilded one'.

## THE KING WITH THE MIDAS TOUCH

It would have been easy to cover King Midas in gold dust; just throw on some ordinary dust and his body would do the rest. Probably inspired by a real king (Mita, a greedy ruler of part of Turkey in the 8th century BC), this ancient Greek myth concerns a wealthy king who was granted a wish by a well-meaning god.

Already happy because he had so much gold, the greedy Midas decided that he'd be even happier if he had a bit more. He thus wished for what became known as the **Midas touch** — the ability to make everything he touched turn to gold. Sounds good, yeah?

Nah. Over the course of the following day, Midas accidentally turned his garden into gold. And then his food. And then his kid.

## THE SAD TALE OF DE SILHOUETTE

Etienne de Silhouette (1709–1767) had a different problem. Everything he touched turned into debt. Appointed French finance minister in 1759, when the country was midway through a ruinous war, de Silhouette inherited an economy on the brink of collapse. And he didn't inherit much help. While France's extravagant ruling classes all wanted something done about the crippling deficit, they didn't want to have to do it themselves. One of de Silhouette's proposed reforms was a heavy tax on all luxury goods, so he got the boot after eight short months.

But that was ample time for a new phrase to enter the language. Since the minister's tax would have meant economising on luxuries, the nobles would say an item was 'of Silhouette' whenever it looked like it was made 'on the cheap'. A snuffbox 'à la silhouette', for example, was one that wasn't made from marble, but (gasp!) wood.

'Shadow' pictures had been around forever, but happened to be back in fashion at the time. Because these pictures were merely outlines, they cost far less than a detailed portrait, so they got called *silhouettes* too.

## THE TARIFFS OF TARIFA

Perhaps Monsieur de Silhouette should have avoided heavy taxes, and pinned his faith in *tariffs* instead? The icy wind-blast of competition is all very well, but economic shelter can be nice.

This financial practice is thought to have begun in the Tarifa, ancient Spain's southernmost port. Just 14 kilometres north of Africa, Tarifa was more or less the doorkeeper of the western Mediterranean: it was every ship's final port of call before they entered or left the Atlantic. But you couldn't call by for free: in the 7th century, Tarifa became possibly the world's first port to charge merchants for the use of their docks. 'Tariff', as coincidence would have it, was at that time already an Arabic word meaning 'fees to be paid'. But it most likely made its way into English via that most businesslike of Spanish ports.

## LAMBERT LE BEGGAR

Those tariffs probably made quite a few people *beggars*—though the term itself is surprisingly recent. People having been pleading and beseeching and imploring for donkey's years, but only seem to have 'begged' since about the 12th century. This may possibly be due to a Belgian priest named Lambert le Bégue ('Lambert the Stammerer') who founded a brotherhood called the 'Beghards'. Unlike most other religious orders of the time, the Beghards didn't spend their days singing hymns in a monastery and their nights trying hard not to wank. They were able to marry and own property, and also walk around wherever they chose.

Walking around, in fact, was the brotherhood's raison d'être, because by doing so they could request alms for the poor. But after a while, they weren't the only ones doing the requesting. Many enterprising poor people decided to cut out the middleman and pretend to be Beghards themselves.

## THE CHEAP SIDE OF CHEAPSIDE

Once upon a time, there was no shortage of poor people in Cheapside. Now home to well-heeled stockbrokers (all busily creating another financial crisis), this London street lies in between St Paul's Cathedral and the Bank of England and was the birthplace of Geoffrey Chaucer.

It also helped produce the word **cheap**. The medieval English word 'cepe' meant 'market' and that's what Cheapside was. England's centre of commerce and home of haggling, this great thoroughfare once housed hundreds of shops. Exactly how it came to be synonymous with 'inexpensive' is unknown. But when businesses are forced to battle one another, it's the customer who tends to win.

## A SHAMBLES OF SMELLY FLESH

Back in the Middle Ages, street names made more sense. Cheapside, for example, bordered Honey Lane, Milk Street and Bread Street—three roads where shoppers knew that what they heard was what they were going to get.

There was no such thing as a 'Meat Street', however. Butchers would instead conduct their trade in 'Fleshammels' ('Flesh shelves'), a street name which in time became shortened to 'Shambles'. Now, in life tastes tend to vary, but on one point most will agree. There would be nothing very pleasant or orderly about a street filled with dead and dying animals. Think blood, guts, bones and offal: giant strips of furry skin and great hunks of smelly flesh.

Ok, now you can think about something else. Perhaps consider why any scene of messiness or chaos is nowadays called a **shambles**.

## LUMBER STREET, LONDON

The origin of the word **lumber** is itself rather shambolic—but it's worth noting that it too stems from a street.

During and after the Renaissance, the Italian region of Lombardy was well known for its many merchants.

Lombard businessmen migrated far and wide, moneylending, banking and pawnbroking. One part of London, which was duly named 'Lombard Street', had dozens of these people's pawnshops. And all of them, in the manner of pawnshops, contained a truly ludicrous amount of junk.

In English, 'lumber' accordingly came to mean a pile of useless clutter. In the US, it later came to mean 'timber'. How this happened, we don't quite know, but one theory is that the heavily forested New World had so much timber that it would clutter up in useless piles.

**WHY IT'S OK TO PLAY BALL IN A MALL**

To find piles of useless junk these days, make your way to a ***shopping mall***. This term comes from a London street too. 'Pallamaglio' (meaning 'mallet ball') was a medieval Italian game not unlike croquet. Renamed 'pall-mall', it became all the rage in London during the 17th century, and the area outside St James's Palace, where Charles II himself played, eventually became known as 'Pall Mall'.

That area later became one of London's great streets, and a great place to promenade. The 19th-century upper classes could think of nothing better

Pall Mall

than walking all the way up Pall Mall with a top hat and cane, and then turning around and walking all the way back. This pastime was so wildly popular that any place given over to walking eventually went by the name of a 'mall'. So when some bright American invented spacious shopping arenas in the 19th century, what better word to call them?

# TIMELY WORDS

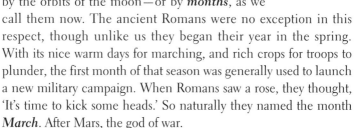

**THE MURDEROUS MONTH OF MARCH**

We all know what it is to spend a long, dull day at work, wearily watching the clock. But consider how workers might have felt a few thousand years ago. All they had to watch was the moon.

Almost every ancient people measured time by the orbits of the moon—or by *months*, as we call them now. The ancient Romans were no exception in this respect, though unlike us they began their year in the spring. With its nice warm days for marching, and rich crops for troops to plunder, the first month of that season was generally used to launch a new military campaign. When Romans saw a rose, they thought, 'It's time to kick some heads.' So naturally they named the month *March*. After Mars, the god of war.

**JUNE AND HER GOATSKIN CLOAK**

The miracles of springtime also account for 'Aprilis' and 'Maius', the Romans' names for the next two months (from which of course we get *April* and *May*). 'Aprilis' most likely comes from 'asperire', a Latin verb meaning 'to open' (just like a budding flower). And Maia was a kind of fertility goddess, who required a sacrifice on the first day of her month.

Juno, being a rather more powerful goddess, required sacrifices all the time. There was no particular reason why *June* should be named after this all-powerful queen of the heavens—it was just generally considered a good idea to honour her whenever you got the chance. Wife of Jupiter, daughter of Saturn and mother of Mars, Juno was warlike, well connected and the personification of womanhood. She could even get away with wearing a goatskin cloak.

## TWO EMPERORS AND AN EGO

**Julius Caesar**

Julius Caesar (100–44 BC), rather more stylishly, liked to wear a laurel wreath. One of those Great Men of History who probably wouldn't make a great husband or son, his Great achievements included the *Julian calendar*, a remodelling of the Roman year so it now began with January and February, and stretched out to a full twelve months. One of his less Great achievements was forgetting to rename September, October, November and December—words that in Latin mean 'seventh month', 'eighth month, 'ninth month' and 'tenth month', but which now apply to months that fall later in the year.

They did remember to rename the 'fifth month', however. After Julius was assassinated, his successor decided to rename Quintillus *July*, to commemorate the month Caesar was born. (And no, he hadn't been born by a *Caesarian section*. 'Caesar' is a Latin word meaning 'to cut'.)

Another successor, Augustus, also wanted to be a Great Man, so he dropped one or two Great hints. And it seems that the Senate picked up on them. Midway through his reign, it declared that Sextillus would henceforth have the name *August*.

Sextillus had been a happy month for Augustus—it had been during that time of the year that he'd conquered Egypt and won Rome's civil war—but in one respect it wasn't a happy choice. It was only thirty days long. Unlike Caesar's month of July, which had thirty-one. So Augustus had a day removed from the new month of February and tacked it on to his own.

## MORE MONTHS

So why call this new month *February*? It's because it happened to incorporate Februa, a traditional festival of ritual purification that was named after a Latin word meaning 'to cleanse'. Many people would simply mark the occasion by having a bath or spring-cleaning their house, but women who were having trouble getting pregnant sometimes used Februa to cleanse themselves. They would sacrifice a goat and get beaten with a whip made from its hide, in order to wash away whatever obstructed their wombs.

Janus also couldn't get pregnant. But since he was a male god, this was probably just as well. The god of beginnings and doorways, his name was a natural choice for **January**, the first month of the year.

**THE NIGHT-WATCHMEN ON YOUR WRIST**

Janus also gave his name to **janitors**, who were once just people who stood guard at a door. Fortunately for those who like law and order, some medieval cities had nightwatchmen as well: sturdy yeomen who patrolled the streets from sunset until sunrise, putting criminals in their place.

Thanks, boys. In the 17th century, I'm happy to report, a new invention made their job easier. Thanks to a new sort of miniature timepiece, nightwatchmen were able to check the time while they made their rounds, and so be near a pub at dawn. It's thought that people associated this new timepiece with the nightwatchmen, and accordingly named it a **watch**.

**THE WAYS WE SPEAK ABOUT DAYS OF THE WEEK**

When it comes to the days of the week, it's a good thing that no-one's ever guarded the English language. It's stolen words far and wide.

It seems to have been the Babylonians that first came up with the idea of a seven-day week — their logic likely being that, since there were five (visible) planets in the sky, plus a sun and a moon, why not have seven days and give them their names? This system being as good as any other, it soon spread to Egypt, and from there to Rome.

And so for centuries, the seven days of the week were 'Saturn', 'Sun', 'Moon', 'Mars', 'Mercury', 'Jupiter' and 'Venus'. All Roman names for the planets, which had come from Roman gods. And three of those days are still so-named today. Next **Saturday**, **Sunday** and **Monday**, spare a thought for Saturn, the sun and the moon.

But when the Roman Empire collapsed, so too did the other four names. The English got rid of the names of those Roman gods and replaced them with gods of their own. In place of the Roman god of war, Mars, for example, they substituted their own god of war, Tiw—with the result that we now say **Tuesday**.

**Wednesday**, in turn, means 'day of Woden'. That god of wisdom had a little bit in common with Mercury, the Roman god of sacred mysteries and hidden things, whose day it had previously been.

The next day on the old calendar had been named Jupiter, after Rome's most powerful god. So the English re-named it **Thursday** after that most powerful of pagan gods, Thor.

Nothing beats the power of love, however. Venus was the Roman goddess of love, so the English swapped her for a similar one. Freya, Woden's loving wife, who we honour every **Friday**.

**Thor, god of thunder**

# SEX & VIOLENCE

## ROMANTIC WORDS

*Lothario, Latin lover,*
*Romance language,*
*Romance, Roam,*
*St Valentine's Day,*
*Erotic, Aphrodisiac,*
*Tantalise, Priapism,*
*Platonic love*

---

## ADVENTUROUS WORDS

*Sadism, Masochism,*
*Sodomy, Lesbian,*
*Sapphic, Bugger,*
*Onanism, Narcissism,*
*Adonis, Gorgon,*
*Oedipus complex*

---

## TAWDRY WORDS

*Hooker, Harlot,*
*Hussy, Wench,*
*Jezebel, Peeping Tom,*
*Nosey parker, Tawdry,*
*Sleazy, Vulgar*

## INTOLERANT WORDS

*Barbarian,*
*Vandalism, Gothic,*
*Philistine, Bohemian,*
*Gypsy, Cannibal,*
*Caribbean Sea, Red*
*Indians, West Indies,*
*Mongoloid,*
*Down syndrome,*
*Caucasian, Neanderthal*

---

## WARLIKE WORDS

*Pistol, Carbine rifle,*
*Bayonet, Big Bertha,*
*Gatling gun, Derringer,*
*Colt revolver, Mauser,*
*Luger, Tommy gun,*
*Uzi, Molotov cocktail,*
*Shrapnel, Tommies,*
*Hun, Digger,*
*Hatchet man, Pioneers,*
*Diehard, Stonewall,*
*Fabian Society,*
*Pyrrhic victory,*
*Lethargy, Lethal,*
*Morgue, Mausoleum,*
*Deadline, Armageddon,*
*Macabre*

## FIGHTING WORDS

*Hooligan, Hoodlum,*
*Plug-ugly, Donnybrook,*
*Skid row, Ghetto, Thug,*
*Pressgang, Shanghaied*

# ROMANTIC WORDS

**LOTHARIO
THE GAY
LOTHARIO**

The musician Sting once claimed that he could make love for eight hours straight. What he didn't say, he later admitted, was that this figure included four hours of begging and then dinner and a movie.

Such, alas, seems to be life for the modern male. Even the velvety-voiced crooners of this world can't just whip it out anymore. Men must woo and charm and quip and emote (then give up, go home and surf porn).

*Lothario* would be turning in his grave. That name for an unscrupulous rake is in fact the name of an unscrupulous rake: Lothario is an Italian character in *The Fair Penitent*, Nicholas Rowe's 1703 play. 'Haughty, gallant and gay,' he seduces said penitent (a sweet innocent named Calista) then betrays her like the bad man he is.

**LATIN
LOVERS,
ROMANCE
AND ROME**

Oh, those **Latin lovers**. For some women it matters not if the heart be black, so long as the hair is too. When their eyes see olive skin, a bad personality can be overlooked.

An annoying state of affairs for the rest of us—and one for which Latinus is largely to blame. According to Virgil's *Aeneid*, he was the founder and first king of the Latins, an ancient tribe of central Italy that settled a series of city-states in the first millennium BC.

The most powerful of those city-states was Rome. Ever hungry for conquest, the Romans swallowed up their fellow Latins in 338 BC, then began feasting on the rest of Europe. In theory, the emergence of the Roman Empire meant that Europeans everywhere spoke Latin, the language of Latinus and Rome. In practice, how-ever, most ordinary people learned *bits* of Latin (enough to get by with their conquerors, at least) but continued to speak their local tribal language, or merge the two where appropriate.

So when the Roman Empire collapsed, in some places Latin did too. In France, Spain, Portugal and the rest of Italy, however, Latin had become tied up with the local languages, and remains so to this day. Which is why (if you've ever wondered) French, Spanish, Portuguese and Italian are called the **Romance languages**.

It's also why we have *romance* itself. In the 14th century, 'serious' books of history, philosophy and theology tended to be written in Latin — by then a long-dead language understood only by the educated elite. Frivolous tales of bold knights and their fair maidens, on the other hand, were for ordinary people, and so they were written in words they could read. That is to say, in the Romance languages: the language of ordinary people. In time, then, the term 'romance' became synonymous with novels of courtly love. And then it simply became synonymous with courtship, that oh-so-complicated art.

(Entirely incidentally, Rome may also be why we **roam**. Since it was the holy home of the Catholic Church, medieval pilgrims often made their way there. That is to say, they 'roamed' — a word that for many years simply meant 'wandering to Rome'.)

**SAINT VALENTINE AND THE CORPSE**

Hopefully none of those pilgrims came in search of St Valentine. The city authorities had killed him off centuries earlier. A Roman priest who 'assisted [Christian] martyrs', Valentine was beaten with clubs and battered with stones on 14 February, 269 AD. And, when that didn't do the job, people beheaded him and then beat up his corpse.

'Good work,' you might say, understandably bitter about the man's life's work. But don't be like that. He can't really be blamed for **St Valentine's Day**. This saint had nothing to do with romance that we know of; he just happened to be martyred on (and so became the Catholic namesake of) a day that was associated with love. Birds begin to pair up and mate around 14 February, so Europeans had long considered it a special day for romance. A time to wear your heart on your sleeve, or at least take off someone's pants.

**APHRODISIAC AND HER EROTIC SON**

This isn't always easy. In Greek mythology, Eros's job is to meddle in affairs of the heart, not necessarily to make them run smoothly. The source of the word **erotic**, Eros's quiver holds two types of arrows. Golden ones with dove feathers arouse love, but next to them sit arrows made of lead, with owl feathers. When they strike, they cause indifference.

Perhaps that owl-arrow's struck you? Sometimes when you've had a long day at work, you just want to watch the news rather than attend to matters of love. But if you find yourself watching the news all the time—or perhaps even sitting through *Two and a Half Men*—you may need an **aphrodisiac**.

For this useful invention, the sexually inadequate everywhere can presumably thank some scientist. For the name, however,

Aphrodite and Eros: an intimate portrait of mother and son

tip your hat to Eros's mother, the mighty Aphrodite. This Greek goddess of sexual rapture was born after somebody cut off another god's testicles and hurled them into the sea. They 'were carried over the sea a long time and white foam ("aphros") arose from the immortal flesh. With it a girl grew'.

Not the sexiest start to life, you might think, but it seems that Aphrodite was wildly desirable, and all the gods wanted to fight for her hand. So the king of the gods, Zeus, quickly married her off to the most peaceable of them—who would look away while she shagged the rest.

**HOW TO TANTALISE KING TANTALUS**

Zeus was full of these sorts of good ideas—but inviting King Tantalus to dinner wasn't one of them. A king of Phrygia (in modern-day Turkey), Tantalus decided that such a special banquet required a very special offering—a nice bottle of red just wouldn't do. So he killed his son, chopped, boiled and garnished the corpse, then served it up on a fancy plate.

The dish was not a hit. Horrified, the gods decided that such a special gesture required a very special punishment: temptation without satisfaction. They placed Tantalus in a pool of water for eternity, just below a sweet-smelling branch of fruit. Whenever he tried to reach for the fruit, the branch would move away. And whenever he tried to take a drink, the water would recede.

King Tantalus being tantalised

Doesn't that sound *tantalising*?

**THE GOD
WITH THE
GIANT
WILLY**

Cursed with 'ugliness and foul-mindedness', Priapus was less tantalising. But on the upside, he did have an enormous penis (permanently erect, for your added convenience). The medical term *priapism* — covering men who definitely don't need an aphrodisiac — is named for this minor rustic god. Notorious for attempting to rape a nymph (only to be 'thwarted by an ass' when its loud braying ruined the mood), Priapus was the divine protector of livestock, fruit plants and gardens. And, yes, willies.

Priapus, the ever priapic

**PLATO'S
PLATONIC
LOVE**

If all this willy talk seems a bit stomach-churning, perhaps ***Platonic love*** is the best option for you. Life would be so much easier if we all kept our clothes on and just played board games in a cosy pub.

Only it probably wouldn't be. 'Amor platonicus', as the Renaissance creators of the term first phrased it, is actually a fairly gruelling process, involving deep and constant consideration of the spiritual. It means not loving any person in particular but loving love in general; appreciating beauty, truth and goodness and thinking about them all nonstop.

Or something along those lines, anyway. The Florentines who thought up the term got it from a passage in Plato.

# ADVENTUROUS WORDS

**A PERFECT MATCH: THE SADIST AND THE MASOCHIST**

Some urges are best repressed. In the novel *The 120 Days of Sodom*, for example, four sexually liberated men decide to get together and hire a castle. They use it to imprison several prostitutes, teenagers and old ladies — and spend a few months raping and torturing their captives, then killing them, one by one. 'Sensual excess drives out pity in a man,' declared the author. 'It is always by way of pain that one arrives at pleasure.'

That author, of course, was the Marquis de Sade (1740–1814). Five foot two, fat and a 'fanatic of vice', he liked to write about paedophilia, necrophilia, bestiality and incest. No book, the Marquis felt, was ever truly complete if at least one character didn't become a sex slave in a monastery.

An illustration from *The Prosperity of Vice* by the Marquis de Sade

**The masochistic Leopold von Sacher-Masoch**

It's a pity that that **sadist** never met Leopold von Sacher-Masoch (1836–1895); they would have made a perfect couple. For while de Sade liked inflicting pain, Leo loved to experience it. A distinguished Austrian academic, he would be remembered for his progressive views on anti-Semitism and women's rights if he hadn't taken one woman's rights too far.

In 1869, Sacher-Masoch and his mistress signed a contract that made him her willing slave. For six months, the academic promised, he would 'comply unreservedly with every one of her desires and commands'. For her part, she undertook to 'wear furs as often as possible, especially when she is in a cruel mood …' and make good use of her nail-studded whip.

The next six months became the basis of Sacher-Masoch's novel, *Venus in Furs*—and, ultimately, of the term **masochism** as well. 'Man is the one who desires, woman the one who is desired,' it contends. 'The wise woman knows how to make him her subject, her slave, her toy, and how to betray him with a smile in the end.'

Not, you might think, the best attitude to take into a relationship—and, as it happens, you might be right. Sacher-Masoch went through quite a few wives. And the last one put him in an asylum.

## THE SODOMITES OF SODOM

Another good way to harm yourself is to step out of the closet: history is full of violent homophobes.

Take God, for example. He seemed to forget about the whole 'love thy neighbour' thing when it came to Sodom and Gomorrah, two ancient cities where 'sin was grievous'. Instead, we read, 'the Lord rained brimstone and fire … out of heaven, and he overthrew those cities, and all of the plain, and all the inhabitants of the city'. Clearly not a fan of **sodomy**.

**THE LESBIANS WHO SLEPT WITH MEN**

The first *lesbians*, luckily, were a little bit more discreet. In fact, they were so discreet that they probably weren't even lesbians. The term comes to us from Lesbos, a large Greek island near the Turkish coast. In the 7th century BC it was home to Sappho, a female poet who founded a school of young women dedicated to the cult of Aphrodite, goddess of love.

In theory, this meant that they sat around and wrote love poems. And in practice, that's probably what they did. There's actually no evidence that any more than the usual amount of homosexuality was happening on Lesbos—and, indeed, far from being *Sapphic*, Sappho may have had a husband and son. But get a bunch of girls together and men's imaginations will do the rest.

**BUGGERY IN BULGARIA**

Get a bunch of heretics together and the Catholic Church will kill them.

The Bogomils were a medieval sect of Bulgarians who were unimpressed by the pope in Rome. True Christianity, they believed, was something a lot more like early Christianity, when there wasn't such an all-powerful church. People should try to form their own individual relationships with God, the Bogomils said, instead of just mindlessly worshipping Him in whatever ways Rome required.

Naturally, Rome then required the Bogomils to shut up. All the usual methods were employed to achieve this—torture, murder, imprisonment, slander—and it so happened that one slander stuck. Since 'heretics' were routinely associated with 'vice', the Church announced that the Bogomils were gay. Depraved, degenerate sinners who would probably sleep with the devil if they weren't so busy worshipping him.

And almost a thousand years later, people are still saying the same thing. Ever wondered why we use the word *bugger*?

Masturbation is another good way to annoy the pope. You don't even have to do it in a church.

Onan supposedly did it in the Bible 'and the thing which he did displeased the Lord: wherefore he slew him'. **Onanism** has been a term for masturbation ever since, but a closer reading reveals that it shouldn't be. In the story, Onan's brother, Er, dies and their father forces him to marry Er's wife. The idea was that, by having children, they would preserve Er's family line, but Onan wasn't so keen on it. 'So whenever he lay with his brother's wife, he spilled his semen on the ground to keep from producing offspring for his brother.'

So not masturbation at all, in fact. Someone probably twisted the tale to prove how much God disapproved of the practice.

Narcissus, on the other hand, probably *did* masturbate. He found himself pretty hot. **Narcissism**, of course, is named after this vain youth from Greek mythology—a raven-haired, pouty-lipped and firm-buttocked hunter who left a trail of broken hearts in his wake.

Narcissus

All this womanising didn't make him very popular with the gods, however. And matters came to a head when one paramour committed suicide (the flighty Narcissus having sent them a sword, with instructions to 'Prove your love!'). So the gods punished this adorable hunk of man flesh by forcing him to adore himself. At a clear spring in Thespiae, Narcissus caught sight of his reflection for the first time—and, entranced, he couldn't turn away. Most versions of the myth then have him slowly dying of starvation. But we all know he would have had a wank first.

*Adonis* too, probably. This name for a strapping young super-hunk also comes from a handsome hunter in Greek mythology. It's said that two goddesses, Aphrodite and Persephone, both hungered after Adonis, and so decided to split the meal. He was forced to spend a third of every year with each of them, and the remaining third with whomever he chose.

He never chose to spend it with the **gorgons**. Nowadays a byword for hideousness, the three mythical sisters Medusa, Euryale and Stheno can best be described as an acquired taste (not unlike gorgonzola). If you like giant fangs, scaly necks and coiled snakes in the place of hair, then you'd *love* the gorgons. If not, best to stay away.

**THE KING WHO LOVED HIS MUM**

Not that the gorgons were the worst shag in Greek mythology. That honour goes to Jocasta, the Queen of Thebes—if only from the point of view of her son. One of those classic 'mistaken identity' yarns, Sophocles's play *Oedipus Rex* sees the title character unwittingly murder his father, and then hop into bed with his mum.

When everyone's true identity is revealed at play's end, not everyone takes it well. Queen Jocasta immediately hangs herself. Oedipus, not to be outdone, takes a brooch from one of his mother's dresses, and plunges it deep in his eyes.

Sigmund Freud would have found this odd. That psychologist thought that *all* little boys want to kill their father and have sex with their mother, which would have made Oedipus a lucky guy. 'Being in love with the one parent and hating the other are among the essential constituents of our psychic development,' Freud wrote (one would hope after his parents had died). 'This discovery is confirmed by a legend that has come down to us from classical antiquity … the legend of King Oedipus,' and his **Oedipus complex**.

# TAWDRY WORDS

**A CITY BUILT ON HOOKERS**

Long before *Sex and the City*, New York City was built on sex. Most scholars believe that **hookers** got that nickname from Corlear's Hook, a coastal area on the Lower East Side of Manhattan that has long been lost to landfill.

But back in the 19th century, it was lost to depravity instead. Separated from the city proper by 'high, uncultivated and rough hills', this hook-shaped piece of marshy waterfront was a veritable 'resort for the lewd and abandoned'. Particularly popular with sex-starved sailors, the streets of Corlear's Hook 'abounded every night with … prostitutes'.

**THE HARLOT OF NORMANDY**

At least they didn't call them **harlots**. That pejorative term probably comes from an Old German phrase meaning 'army loiterer' ('hari-lots' could make a pretty deutschmark following soldiers) — but a more interesting story concerns William the Conqueror.

Also known as 'William the Bastard', this medieval warlord had a father named Robert the Magnificent, a blueblooded duke of Normandy. Noble scion of a noble house and wise ruler of his people. But his mother was not so magnificent. She was Arlette, an unmarried tanner's daughter. The story goes that Robert was cantering through a village one day, saw her bathing naked and thought 'Mon Dieu!' Medieval folk thought this a shameful tale, and called any loose woman an 'arlette'.

**WHY YOUR MUM'S A HUSSY AND YOUR SISTER'S A WENCH**

But whether or not Arlette was a harlot, no-one could call her a *hussy*. This is because she was unmarried. The word 'hussy' is a contraction of 'housewife' and for a long time that's all it meant. Not a bad housewife or a shameless housewife or a brazen housewife but *any* housewife. Just a married woman who lived in a house.

Seventeenth-century England was a land of subtle social distinctions, however, and language was a good way to express them. So snobbery slowly took hold of the word, making it mean a woman of low rank. And then, about a century later, sexism had a go too.

It had long since affected the meaning of *wench*. In the 13th century, not even the most pure-minded, delicately scrupled bishop would have objected if a hussy gave birth to a wench. All this meant, after all, was that a married women had given birth to a *girl*. Which was not, of course, as good as having a boy, but nonetheless formed part of God's plan.

By the 14th century, however, everyone had realised that there was nothing good about being a girl, so 'wench' came to mean something bad.

**JEZEBEL AND THE DOG'S BREAKFAST**

A *jezebel*, on the other hand, is an *exceptionally* bad girl—the sort of brazen, shameless floozy who not only has sex (gasp!) but has been known to enjoy it too.

The original jezebel, strangely enough, was Jezebel, a Phoenician princess in the Old Testament. This 'wanton woman' spent her time sponsoring false prophets in Israel, in between bouts of 'whoredom and witchcraft'.

Bad, very bad. But you'll be glad to know she get her just desserts. Enraged by the way she had 'painted her eyes and adorned her head', some soldiers threw her out of a window. Her corpse was trampled by horses and eaten by dogs, so that all that remained was 'the skull and the feet and the palms of her hands'.

A tasty Jezebel ... being eaten by dogs

**WHY PEEPING TOM WENT BLIND**

You'd hope that Lady Godiva's body was in better shape. This 11th-century noblewoman is best remembered for riding naked through the streets of Coventry. True or not, the story goes that Godiva was a champion of the people, constantly petitioning her husband, the Earl of Mercia, on behalf of the poor and oppressed. But she didn't make much progress when it came to one particularly oppressive tax. The earl simply refused to reduce it, no matter how hard she nagged.

Eventually—and, it's presumed, jokingly—the earl suggested a deal. He would agree to cut the tax if Godiva rode through town on a white horse … wearing nothing but a smile on her face. So that's what she did. First, however, she issued a canny proclamation: all the townspeople had to stay indoors, with their shutters firmly closed.

But who can resist checking out a nude noblewoman? Not Tom, that's for sure. The town's tailor supposedly bored a hole in his shutters in order to catch a sneaky peek. His reward was to be struck blind—God doesn't like a **Peeping Tom**.

Archbishop Nosey Parker

### ARCHBISHOP NOSEY PARKER

On the other hand, God *does* like a *nosey parker*. Or at least, so we must assume. This term most likely comes from one of His chosen representatives, an officious Archbishop of Canterbury named Matthew Parker (1504–1575), who had a rather lengthy nose.

Appointed by Elizabeth I to manage the Church of England, Parker introduced a vast number of administrative and ceremonial reforms. And then he introduced some more. The good Bish was notorious for zealously micromanaging every single detail of clerical life. He was forever asking employees what they were doing, and noting down every word that they said.

### THE SAD TALE OF ST TAWDRY

Another one of God's favourite children might have welcomed some advice, but by Parker's time it was all too late. St Audrey (636–679) did one thing wrong in an otherwise chaste and righteous life, and paid a terrible price.

Born in what's now Cambridgeshire, Audrey was the daughter of a local king and a humble servant of our Lord. Serving God, for Audrey, meant keeping her pants firmly fastened: she made a vow of virginity and somehow managed to keep it, despite getting married twice. Forced to flee her second husband, who had begun to get a little sexually frustrated, she ended up founding a monastery on the island of Ely, and was made a saint a few years after her death.

To commemorate Audrey's sainthood, the Ely islanders used to hold an annual fair in her name. One of the main attractions at St Audrey's Fair was a local product called 'St Audrey's lace': a fairly cheap and gaudy-looking scarf that tended to fall apart after a couple of wears. And in that fluid, ever-changing medium that is the English language, phrases can fall apart too. So 'St Audrey lace' slowly became 't'Audrey' or *tawdry* lace. And nowadays, any product (or, indeed, sexual preference) can be described as 'tawdry' if it seems tacky or cheap.

**SLEAZY CLOTH AND VULGAR ROMANS**

You wouldn't get such shoddy fabric in Silesia. Once an eastern province of Germany, and nowadays part of Poland, Silesia used to be famous for its high-quality, beautiful linen. For English-speakers in the 17th century, *sleazy* cloth meant good cloth.

Until, that is, it turned bad. Capitalism being capitalism, rival manufacturers started to pretend that *their* linen came from Silesia too. Customers ended up being hoodwinked so often—paying top dollar for bottom-of-the-barrel products—that 'sleazy' became a synonym for 'shoddy'. The current sense of the word ('squalid, sordid, vulgar') evolved fairly naturally from there.

For the origins of *vulgar* itself, however, we must go further back in time, to the glories of ancient Rome. Only we have to ignore the glorious bit. 'Vulgus' is Latin for 'the common people'. The smelly, unwashed hordes who didn't win wars and wear wreaths, but just dug fields, planted stuff and died.

# INTOLERANT WORDS

Once upon a time, no Greek could be a *barbarian*, however much they might grunt or fart. Someone from Athens could dress in fur, live in a cave and use the wrong kind of fork for his fish course, yet still be considered a wholly civilised chap.

This is because the word comes from 'baraophononoi', an ancient Greek term meaning 'a babbler'. And 'babblers', as far as those toga-wearers were concerned, were any and all people who didn't speak Greek.

So why, then, does 'barbarian' now mean not just any old foreigner, but specifically those shaggy-haired Germanic tribal types who tore down ancient Rome? The answer is racism. To not be Greek, the ancient Greeks thought, was to not be sophisticated, so 'baraophononoi' slowly came to mean the most primitive foreigners—the ones who didn't read or write or nibble the right kind of cheese with their wine. And during the 5th century, no foreigners were considered more primitive than the tribal hordes stomping towards Rome.

One of those tribes was the Vandals: 80,000 hairy-chested Scandinavians who had already ransacked North Africa, France and Spain, plundering whatever they pleased. In 455, famously, it pleased them to plunder Rome. And while they could only spend a few days there, they did manage to pack in a lot of senseless destruction: burning buildings, smashing statues and destroying works of art in what became known as 'the sack of Rome'.

Unfortunate but not unusual—over the next thousand years or so, Rome was actually sacked quite often. But with the 14th century came the Renaissance: a period where a bunch of influential artists and thinkers decided to try and renew the cultural glories of ancient Rome. One of them put the blame for the thousand-year-long 'Dark Ages' firmly at the feet of the Vandals. The wanton destruction of 'civilised' things, he said, should henceforth be known as *vandalism*.

**WHY
GOTHIC
ARCHITEC-
TURE ISN'T
GOTHIC**

But when it came to denigrating barbarians, Renaissance intellectuals didn't like to stop there. A tribe called the Goths got a bad review too. Hailing from Poland and Germany, these Goths also did a bit to bring down Rome—looting here, raiding there and killing everywhere—before dispersing all over Europe, blending into various other cultures, and more or less ceasing to exist.

During the Renaissance, however, the word 'Goth' was dredged up from the dead. Snooty types despised the distinctly un-Roman architecture of the Dark Ages (wanting to replace it with 'classical' arches and the like), so they took to calling medieval castles 'Gothic'. Not because the Goths had made them (they hadn't) but because the word helped express how barbaric such buildings were—how uncultured and crude and rude.

So that's why we have *Gothic* architecture. And here's why we have 'Gothic' culture. In 1764, Horace Walpole wrote what was probably the world's first horror novel. Set in a crumbling, spooky ruin of a Gothic castle, filled with vampires, graveyards and ghosts, *The Castle of Otranto* led people to associate Gothic architecture with horror and doom and gloom. Eventually the word 'Gothic' got that association too.

## THE PHILISTINES OF JENA

So there you have it: the dark side of Enlightenment. When snooty intellectuals don't want to seem *philistine*, racism is what usually results.

Want more proof? Ok, then: 'philistine' is a racist word too. It first described, if you recall your Old Testament, a Bronze Age tribe from the Gaza strip. Possibly hailing from Cyprus, Goliath & Co lived in what was then known as Philistia—and they didn't really get along with their neighbours. Just like their descendants in the area, the Palestinians, they were constantly bothering the Israelites. (To be fair, the warmaking was mutual.)

And that's about all there is to the story: the Philistines were no more or less 'unintellectual' than anyone else. Their name only acquired its present meaning in the 17th century, thanks to an incident in the German university town of Jena. At the time, there was a great deal of hostility between the students and the townspeople, which occasionally broke out into violence. So a local preacher delivered a sermon in which he likened the town's situation to the Gaza strip. His speech didn't do much to heal the rift, but it did at least inspire a new insult. The students took to calling any 'enemy' of the university a 'philister'—and the term eventually came to mean any enemy of learning per se.

## BOHEMIANS AREN'T FROM BOHEMIA

What that uni really needed was some *bohemian* students. Art lovers, rather than fighters, who would much sooner have some group sex than get involved in a pointless brawl. So would that have meant a foreign exchange program? Bohemia is a region in the Czech Republic, after all, so a 'Bohemian' is technically someone from there. But are all of them really painters and poets? How many actually starve in garrets or wear their hair all dirty and long? What makes Bohemians so bohemian?

Nothing, really. We now know that the Romany people came to Eastern Europe from India in around the 11th century, and then gradually made their way west. But Western Europeans didn't know this at the time. In France, it was thought that these rather groovy vagabonds—these players of kooky music and wearers of colourful clothes—actually came from Eastern Europe. Specifically, from around Bohemia.

Oh those French. The English would never have been so stupid. *They* thought that the Romany people came from Egypt. And therefore called them **gypsies**.

**WHY CANNIBALS ARE MIS-UNDERSTOOD**

Such misunderstandings abound, sad to say. It's hard enough to understand your own culture sometimes, let alone anyone else's.

Christopher Columbus, for example, was a little confused by the Carib Indians, who lived near what became known as the **Caribbean Sea**. (Though he tended to get confused rather a lot, actually. If you've ever wondered why the Americas have **Red Indians** and the **West Indies**, it's because Columbus thought he'd landed somewhere near Delhi.)

Anyway, what confused the easily confused Columbus was the fact that (instead of eating something logical, like curry) the Carib Indians ate human flesh. Never more than the occasional nibble of a much-revered enemy, mind you. A slice that, once nibbled, would be spat back out. For the 'carribals', the snack was a way of honouring, and hopefully absorbing, their enemy's bravery— something they also hoped to achieve by decorating their house with his bones.

**Some Carribals**

Columbus's men saw all the bones, however, and assumed that they were seeing the leftovers of some hearty meals. So when they headed back to Europe, they brought a new word with them: *cannibal*.

**MONGOLOIDS, CAUCASIANS AND THE GERMAN RACE SCIENTIST**

Today's Carib Indians don't much care for the term, and I'm told that Mongolians don't really like *mongoloid*. For that one, they can blame a German race scientist (a job that's lost some of its social cachet in recent years). Johann Blumenbach (1752–1840) divided humans into five races based on the shape of their skulls. One of these impeccably scientific categories was 'the Mongolian or yellow race', people from 'beyond the Ganges and below the river Amoor'.

So far, so blah. But in 1866, an Englishman named John Langdon Down enters our story. He discovered what we now call **Down syndrome**, but modestly preferred to use the term 'mongoloidism'. 'I have for some time [wanted to develop] a classification of the feeble-minded, by arranging them around various ethnic standards,' wrote the enlightened Doc. With their 'shortened foreheads, prominent cheeks, deep-set eyes and slightly apish nose', he decided that 'a very large number of congenital idiots [resemble] typical Mongols'.

Charming. Another one of Blumenbach's race classifications, should you be wondering, was **Caucasian**, a term that essentially means white people. Each race of human being, said Professor Head-Shape, had been at its pure-blooded best when God first created it. The 'inbreeding' brought on by migration, then, was quite bad news, genetically speaking.

With this theory in mind, Blumenbach cast his eyes around for the best-looking white folk, and decided that he'd found them in the Caucasus Mountains, an area near the Caspian Sea. Since that region 'produces the most beautiful race of men', he reasoned, it was most likely where whites first lived.

**NEANDER-
THAL MAN
WROTE
POETRY**

The **Neanderthals** were a less beautiful race of men, at least to our *Homo sapiens* eyes. But it's worth noting that these hulking, hairy 'pre-humans' actually owe their name to a poet. A really poncy poet, in fact: one of those spindly aesthetes who spent their days prancing amongst daffodils, singing the praises of morning dew. 'See how He hath everywhere / Made this earth so rich and fair,' proceeds one typical Joachim Neander (1650–1680) ode. 'Hill and vale and fruitful land / All things living show His hand.'

Lovely, if you like that sort of thing, and it appears that the people of the Germany's Düssel River region did. At least, they named the limestone canyon where Neander did his flower-gazing 'Neanderthal' ('the Neander Valley') in his honour.

Daffodils don't pay the bills, however, and a few centuries later, some soulless miners dug up that hill and vale and fruitful land. And found a set of bones. First thought to belong to a bear, they were eventually found to belong to an entirely new species: good old Neanderthal Man.

# WARLIKE WORDS

**ARMED BUT
ARMLESS:
THE
PISTOLS OF
PISTOIA**

'We must realise that no arsenal, or no weapon in the arsenals of the world, is so formidable as the will and moral courage of free men and women,' declared US president Ronald Reagan in his inaugural address. Someone shot him a few months later.

Reagan survived the attack but in Pistoia, people often didn't. Described as 'enemies of heaven' by Michelangelo, the people in this famously violent Italian region liked to give war a chance.

In one illustrative story, two Pistoiese children were playing with swords when, inevitably, one got hurt. The uninjured kid dutifully apologised to his friend's father—but the apology was ignored. 'Iron, not words, is the remedy for sword wounds,' said the father, and cut off the child's right hand.

I guess the kid was lucky he didn't get shot. Pistoia was naturally a big market for *pistols*—and that may well be why they're so named.

**MORE GUN FUN**

*Carbine rifles*, as good segues would have it, are also named after a region in Italy. Located at the 'toe' of that country's 'boot', Calabria had a pretty groundbreaking cavalry in the 16th century. Armies all over Europe liked to recruit Calabrian horsemen, who would arm themselves with a distinctive short rifle.

Of course, these early rifles had one little problem: they could quite often jam or break. In the middle of a fight, this could turn into quite a big problem, pushy enemy soldiers not being inclined to wait while you painstakingly gathered up more gunpowder, cleaned out the barrel and tweaked and twiddled this and that. Several dead riflemen later, a solution arrived from Bayonne, where hunters had long used a *bayonet*. With a long steel blade on the end of his rifle, a soldier with a faulty firearm could now stab people as well as shoot them.

For all the 'bayonets' and 'carbine rifles' of this world, however, most firearms aren't actually named after places. It's mainly people who live on as guns. A woman was so honoured with Germany's WWI gun, the *Big Bertha* (Bertha Krupp was the granddaughter of Alfred Krupp, the manufacturer) but most of the names come from male manufacturers who instead chose to honour themselves. Hence we have the (Richard) *Gatling gun* and the (Henry) *Derringer*, the (Samuel) *Colt revolver* and the (Paul) *Mauser* and the (Georg) *Luger*. John T Thompson, slightly less obviously, gave us the *Tommy gun* and Usiel Gal came up with the *Uzi*.

**FOOD PARCELS AND MOLOTOV COCKTAILS**

Having a weapon named after you isn't always intended as an honour, however. Take the **Molotov cocktail**, a simple homemade bomb made out of a bottle filled with petrol and a fuse. Its name comes from Stalin's foreign minister, Vyacheslav Molotov (1890–1986), a man Trotsky described as 'mediocrity personified'. When the Soviet Union started bombing Finland in 1939, one of Molotov's many diplomatic masterstrokes was to inform the wider world that it wasn't actually dropping bombs at all. No, silly. They were food parcels.

The Finns who weren't being blown to bits by these food parcels decided to fight back with some homemade bombs. They satirically dubbed them 'cocktails', as they would 'go with all the food'.

**LIEUTENANT HENRY SHRAPNEL**

The problem with all bombs, however, is that, every now and then, they miss. And, really, what's the point of a weapon if it doesn't lead to pain and death?

In 1804, a British lieutenant called Henry Shrapnel (1761–1842) nobly solved this problem. By inventing, yes, **shrapnel**. Now soldiers could throw hollowed-out bombs that were filled with little lead pellets; even if they missed, they'd scatter their bits far and wide, ensuring that someone somewhere would at least get maimed. He was quickly promoted to lieutenant-colonel.

**FACING DEATH WITH A SMILE: THE FIRST BRITISH TOMMY**

Shrapnel, of course, is not the only way to cause pain and death. 'Fighting' during WWI, for example, basically involved walking very, very slowly towards a machine gun while it spread your organs over a muddy field.

England's **Tommies** were particularly good fighters—but where exactly did they get that name? The tradition probably began with an 1815 War Office publication that showed how soldiers should fill out their pocket book. In the space where they were supposed to put their signature, it provided the sample signature 'Tommy Atkins'.

Which leads to the question: was there a real-life Tommy Atkins? The tentative answer is 'yes'. The story goes that he impressed the Duke of Wellington one day by dying with an appropriately patriotic cheerfulness. 'It's all right, sir. It's all in a day's work,' were Private Atkins's final words.

**CAUSING DEATH WITH A SMILE: THE FIRST GERMAN HUNS**

German patriots weren't called Tommies, of course. They *killed* Tommies. But before that, they kept busy killing Chinese people. In 1900, Kaiser Wilhelm II dispatched his forces east to help deal with China's Boxer Rebellion. His farewell speech to the troops may not have been a public relations masterstroke — likening, as it did, the German soldiers to a famously savage horde of tribesmen. 'When you meet the enemy, he will be defeated!' the bullish Kaiser bellowed. 'No quarter will be given! No prisoners will be taken! Those who fall into your hands are forfeit to you! Just as a thousand years ago, the Huns under their King Etzel made a name for themselves that make them appear awe-inspiring in tradition and myth, so shall you establish the name of Germans in China for a thousand years, so that a Chinese will never again dare to look askance at a German.'

The Kaiser's speech was widely reported, and didn't do much for Germany's image. The land of Hegel and Heidegger came to be seen as the land of the **Hun**.

**DIGGERS, PIONEERS AND HATCHET MEN**

Australia's soldiers have also had a few nicknames — 'ANZACs', 'Colonials', 'foul-mouthed hooligans' — but the most famous is undoubtedly **digger**. While this slang term was clearly linked to their duties digging tunnels and trenches, it's thought to have begun well before WWI, in the Victorian goldfields of the 1850s.

Through the process of 'working together in the otherwise solitary bush', as one contemporary observer put it, 'habits of mutual helpfulness arise, and these elicit gratitude, and that leads on to regard. Men under these circumstances often stand by one another through thick and thin'. To be a 'digger', then, was to be a good bloke. 'A man for whom freedom, comradeship, a wide tolerance, and a strong sense of the innate worth of man count for more than all the kingdoms of the world, and all the glory in them.'

Not everyone who dug was 'a digger', however. In the US, he might have been called a **hatchet man**. Nowadays used to describe any sort of goon who does their employer's dirty work, this name once belonged to a specific sort of soldier who quite literally worked in dirt. Employed by the US military in the 19th century, hatchet men would use their hatchets to fell trees and build fortifications, and their spades to dig trenches and tunnels.

They would have been better off working in Europe. There the soldiers who marched ahead of the army to build fortifications were given what now seems a much better name. **Pioneers**.

**BEING A DIEHARD WAS QUITE HARD**

If a soldier wants a *really* good nickname, however, they must be prepared to suffer for it. The 57th, a British regiment of foot soldiers, earned a really good nickname in 1811. Surrounded and outnumbered by Frenchmen on horseback, thanks to a tactical blunder, the regiment was on the verge of meekly surrendering, instead of dying needlessly for the cause.

Then something happened. The regiment's leader was shot. He tumbled, dying, into the mud, blood spurting from his neck, his body convulsing from pain. No surprises there—it was happening to everyone—but the colonel's fighting spirit stayed alive and well. As blood flowed and numbers dwindled, he lay there repeating 'Die hard 57th! Die hard!', and so die hard they did. Of the 570 troops,

422 were killed or wounded. But the French, being French, eventually retreated, and *diehard* became the regiment's nickname.

A few decades later, when the upper echelons of British army proved stubbornly resistant to reform, they were called the 'diehards' too—and the term eventually came to mean anyone who will not be swayed from a belief.

**TWO STONE-WALLERS**    General Thomas Jackson (1824–1863) would not be swayed from *any-thing*—or such, at least, became his reputation after the Battle of Bull Run. This crucial encounter in America's Civil War was going badly for the outnumbered Confederate soldiers—all of them, that is, except Jackson's troops, who were holding firm against all odds. Another general pointed this out to his men—shouting, 'There is Jackson standing like a stone wall. Let us determine to die here, and we will conquer.'

**Stonewall Jackson looking stony**

They did *not* conquer, as it happens, but Jackson was renamed 'Stonewall Jackson' and to *stonewall* became a handy verb.

Jackson certainly wasn't the first general to stonewall. The tactic of not budging either backwards or forwards dates back to ancient Rome. In around 230 BC, the Eternal City was looking rather temporary, thanks to a crazy Carthaginian general named Hannibal. Having marched not only troops but elephants over Italy's icy Alps, this unstoppable warrior was storming towards Rome and smashing every army the city sent out to fight him.

General Fabius's (280–203 BC) solution? Stop sending Hannibal armies to annihilate, and instead fight a war of attrition. That canny soldier simply set up Rome's defences and waited for the enemy to leave.

Two thousand years later, the likes of George Bernard Shaw, HG Wells and Virginia Woolf joined a left-wing group founded on much the same principles. Socialism, they felt, should be achieved by gradual attrition, not sudden revolution. A little more conversation and a little less action. 'For the right moment you must wait, as Fabius did most patiently,' read the first pamphlet of the **Fabian Society**.

**OOPS. THE FIRST PYRRHIC VICTORY**

Pyrrhus (318–272 BC) could have done with some of that caution. This king of Epirus in northern Greece, he was, like Hannibal, no fan of Rome. And, like Hannibal, he was anxious for glory, leading his troops to battle against the empire in 279 BC.

They won, somewhat miraculously, but the triumph came at a cost. While Rome still boasted dozens of legions, this small-time king had lost more than half of his men. 'Another such victory and we are lost!' he ruefully exclaimed, thus giving us that neat term, *pyrrhic victory*.

**THE LETHAL RIVER OF LETHARGY**

Being Greek, Pyrrhus would have believed in the afterworld. According to Greek tradition, five rivers feed into this ancient abode of the dead, including Styx ('the river of hate') and Phlegethon ('the river of fire'). But the one that concerns us here is Lethe. A 'lazy stream' that flowed under a mountain that the sun's 'beams can never reach', its name means 'the river of oblivion' and its job was to reconcile people to death. When they drank Lethe's water, the dead would become drowsy, and then slowly forget all about their past life.

Western civilisation, on the other hand, tends to remember its past life. We recall the River Lethe whenever we say *lethargy* (meaning a state of drowsiness) or indeed *lethal* (causing death).

**A HOLIDAY AT THE MORGUE**

However much we might honour the Greeks in our language, we don't have much time for their theories. Dead people, we know, rarely end up in a river. They generally get bunged in a *morgue*.

Once upon a time, however, this could only be said of dead French people. All morgues get their name from the Paris Morgue, a now long-gone building that got its name from a verb meaning 'to stare'. That morgue, however, wasn't the sort of boarded-up bureaucratic institution we associate with the term these days. It was no shiny clinic reserved for forensic pathologists in bright white coats.

The Morgue's halls were instead filled with sightseers, all keen to stare at the latest corpse. Built as a house for unidentified bodies in 1804, in the hope that someone would come along and claim them, the Morgue was one of France's most popular tourist attractions by early 1805. Around 10,000 visitors came along every day to see the naked rows of the dead. When it was finally closed to the public in 1907, several local merchants went out of business.

**CANNIBALS, INCEST AND THE FIRST MAUSOLEUM**

King Mausolus went out of business in about 353 BC. A minor, war-mongering governor of Caria (a region in what's now Turkey), this monarch didn't do anything particularly noteworthy with his life, but in death he really came into his own.

When he died, it's said that his wife (and, um, sister) was so upset that she drank a little bit of his ashes with all her daily meals, before dying herself from grief (and an ash-heavy diet). A rather more lasting expression of her anguish, however, was an enormous marble monument she built in her husband's memory: a showy, statue-filled super-tomb 30 metres high and 76 metres wide that became one of the Seven Wonders of the Ancient World.

We can't know if it really was so wonderful, as it was destroyed in an earthquake in 1304. But we do know that it gave us a wonderful word: *mausoleum*, meaning an ornate tomb.

## A DEADLINE YOU'D RATHER MISS

Camp Sumter definitely wasn't wonderful. 'There is so much filth about the camp that it is terrible trying to live here,' wrote one inmate of that Confederate military prison in the US Civil War. 'With sunken eyes, blackened countenances from pitch pine smoke, rags, and disease, the men look sickening. The air reeks with nastiness.' Nonetheless, Sumter did end up functioning as a tomb of sorts. Almost 13,000 Northern soldiers died there from disease, malnutrition or other causes.

One of those other causes was a small fence around the perimeter of the camp. It stood about 6 metres from the enormous main wall, which had several 'pigeon roosts' of sentries standing guard. Should a prisoner cross the *deadline* marked out by this small fence, the sentries looking on from the main wall would immediately shoot him down.

The deadline at Camp Sumpter

## ARMAGED-DON OUT OF ISRAEL

Of course, we all have a rather pressing deadline hanging over our head these days: *Armageddon*. According to some readings of the Bible, the Messiah will one day return to earth and preside over the final battle between good and evil. Satan will be defeated (hurrah!) and dispatched into a 'bottomless pit'. According to other readings, though, Armageddon will instead involve us humans in some kind of apocalyptic war. Which will lead to all of our deaths.

Hmm … food for thought either way, really. And Israelis who live near the ancient ruins of 'Megiddo' city have even more to think about than the rest of us, as it's on their turf that the war will be waged. 'Armageddon' literally means 'Fort of Megiddo'. Located on the Via Maris, a sort of ancient superhighway that once connected Egypt with the Levant, Megiddo may have hosted more battles than any site in history. Assyrians, Canaanites, Egyptians, Greeks, Israelites, Persians, Philistines and Romans all conquered the strategically vital city at one point or another, and then managed to get conquered themselves. The result was that, when people wrote the Bible, the name was more or less synonymous with war.

**DEATH BEFORE PORK! A MACABRE MUM'S LOVE FOR HER SONS**

If you think this whole Armageddon thing sounds a little *macabre*, I'm sorry but you're wrong. It sounds a little 'Maccabee'.

The Maccabees were an ancient Jewish family who took their Judaism very seriously. Legend has it that they were all arrested by some tyrant who sadistically tried to make them eat pork. Fearing God more than any man, they refused, so he tortured and killed each of them, one by one. The mother, we're told, 'was the most remarkable of all, and deserves to be remembered with special honour. She watched her seven sons die in the space of a single day, yet she bore it bravely because she put her trust in the Lord'.

Mmm … heartwarming. Anyway, come the 14th century, someone wrote a morality play about the Maccabees. Each performance would finish with what eventually became an iconic and standalone piece of medieval theatre: the 'danse macabre', or 'dance of death'. Decidedly macabre, it involved some personification of death summoning up representatives from all walks of life—popes, princes, peasants; the rich and the poor; the old and the young—and leading them on a merry dance to the grave.

In theory, this was supposed to remind people that life is fleeting and all earthly circumstances merely temporary. In practice, it just gave us a new word.

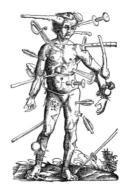

# FIGHTING WORDS

**HOULI-HAN THE HOOLIGAN**

Ireland is the land of Joyce and Yeats, Wilde and Shaw—but to that exalted list we must add some Houlihans. Less bookish than their aforementioned countrymen (unless we're talking about some kind of heavy book that you could use in a fight), the Houlihans were the sort of people who would punch a poet if they ever met one, then stab him a few times in the testicles, and set fire to his poncy beret.

This motley crew of thieves and thugs was led by a man named Patrick Houlihan. A part-time bouncer and full-time nutjob, he 'walked among his fellow men robbing them and occasionally bashing them'. 'The man must have had a forceful personality,' wrote one observer in 1899. 'It was doubtless the combination of skill and strength, a certain exuberance of lawlessness, an utter absence of scruple in his dealings, which marked him out as a leader among men … He established a cult.'

Patrick's illustrious career came to an end in jail. (He had gotten into an argument with a policeman. Which obviously meant that the policeman had to die.) But he lives on in the word *hooligan.*

## THE HOODLUMS OF SAN FRANCISCO

It's probably best not to say 'hooligan' in a dark alleyway, should you ever be surrounded by street toughs. Instead try 'Help, police!' or perhaps a 'Please don't hurt me!' Afterwards, however, while lying about the incident to your friends, you may like to use the word *hoodlum.*

Scholars can confidently trace 'hoodlum' to San Francisco, where it first appeared in 1871, but that's where their agreement ends. Some say the word came from German immigrants ('hodalump' means 'gangster' in a Bavarian dialect), others from a local gang who would yell 'huddle-'em' as a (confusing) kind of war-cry when brawling.

The oldest and most popular theory, however, is that 'hoodlum' was first used to describe another notorious San Francisco gang, one led by a burly psycho called Muldoon. A newspaper journalist wrote a series of articles about the gang, but (whether out of fear for his safety or a concern about litigation) in them spelled the thug's name backward. 'Muldoon' thus became 'Noodlum'. And then 'Hoodlum' after a subeditor mistook the 'N' for an 'H'.

## ELECTION-EERING WITH THE PLUG-UGLIES

No reporter could have done this in Baltimore. Newspaper-buyers don't want to read about the 'seilgu-gulp' gang. Spelled the right way around, for your ease and convenience, that would read the *Plug-uglies* gang—a notorious 'political club' that operated in the west side of Baltimore from 1854 till 1860.

A vital campaign tool on election days, which no corrupt politician could do without, the club's contribution to democracy involved 'bringing out the vote' by 'plugging people ugly'. Changing the minds of voters by changing their faces into a bloody mess.

The gang also dabbled in rioting, bringing the word 'plug ugly' to national attention after one particular rampage resulted in ten deaths.

**THE DUST-UPS AT DONNY-BROOK FAIR**

On the other side of the Atlantic such a disturbance might be dismissed as a ***donnybrook***. Lively exchanges of opinion are fairly common in Ireland, a land where small talk involves criticising somebody's politics, then going on to denounce their religion. And things could get particularly spirited in Donnybrook, a boggy stretch of Dublin marshland that was once home to an annual fair. First held in 1204, and closed down 650 years later (after someone invented a new concept called 'public safety'), the fair was synonymous with wild, drunken brawls. A typical day, if a police report from 1822 is anything to go by, involved 'broken

The delights of Donnybrook Fair

heads, black eyes, bloody noses, squeezed hats, singed, cut and torn inexpressibles, jocks and upper benjamins, loodies, frocks, tippets, reels and damaged leghorns, together with sundry assaults, fibbings, cross buttocks, and ground floorings too numerous to mention'.

**SKID ROW, VANCOUVER**

Ouch. But such, I guess, can be life when you're down and out on the wrong side of the tracks. Cross buttocks and singed upper benjamins are just two of many potholes when life's journey takes you to ***skid row***.

Only the people of Donnybrook weren't on skid row. That's not in Ireland, but Canada. To explain, let's backtrack 600 years or so, when skid *roads* first began to be used. Usually found in timber forests, they are basically roads made out of logs—a heap of them packed together like a raft and placed on the ground to make a path. They are used to drag (i.e. 'skid') other logs that would otherwise be too heavy to move, or too likely to sink in a marsh.

The Canadian city of Vancouver began life around one such skid road, as its first major business was a sawmill. In time, of course, that road was paved over with concrete but the area around it continued to be called 'Skid Road' or 'Skid Row'—and in increasingly disapproving tones. Forestry work, you see, is very seasonal. So with nothing else to do in the off-season, the area's loggers took to boozing, fighting and whoring. And drug use soon became popular too. Vancouver was for a long time the main port-of-entry for the North American opium supply and the area around Skid Row still has some of North America's highest rates of hepatitis and HIV.

**GHETTOS, SMELTING AND SLAG** Not the sort of thing you associate with Venice, but, actually, perhaps you should. That picturesque city isn't just home to charming canals and gondolas (all filled with shell-shocked honeymooners getting systematically fleeced). It also boasts the world's first **ghetto**.

Now used to describe any sort of overcrowded, ultra-poor urban area that's dominated by one ethnic group, 'ghetto' started out as a Venetian word for 'slag'. (Slag being 'a partially vitreous by-product of smelting ore', if that means anything to you.) And since the city's iron foundries, where such smelting took place, could all be found on the one island, it became known as 'Il Geto' too.

Enter the anti-Semites. In 1516, the city authorities decided that, rather than living wherever they pleased, all Venice's Jews should be made to live on a single island. You can probably guess which one they chose.

**THE GODDESS OF DESTRUCTION AND HER THUGS**

Such bigotry is an ugly thing, but it does have its time and place. In the 1830s, for example, British colonialists outlawed Thuggee, one of India's religious cults. They hanged 400 of its practitioners and imprisoned a few thousand for life.

'Bad,' you mutter, 'very bad. Amnesty International should write a strongly worded letter.' True, perhaps, but let's learn a bit more about this cult. Named after 'thag', a Hindustani word for 'cheat', the Thuggees worshipped Kali, the goddess of destruction, and liked to practise what she preached. Worshipping Kali, they decided, involved putting on disguises, blending into large groups of travellers and slowly winning everyone's trust. Then finding a lonely spot in which to strangle the lot of them, and quietly slipping away with the loot.

*The Guinness Book of Records* estimates that the Thuggees were responsible for the deaths of up to two million travellers, somewhat pushing the boundaries of religious tolerance. Whether or not that's true, there's no doubting that they were ***thugs***.

**Some thuggish thuggees**

**HOW TO GET SHANGHAIED INTO A PRESSGANG**

Travelling could often be unpleasant back in the day, even when there were no thugs in sight. *Pressgang*, it's worth mentioning, didn't start out as a verb. From 1664 until Napoleon was defeated in 1815, it was very much a noun.

During wartime, the British Navy often found itself short on numbers (people being strangely unwilling to toil for King and Country in return for floggings and scurvy). To solve this problem, some bright spark came up with 'impressment': a deeply unconstitutional law that allowed gangs of officials to seize random men in sea ports and press them into naval service.

Once 'pressed', we should note, you still did have a choice. You could sign up as a 'volunteer' and receive payment (such as it was). Or you could go to sea 'under protest' and receive nothing at all.

The good news, I guess, is sailors got to see the world. If you've ever wondered why someone forced to do something against their will has been *shanghaied*, it's because China was a major trading destination for British ships. Once he'd had the misfortune to stumble into a pressgang, a recalcitrant sailor often sailed to Shanghai.

**Getting pressganged**

# PEOPLE

## SHADY WORDS

*Charlatan, To fudge,
Pariah, Villain,
Blackguard, Turncoat,
Welsher, Bogus,
Smart Alec, Shyster,
Flashy, Furphy*

## STOUT-HEARTED WORDS

*Jovial, Serendipity,
Stoic, Spartan, Laconic,
Maudlin*

## INTELLIGENT WORDS

*Academia, Boffin,
Brainiac, Poindexter,
Brains trust, Muse,
Museum, Boofhead,
Drongo, Cretin,
Nincompoop, Dunce,
Silly Billy, Moron,
Ignoramus*

## SMALL-MINDED WORDS

*Bigot, Doctrinaire,
Martinet, Chauvinist,
Jingoism, Gosh,
Cor blimey, Zealot,
Fascism, Aryan, Iran,
Quisling, Redneck,
True Blue*

## MAD WORDS

*Lunatic, Dollally,
Juggernaut, Batty,
Barmy, Bedlam,
Pandemonium, Berserk,
Panic, Psychology,
Hypnotism, Mesmerise,
Svengali*

## SUBSERVIENT WORDS

*Whipping boy,
Namby-pamby,
Pandering, Quixotic,
Goody-two-shoes,
Brownie point, Toady,
Sycophant, Slave,
Maverick, Piker,
Hillbilly*

# SHADY WORDS

*I'n qui ne se présente plu*:

**THE FIRST CHARLATANS** Back in the Renaissance, medical services weren't quite what they are today. Instead of shiny hospitals, soothing drugs and nurses in crisp white uniforms, all ill people had to look forward to was leeches, followed by some more leeches, and then a long, slow, painful death.

When a patent medicine salesman in Cerreto wandered by, however, things were very different. Ill people could instead spend vast sums of money on a hitherto unknown miracle cure — and *then* suffer a long, slow, painful death.

A small Italian town packed with 'sellers, beggars and cheats', Cerreto was once notorious for its travelling doctors: smooth-talking shysters who would saunter through town singing the praises of a brand-new ointment, then scurry out the moment it sold. Unfortunately for their business model, however, the word 'cerettan' eventually became synonymous with 'hustler'. In English, we know it as ***charlatan***.

**THE CAPTAIN WHO FUDGED HIS FACTS** Of course, doctors aren't the only kind of travellers who've been known ***to fudge*** a fact. According to a letter written in 1664, there was once 'one Captain Fudge, who upon his return from a voyage … always brought home his owners a good cargo of lies'. This happened so much, the story goes, that 'sailors, when they hear a great lie told, now cry out, "You fudge it"'.

We don't know whether Fudge *did* in fact tell tall tales (the phrase 'to fudge' could simply be a version of 'to fadge'). But, given he was such an accident-prone sailor, lying probably would have seemed like a good idea. The good captain's last journey, records tell us, ended with his ship being captured by the Dutch. Though not before twenty-seven of his crew had died from disease, everyone left had mutinied, and Fudge himself was arrested for debt. Good luck fudging your way out of that!

**PARIAHS ARE PEOPLE TOO**

A sad end for a sailor: from seadog to social outcast. But at least Captain Fudge wasn't *born* a social outcast, like quite a few million people in India. Named for the 'parai', a kind of drum they beat at festivals, those of the Paraiyan caste were considered 'untouchable' by their fellow countrymen, which wouldn't do much for their self-esteem.

Non-Indians weren't very supportive either. When British empire-builders arrived in the 17th century, they employed vast numbers of Paraiyars as domestics, nobly allowing these 'lowest of the low' to cook, clean and fetch for them in return for a lowest-of-the-low wage. Among their employers, these competitively priced slave-folk came to be known as *pariahs*—a word we now apply to any poor soul who is despised by society at large.

**WHY VILLAINS DESERVE OUR SUPPORT**

Ah, England. Land of hope and glory for those who can afford it, and mud, cold and damp for the rest. In medieval times, it's important to remember, most people never saw the inside of a palace. The life of your average serf (commonly known as a 'villein') basically involved slaving away on someone else's land until they caught either smallpox or plague.

Not such a good job, then, all things considered: on the social scale, villeins ranked one or two degrees below headlice, and more or less alongside pus. And they're still not getting much love. In French, a 'villein' is someone who's ugly, and in Italian, a 'villein' is uncouth. In English, even more demeaningly, it means criminal. If someone's wicked, we might say they're a *villain*.

**BLACK-
GUARDS
BELONG
IN THE
KITCHEN**

*Blackguards* also can't be trusted, if you go by the average 19th-century novel. They're the sort of scoundrelly knaves who compromise some fair maid's honour, and so get challenged to pistols at dawn. In medieval times, however, a blackguard's life wouldn't have made such racy reading. Back then, they were just another kind of smelly serf: the kitchen servants who cleaned all the blackened crockery, and guarded it wherever they went.

**TURNCOATS
AND
WELSHERS**

Their masters, on the other hand, kept busy by guarding themselves. One ruler of Saxony may have been particularly diligent in this regard. In the first half of the 17th century, Saxony was a thin sliver of land dividing the possessions of Spain and France—two European superpowers that were fighting a thirty-year-long war. Tough to stay on everyone's good side, you might think, but the good lord did his manly best. According to legend, he had his tailor make him a reversible coat: one side blue (the colour of Spain) and the other side a very French white. As the fortunes of war changed, so did the colour of his coat.

Noble, perhaps, but not so loyal. These days, we'd call him a *turncoat*.

Even *he* might have drawn a line at supporting Wales, however. That nation, if the English language is to be believed, is simply crawling with no-good *welshers*.

This damning term for people who don't pay their debts is thought to have begun with a few Welsh bookies. Back in the 19th century, it's said, some of them were known to quietly slip away from the racecourse when things hadn't gone their way, and hotfoot it back to Wales.

**DOING BUSINESS WITH MR BOGUS**

When a heavily backed outsider came through at especially long odds, a few other bookies probably fled to the US. While there, we can only hope that they came into contact with Mr Borghese, a businessman with a big, broad outlook. According to an 1857 edition of *The Boston Courier*, this Borghese was 'a very corrupt individual, who twenty years ago or more did a tremendous business in the way of counterfeit bills and also bills on fictitious banks. People fell into the habit of shortening the name of Borghese to that of **Bogus**, and his bills, as well as all others of like character, were universally styled by them "bogus currency"'.

**SMART ALEC DID A DUMB THING**

**Smart Alec** preferred real currency. Alec Hoag was a conman and pimp from 1840s New York who sometimes did both jobs at once. In what police dubbed the 'panel game', one of his prostitutes 'would make her victim lay his clothes … upon a chair at the head of the bed near a secret panel, and then take him to her arms and closely draw the curtains of the bed. As soon as everything was right and the dupe not likely to heed outside noises, the traitress would give a cough, and the faithful Alec would slyly enter, rifle the pockets of every farthing or valuable thing, and finally disappear as mysteriously as he entered'.

Smart. But Alec then got a bit too smart for his own good, when he decided to cut costs by reducing bribes to police. A short time later, he found himself in jail.

**SOME SHYSTERS AT YOUR SERVICE**

We can only hope that he got a good lawyer: New York had plenty of bad ones. Originating from 'scheisser', the German word for 'one who shits', the word **shyster** was first used to describe the thousands of unqualified 'lawyers' who infested New York prisons in the 1840s, hoping to con a convict into giving them a case.

For Mike Walsh, the journalist who coined the term, this 'disgraceful gang' of would-be lawyers was mostly made up of 'ignorant blackguards, illiterate blockheads, besotted drunkards, drivelling simpletons, deviant mountebanks, vagabonds, swindlers and thieves'. (None of which looks good on a tax return.)

### A GOOD PLACE TO BE FLASHY

Such *flashy*, unreliable lawyers are alas all too common these days (though if we made up a word about *them*, they'd be quick to sue). In our litigious culture, it's much safer to slander a place. A place like Flash, for example.

Sitting on the border of three different counties, this hilltop English village had long been considered faintly dodgy, as it started out as a sort of camping spot for travelling salesmen. But it became a Mecca for the seriously dodgy in the 19th century, when a new law prevented the police of each county from acting outside their borders. In the charmed village of Flash, this meant that a criminal could simply keep an eye open for any policemen travelling up the hill, and stroll over to another county before they reached the top.

Bad news for cops and even worse for economists: Flash soon became Britain's counterfeiting capital. In time, all fake money became known as 'flash' money— and eventually, anyone dishonest, or at least deceptively showy, could stand accused of being a little 'flashy' himself.

### TELLING FURPHIES IS THIRSTY WORK

In Australia, such flashy types might tell *furphies*. This slang term for an unlikely rumour most likely came from one John Furphy (1842–1920), a perfectly respectable blacksmith who dedicated his life to the fight against thirst. Among other

A Furphy water cart

products, Furphy manufactured giant iron water carts (displaying the Furphy name in bright, bold letters).

These water carts were used a lot during WWI. Typically placed near the toilets (and so away from officers' prying eyes), they were a place where Australian soldiers could gather together for a bit of a gossip, much like water coolers in an office today. Tall tales would often be told—and then the driver would take the water cart to another military camp, and repeat whatever he'd heard. 'Is that true?' troops would ask him. 'Or are you telling a furphy?'

# STOUT-HEARTED WORDS

**JOVE
THE JOVIAL
GOD**

A cloudy day is no match for a sunny disposition, as some chirpy soul once put it. Smile and the world smiles with you; frown and you just get wet.

But having said that, we shouldn't necessarily blame the frowners of this world for being so dark and stormy. The Romans, so wise in so many respects, thought that our personalities were predetermined by when we are born. The best time to leave the womb, they believed, was when Jupiter was high in the sky, as this planet belonged to Jove, the king of the gods. Being so conspicuously blessed by the high and mighty one, such people tended to go through life very cheerful. Or very *jovial*, to use a more technical term.

**THE THREE PRINCES OF SERENDIP-ITY**

Perhaps it's also lucky to be born in Sri Lanka. In 1754, the author Horace Walpole wrote to a friend about 'a silly fairy tale' from that country (which among Arabs was once known as 'Serendip').

Called *The Three Princes of Serendip*, the tale saw the three said princes go on a long and extremely rewarding journey. They 'were always making discoveries, by accident and sagacity, of things they were not in quest of'. This kind of lucky knack should have a name, Walpole said. So he coined one: *serendipity*.

**THE STOIC PORCH**

Of course we can't all be so lucky: in life, it pays to be *stoic*. One must face the world with a cool, steady gaze and stiff upper lip, even if you've just done a fart.

Such at least was the attitude of the Stoics, a group of ancient Greek philosophers named after a 'stoa poikile' ('painted porch') where their leader taught. 'Let no-one break your will,' Zeno would lecture. For that philosopher, happiness essentially involved being indifferent to every circumstance. A stoic can be 'sick and yet happy, in peril and yet happy, dying and yet happy, in exile and yet happy, in disgrace and yet happy … The wise man is sufficient unto himself in all things … and will be happy even when stretched upon the rack'.

Excellent news. Though it should be noted that Zeno didn't seem very happy one day in 430 BC, when he tripped over and broke a toe. 'I come God, why dost thou call for me?' he cried, somewhat less than stoically, and then proceeded to strangle himself.

**BABY-SITTING SPARTAN-STYLE**

Less philosophical ancient Greeks could also be pretty stoic. Take the natives of Laconia. In stark contrast to the hyper-civilised Athenians, they were stab-now, think-later types: an entire culture devoted to military excellence at the expense of, well, culture.

When a male child was born in Sparta, Laconia's capital city, they were immediately bathed in wine. This wasn't designed as a health measure, but to see if they were strong. If they died, they weren't. Should a baby survive that ordeal, it would be inspected by a council of high-ranking warmongers … and be thrown off a cliff if it was judged 'puny and deformed'.

Shortly after that, it was time to begin military training and life from then on was, yes, *spartan*. Military trainees made do on the barest necessities of life, and got slaps, not hugs, from their mums. Austerity, hardship and deprivation killed the weak, went the theory, and strengthened the character of those who remained.

And perhaps there's something to be said for this. Once, it's said, a young soldier became so sick of Spartan fare that he stole a fox and hid it under his cloak, intending to enjoy a furry snack later on. The fox soon woke up, however, and started having a snack of its own, gnawing away at the boy's vital organs. But since he was busy on a military parade, he simply stood there and suffered in silence. And then, ever so quietly, died.

Of course, he probably could have said *something*. Though they preferred bleeding and fighting to reading and writing, the people of Laconia were quite famous for being *laconic*. By using just a few words, they could often say rather a lot. One particularly famous example of this terse, tight-lipped style of speaking occurred when a neighbouring superpower was making preparations to invade. 'If I bring my army into your land, I will destroy your farms, slay your people and raze your city,' threatened the all-powerful Philip of Macedonia (382–336 BC). The Spartans' reply was a laconic 'If'.

---

**WAS MARY REALLY SO MAUDLIN?**

Mary Magdalene probably would have burst into tears. Pronounced Mary 'Maud-lin', Jesus's repentant prostitute buddy from the New Testament has never been known for her steely-eyed fortitude.

In large part, however, this is due to the work of medieval and Renaissance portrait painters, not to any blubbiness from Mary herself. The all-powerful medieval Church was always anxious to reinforce the moral codes of the day (prostitution bad; chastity belts good), so it tended to tell its painters that they had to emphasise Mary's repentance. That sinner would thus always be shown with red, swollen eyes and pale, teary cheeks, hands clasped in a plea to God on behalf of soiled womankind.

**Mary Magdalene looking maudlin**

A little over the top and sappily sentimental, some would say. Though others might use the word ***maudlin***.

# INTELLIGENT WORDS

**THE FIRST ACADEMICS**

*Academia* can be pretty tough these days, but once upon a time it was a walk in the park. In 387 BC, universities hadn't been invented yet, so Plato and his followers had to create their own. Whenever those toga-wearing philosophical types wanted to discuss good and evil or life and death or sandals and olives, they would gather together at Akademia, a public park just outside Athens which had been named after Akademos, a hero of the Trojan War. These informal gatherings eventually became semi-formal, and then morphed into a sort of philosophical school. Greeks dubbed it 'the academy'. And by the 15th century, pretty much any place of higher learning was called an 'academy', regardless of the state of the grass.

**THE BOFFINS OF BAWDSEY**

Most *boffins* have had some higher learning. One or two scientists may have been born knowing all about beta particles, transverse waves and Planck's constant, but most of them need to study a bit before they can wear a white coat.

The first boffins, however, went to the School of Hard Knocks and then had to graduate from the University of Life. The term was born on the battlefields of WWII. Or perhaps not *on* the battlefields so much as *near* them: the first 'boffins' were a team of British scientists and engineers at Bawdsey Research Station who worked on new military technologies like the radar. It's said that they would meet for lunch at an eatery called 'Boffins', though it's more likely that the term was just an acronym for 'Back Office Intelligence'.

**SOME SOCIALLY AWKWARD SUPER-VILLAINS**

The original *brainiac* wouldn't have been impressed by their work. *His* inventions, after all, were able to shrink cities (not to mention clone things and travel through time). An alien with a 'tenth-level intellect', 'Brainiac' debuted in *Action Comics* #242 and quickly became one of Superman's most formidable rivals. Though, with those red diodes protruding from his bald green head, he was probably a bit less competitive when it came to the ladies.

*Poindexter* knew just how he felt. Short, bald and with big, thick glasses, that *Felix the Cat* character combines an IQ of 222 with the social skills of a turnip. As the nerdy nephew of Felix's archenemy, The Professor, Poindexter spends his time doing dastardly deeds in his laboratory, and stays well away from the nightclubs. His name's been a term of abuse for geeky prodigies since the 1960s.

**THE FIRST BRAINS TRUST**

Which was lucky timing for Raymond Moley, Rexford G Tugwell and Adolf A Berle. They were geeky prodigies much earlier. After going to school in the late 19th century (where they probably enjoyed pleasingly archaic taunts like 'bookworm' and 'swot'[†]), those three men became professors at New York's Columbia University.

Come 1932, the governor of New York, Franklin D Roosevelt, decided that his run for president could do with a bit more academic input, so he recruited that trio to write his campaign speeches. They were subsequently dubbed Roosevelt's **brains trust** in a *New York Times* article, and the term eventually came to mean any group of highly credentialed advisors.

**WHY MUSEUMS ARE SACRED TURF**

Ancient Greek artists had a different word for *their* brains trust. Anyone who wanted to accomplish anything in the arts back then first of all had to look to the Muses. Nine gorgeous goddesses with names like Melpomene, Terpsichore and Erato, the Muses were the sacred source of all poetry, literature, dance and song—and the obvious origin for our modern term, *muse*.

Less obviously, they also gave us *museum*. Directly translated, that word means 'shrine of the muses'. The ancient Greeks built many such temples for Melpomene and the gang, and would frequently use them for cultural purposes, like housing works of art.

---

† Although those names were probably the least Tugwell had to contend with.

The Muses of ancient Greece

**BOOFHEAD
AND THE
DRONGO**

The original ***boofhead*** would have preferred a pub. The bumbling, stumbling star of a cartoon strip in Sydney's *Daily Mirror*, Boofhead made it very hard for Australians to overcome their cultural cringe. The 1941–1970 strip was 'amateurish and the humour mundane', sniffs one historian, 'but there can be no disputing its popularity'. And there's no disputing that it gave us a word.

Drongo was also a little amateurish, despite the high hopes of his owners. With his sleekly muscled forelegs and pure, noble bloodlines, this highly credentialed racehorse could do just about anything … except actually win a race. After thirty-seven starts led to thirty-seven losses, he was retired in 1925, but the word ***drongo*** was only beginning its career.

**WHY
CHRISTIANS
ARE
CRETINS**

Not all drongos live in Australia, however (whatever *Neighbours* and *Home and Away* might lead you to think). Some also live in Switzerland. Around the rocky slopes of the southern Alps, you see, the soil is low in iodine. And this means that the plants and the animals that live off that soil are a little lacking in iodine too.

So? Well, iodine, scientists now know, is essential for human development. A lack of it can lead to congenital hypothyroidism, a condition that stunts physical and mental development. In the 1700s, scientists didn't know this—and so travellers to Switzerland who came across entire villages of hypothyroidic people would often conclude that they were in some way subhuman. More enlightened types, on the other hand, called them 'chréteins', the French word for 'Christian'. Their point was that these were God's children too, and so deserved of a bit of compassion.

These days the word has rather less compassionate connotations. English-speakers know it as *cretin*.

**DR DUNCE WAS NO NINCOMPOOP**
Being Christians, the cretins might have known about *nincompoop*. This word for a muddle-headed blunderer mostly likely derives from Nicodemus, a character in the Bible who asks Jesus some naive questions in the Gospel of St John.

John Duns Scotus

If John Duns Scotus (1265–1308) had ever had a chance to cross-examine Jesus, his questions would have been a bit tougher. Over the course of a distinguished career at Oxford and Cambridge, this theologian was known as 'Dr Subtilis', so subtle were the finely shaded nuances of his delicate, carefully reasoned prose. 'Dunsmen' everywhere enthusiastically embraced Duns's complicated metaphysical concepts like 'haecceitas' and 'the univocity of being'—though whether they actually understood them is anyone's guess.

By the 16th century, however, there was a new gang in town. To the 'Thomists'—the followers of a rather more plainspoken theologian called Thomas Aquinas—'Dunsmen' were just plain silly. For this new generation, a *dunce* was no more than a pedant: a person preoccupied with irrelevant details and devoted to the needlessly complex. Eventually the word simply came to mean a dimwit, which all in all seems a little unfair.

**TIME FOR A REPUBLIC: KING SILLY BILLY AND THE MORON**

Of course, not all dopey people wear a dunce cap. William IV (1765–1837) wore a crown. After five decades of overeating and bedding stage actresses, this elderly British alcoholic woke up one afternoon and unexpectedly found himself on the throne. Endlessly boorish and fond of pointless, rambling speeches, William 'was in no hurry to take upon himself the dignity of king nor throw off the habits and manners of a country gentleman', as one biographer tactfully put it. Less tactful people called him *Silly Billy*.

A rather more intelligent royal was La Princesse d'Elide, the title character in a play by Molière. The same can't be said of one of her fellow characters, however—a dim-witted court jester named *Moron*.

Molière was having his little joke here ('moros' is an ancient Greek word for 'dull') but the name soon became deadly serious. At a scientific conference in 1910, 'moron' was formally adopted as a term to describe people with an IQ of 51–70. Which made them considerably smarter than imbeciles (26–50) and intellectual superstars compared with an idiot (0–25).

King William IV, England's Silly Billy

**IGNORAMUS AND THE INTERMINABLE PLAY**

We don't know what IQ an *ignoramus* has—and *he* doesn't know anything at all. For that term, we can thank another playwright who liked to play with ancient languages. A Latin term meaning 'We do not know', 'Ignoramus' was the name given to a dim-witted lawyer in a 17th-century play. It 'was full of mirth and variety and had many excellent actors', said one reviewer, 'but was more than half spoiled by its extreme length of six hours'.

# SMALL-MINDED WORDS

**BY GOD, HERE COME THE BIGOTS!**

'A great many people think they are thinking,' said William James, 'when they are merely rearranging their prejudices.' But is this really such a problem? Consider how many other people prefer to keep their prejudices right where they are.

The Normans, for example, had a prejudice against other people owning property. Just like their Viking ancestors, these widely travelled medieval warriors were fond of conquering whatever they could. And the best-known Norman was particularly keen on it: William the Conqueror snaffled up all of England in 1066. His soldiers also stole a few English words and phrases. One of them was 'By God!' (a sort of ye olde 'God damn it!')—or 'Bi Got!', as their Norman conquerors would pronounce it.

Now, the Normans also liked to invade France from time to time, which tended to make them a little unpopular. The French, being French, didn't do much when it came to actually resisting these invasions, but they did fight back with some abusive nicknames. One of them was **bigot**.

**IS BEING DOCTRI-NAIRE REALLY SO WRONG?**

Such name-calling, alas, appears all too common in France: Pierre Paul Royer-Collard (1763–1845) got lumbered with one too. A politician after the Revolution, he was a supporter of constitutional monarchy: a carefully wrought marriage of liberalism and royalty that would bring a little moderation to the country after a century of sliced heads and strife.

But such a policy was considered unworkable, the naive doctrine of an unworldly idealist. Royer-Collard and the party he founded were mockingly known as the 'Doctrinaires'. And **doctrinaire** soon came to mean any kind of inflexible theorist (unless their theories happen to line up with your own).

**MARTINET THE MARTINET**

Inspector General Jean Martinet (ca 1620–1672) was also considered rather rigid. Charged with converting Louis XIV's ragtag band of mercenaries into a professional standing army, he was one of those autocratic, knuckle-rapping, straighten-your-tie types who bark out lines like 'It's my way or the highway'.

Martinet's way, we are told, involved rather a lot of drilling. His soldiers would be woken at dawn for some drilling, then do a couple of quick drills after breakfast and an extra-long one just before lunch. Most of the afternoon would be set aside for more drilling, though Martinet would also make time for saluting, boot-polishing and goose-stepping, as well as severely punishing whoever stepped out of line.

France did eventually get a very disciplined army out of this, full of men who were more than happy to be slaughtered. But Martinet never really got to see it, as some of those same men shot him in the back. This 'friendly fire' incident meant that he also never got to hear a new word: **martinet**, meaning crazed disciplinarian.

**CHAUVIN THE CHAUVINIST**

One hundred and fifty years later, however, someone took French discipline to a whole new level. If a superior officer had asked Nicholas Chauvin to shoot himself for the glory of France, he might have hesitated for a fraction of a second. But this would only have been so he could shout out 'Yes, sir!' and give that officer a respectful salute. A veteran of Napoleon's Grande Armée, Chauvin was wounded seventeen times in the line of fire and his only regret was that he wasn't hurt more.

Gruesomely disfigured, (the possibly apocryphal) Chauvin lived out his days with a tiny military pension—and a ludicrously overgrown sense of patriotism. He could never shut up about the nobility of Napoleon, the infallibility of France, or the desirability of ceaseless war. By 1831, the story goes, Chauvin's neighbours weren't the only ones laughing at him. Thanks to *La Cocarde Tricolore*, a popular play featuring a thick-headed, blood-and-guts nationalist named 'Chauvin', he had become a national figure of fun. From that play came **chauvinist**—a word that can today mean any kind of bigot, but originally meant warmongering patriot.

**JINGOISM AND THE RUSSIANS**

In England, this kind of flag-waving bloodthirstiness generally goes by another name. **Jingoism** is a reworking of 'By Jingo'—a phrase that, much like **gosh** ('God') and **cor blimey** ('God blind me'), was designed to let people say something vaguely controversial (like 'By Jesus') without immediately getting sent to hell.

In the 1870s, on the other hand, one thing was *not* controversial: England was going to finish the Russo–Turkish War. It was time to take the swishy cane out of the cupboard and give those Russian bounders a damn good hiding. London's red, white and blue music halls frequently shook to the following song: 'We don't want to fight but by Jingo if we do / We've got the ships, we've got the men and we've got the money too'.

'Jingoism' was born. Sadly, it's yet to die.

**DEATH TO EVERY-BODY! THE FIRST ZEALOTS.**

The original *zealots*, on the other hand, had absolutely no problem dying. It was more or less the only thing they did really well.

A militant sect in 1st-century Judea, the Zealots were deeply opposed to the Roman Empire's rule over the region, and expressed the way they felt with some old-fashioned terrorism. Described in the Talmud as 'boorish … ruffians', the Zealots' policies ultimately boiled down to (1) killing every Roman, (2) killing every Jew who didn't want to kill every Roman and (3) killing anyone else who happened to get in the way.

When these policies didn't work out, they resorted to (4) killing themselves. Cornered by the Roman army in a desert fort in 70 AD, 960 zealots chose to commit suicide rather than be captured.

**WHY FASCISTS WERE ONCE QUITE NICE**

Hitler and Goebbels went the same way. Though their zealousness was of course in the cause of *fascism*: an ideal ideology for dictators who got teased at school and not enough cuddles at home.

Originally, however, fascism was just for Sicilians. Mussolini may have founded the first 'Fascist' party in the sense used today, but he borrowed the term from a Sicilian workers group of the 1890s. Democratic socialists, as opposed to goose-stepping psychopaths, the Fasci Siciliani in turn got the name from the 'fasces', a tightly bound bundle of sticks with an axe in the middle that in ancient Rome symbolised 'strength through unity'. But the Fasci Siciliani simply wanted to use their strength to develop some workers' pension schemes, and improve conditions on Sicilian farms.

**QUISLING WASN'T REALLY AN ARYAN**

Hitler, on the other hand, wanted to improve conditions for **Aryans**. But it was only really in his mind that this term meant blond-haired Nordic types who can't get enough sausage and Wagner. For thousands of years before he was born, 'Aryans' were simply people from Persia.

Derived from 'arya', the Sanskrit word that also gave us **Iran**, the Aryans were an ancient Indo-Iranian tribe. An obscure Anglo-German language scholar borrowed their name in the 19th century to describe the Indo-European family of languages, and a few crackpot race theories started from there.

Major Vidkun Quisling (1887–1945) would have loved them all. More or less the only Nazi in 1930s Norway, he started up his own fascist party in that country, but could never achieve more than 2 per cent in the polls. Good news for Norway, of course, but rather frustrating for Quisling himself.

Exasperated by everyone's failure to see what was good for them, Quisling secretly met with Hitler in 1940 and gave him some information that would help Germany invade. And invade the Nazis duly did, three days later. They marched in to the sound of Quisling on the radio, urging his fellow Norwegians to lay down their arms. His reward was to become Norway's puppet dictator until the end of the war: four glorious years spent on a bombproof island palace with 150 bodyguards and food tasters.

And it seems like he needed them all. The desperately unpopular dictator was arrested the day the war ended and executed within months, despite Norway having a law against capital punishment. But the word **quisling** still survives.

**WHY RED-
NECKS ARE
TRUE BLUE**

Religious diversity lives on too. In part, this is thanks the Scottish Covenanters, a group of Presbyterians who wanted to keep the Church of England out of Scotland— but having said that, they were *rednecks*. In 1639, the Covenanters signed a 'National Covenant' in their own blood. Many then began to wear a red scarf around their neck to remind people of their commitment to this 'blood oath', and willingness to lose a head for the cause.

Some Covenanters signing up

Over the following centuries, many Scots settled in the more rural parts of the US, and some of them inherited the nickname. By 1893, the term had come to mean rural people generally (as 'men who work in the field generally have their skin stained red by the sun, and this is especially true of the back of their necks'). And by the 1970s, people had noticed that such men are sometimes also stained by bigotry, so 'redneck' took on the meaning that it still has today.

In some rural regions of Australia, rednecks are called **true blue**. (i.e. it's ok to be homophobic and racist, so long as you call everyone 'mate'.) Strangely enough, this term may come from the Scottish Covenanters too.

The phrase 'as true as Coventry blue' seems to have already been around during the 17th century. It described how the blue dye made by the weavers of Coventry didn't run (and thus stayed fast and 'true'). But, being such steadfast moralisers, some Scottish Covenanters may have stolen it. They called themselves 'true blue' to describe the way they stayed loyal and true to their cause.

# MAD WORDS

**LUNATICS NEED MORE SUN**

'I can calculate the motion of heavenly bodies,' Isaac Newton once remarked, 'but not the madness of people.' But did it ever occur to him that they could be one and the same thing? When we gaze at the sky, might we being seeing inside our own heads? Could the motion of heavenly bodies actually make sane people mad?

Well, no. Stupid idea, frankly. But for a long time, people thought just that. On a night with a full moon, it was best to stay inside or you just might go a little kooky. Werewolves, of course, reflect this piece of folk wisdom—they are normal folks by day, hairy lunatics by moonlight—but so too does the word *lunatic* itself, originating in the 13th century. 'Luna' is the Latin word for 'moon'. A lunatic is quite literally 'moonstruck'.

**GOING DOLLALLY IN INDIA**

Other people could get Deolali-struck. A hot, dull, dry and dusty outpost in British colonial India in the early 20th century, Deolali was not an ideal place for a holiday. It was, however, the ideal place if you were a mentally ill British soldier, as it had India's only sanatorium.

According to some historians, it was also the ideal place to *become* a mentally ill British soldier. Perfectly well troops were sometimes sent to Deolali when their tour of duty had finished, in order to await the next ship home. And quite often they had to wait for a while. It's said that the endless sitting around with nothing to do, except wipe away sweat and drink buckets of gin, could send all but the hardiest solider a little bit nuts. Or, in other words, a little *dollally*.

**JAGANNATH THE JUGGERNAUT**

Though some Brits, we should note in fairness, thought that Indian people could be dollally too. The word *juggernaut*, coined around 1850, can be traced to Jagannath, a Hindu god worshipped in Puri. Every summer, as part of a worship festival, locals would place a giant statue of that god on a still-more-giant cart, and drag it several kilometres through a densely packed crowd.

If you think that that sounds dangerous, you'd be right. Quite a few devotees got run over and died. They were helpless before the power of a juggernaut—a crushing, ruthless, unstoppable force, carried along on a wave of emotion.

The juggernaut of Jaggernath

**MR BATTY, ST BARMY AND BEDLAM**

India wasn't the only colonial outpost that could have done with a few psychiatrists. Jamaica, for example, was once home to one Fitzherbert Batty, a prominent but profoundly loopy English barrister, who was certified as insane in 1839. Some theorise that his notoriety helped give the language the word *batty*, though it's more likely it comes from the old saying 'bats in the belfry' ('belfries' being the head-like bell tower sticking out from the tops of churches, which were quite often home to bats).

Many batty Brits over the centuries have made their home in St Mary's of Bethlehem. Still open for business today, this London asylum would once chain its more violent patients up in little dungeons and feed them on sermons and gruel. The more harmless patients could be found in two comparatively luxurious wards, however—a smallish one called 'Abraham's', or a larger, more publicly accessible one called 'St Bartholemew's'. Since 'St Bartholemew's' was a bit of a mouthful, visitors tended to call it 'St Barmy's'. And call the people in it *barmy*.

The hospital itself got its nickname much earlier. Short for 'St Mary's of Bethlehem', 'Bed'lam' was a word on many lips in 13th-century England, for the medieval Londoner loved a good laugh. When the delights of bear-baiting and cockfighting began to pall, and there were no public hangings scheduled that day, fun-hungry folk would often take a trip to the madhouse and have a giggle at a few of the loons. For just a penny, they could enjoy all sorts of chaos, and quite possibly see someone who thought they were a duck. So popular was this kind of sightseeing that any kind of noisy chaos became known to as *bedlam*.

**PANDE-MONIUM AND PURE EVIL**

Though *pandemonium* is an equally good word, when you're looking to describe the disorderly. The poet John Milton (1608–1674) would probably say it's an even better word, but he's not such an objective source. Pan*demoni*um first entered the language in *Paradise Lost*, an epic poem by John Milton. A Greek phrase meaning 'every little demon', he used it as the name of hell's biggest city, 'the High Capitol of Satan and his Peers'. 'Abandon hope all ye who enter here … Through me you pass into the city of woe. Through me you pass into eternal pain.'

**THE DRUG THAT SENT VIKINGS BERSERK**

Hell probably contains a few Vikings (big fans of eternal pain). While these Scandinavian seafarers specialised in raping, looting and pillaging, they were also very good at stabbing, hacking and torturing. Pretty much any European who lived near a port during the 8th century was just filling in time until their blood-splattered death.

The best blood-splatterers were the berserkers: Vikings who wore animal skins rather than armour ('ber-serkr' meaning 'bear coat') because they were completely impervious to pain. 'As mad as dogs and as strong as bears', they fought in a kind of savage, unstoppable battle frenzy that was most likely brought on by hallucinogenic mushrooms.

One observer wrote about a berserker who was in the grip of a typical 'frenzy'. 'He furiously bit and devoured the edges of his shield; he kept gulping down fiery coals; he snatched live embers in his mouth and let them pass down into his entrails; he rushed through the perils of crackling fires; and at last, when he had raved through every sort of madness, he turned his sword with raging hand against the hearts of six of his champions.'

In other words, he went ***berserk***.

**DON'T PANIC, IT'S ONLY PAN**

How do you think you'd go, if you had to fight a berserker? Personally, and without wishing to big-note myself in any way, I think I'd probably ***panic***.

The ancient Greeks often panicked too. Chiefly when they got teased by Pan. Half-man, half-goat and all brat, this rascally forest god liked to get up to a bit of mischief when a traveller wandered through his woods.

'Hiding behind a tree, he would gently rustle the bushes, engendering a sense of apprehension … then scurry through the forest to intercept his quarry at the next dark turn of the path. There he would rustle some more vegetation, and the traveller would make even greater haste … Never would the unsuspecting traveller re-enter the forest without experiencing a wave of apprehension.'

Don't panic, it's only Pan

**PSYCHE, HYPNOTISM AND THE UNDER- WORLD: A TALE OF TWO GREEK GODS**

Ah, the mysterious world of *psychology*. Though it's not such a mysterious word. 'Psychology' comes from Psyche, a mythological princess who had an affair with Eros, the Greek god of love. Several bafflingly complicated plotlines later, she gets banished to a sort of deep, dark underworld—and then rises up from it, all radiant and enlightened. Not a bad metaphor for the subconscious.

Hypnos also lived in the underworld. The Greek god of sleep, he inhabited a dark cave filled with poppies, and a few other mind-altering plants. 'Ah, one of those no-good drug-taking types,' you think, but no, you do him wrong. Hypnos was a drug *dealer*. Armed with his poppy stem and horn of sleep-inducing opium, this gentle god performed an important public service, distributing slumber and sweet dreams.

In the 19th century, Hypnos was dragged out of the underworld and placed at the forefront of science. A new medical technique was renamed *hypnotism*, after people came to realise that 'animal magnetism' didn't actually require magnets at all.

Psyche emerges from the underworld, and starts to see the light

**THE MESMERIS- ING HERR SVENGALI**

The original practitioner of this 'animal magnetism' was Franz Mesmer (1734–1815). Essentially a bit of a charlatan, Mesmer was an Austrian doctor who liked to dress in the long, flowing robes of an astrologer and perform his 'cures' in front of big crowds. He would make his patients swallow a solution of iron, and then rub their bodies with a magnet, murmuring soothing words in a soft, steady voice.

**Franz Mesmer**

And the thing was, it sometimes worked. In that dimly lit room with its gentle, eerie music, patients with psychologically based illnesses could quite often find themselves cured. What we now know is that they'd been hypnotised. The good Mesmer may not have known much about magnets, but by God he could certainly *mesmerise*.

As, indeed, could **Svengali**. Now a journalist's term for a shadowy puppet master, 'Svengali' was the name of the hypnotist in *Trilby*, a bestselling 19th-century novel. A man who knows everything about music, except how to make it himself, this sinister character hypnotises an innocent artist's model, who is tone deaf but has an excellent voice. Unwittingly placed under his control, she becomes a famous opera diva and the feted darling of Paris. Then gets publicly humiliated, goes mad and dies. Good times.

# SUBSERVIENT WORDS

***EVERY PRINCE NEEDS A WHIPPING BOY***

Every teacher needs a degree of obedience, so how exactly can you teach a prince? Only a king could lay a hand on a king's son in the palaces of 16th-century Europe, which left their tutors without any hand at all.

The solution was to assign each princeling what was called a 'proxy for correction': a boy of his own age to share the same classroom … and get whipped when the prince did wrong.

The idea was that if his royal naughtiness saw someone else suffer for his wrongdoing, he might be shamed into behaving well. For the sake of the *whipping boy*, let's hope this was right.

**THE NAMBY-PAMBY POET**

The poet Henry Carey (1687–1743) also had a whipping boy: his fellow scribbler, Ambrose Philips (1674–1749). Politics was the main reason for this literary rivalry (Carey was a Tory, Philips an active Whig), but poetry played a role too. Carey hated Philips's poems for children — sweet, soppy odes about fairies that most modern readers would splatter with vomit — and gave him a nickname that expressed his disgust. Taking the 'Amb' sound from 'Ambrose' and the 'P' from Phillips, it proved so damaging that, after a while, it began to be applied to anyone who seemed a little insipid or wishy washy or bland. No-one wants to be *namby-pamby*.

**PANDERUS THE PANDERER**

Shame, Henry Carey. Shame. *Pandering* to low public tastes like that seems unworthy of a poet.

For Panderus, however, pandering was par for the course. This sleazy character in the ancient story of Troilus and Cressida is essentially a bit of a pimp. He acts as a sort of go-between for the two title characters, cynically persuading Cressida to hop into Troilus's bed. 'Since I have [been at] such pains to bring you together,' requests Panderus in Shakespeare's version of the story, 'let all pitiful goers-between be call'd to the world's end after my name. Call them all Pandars.'

**THE QUIXOTIC DON QUIXOTE**

Don Quixote, on the other hand, would never pander to anyone. He was too noble and good and true. The title character of Miguel Cervantes's classic 1605 novel is a slightly deranged Spaniard who sets out in some rusty old armour to right wrongs like the knights of old.

Accompanied by a frail, skinny horse and pot-bellied squire, this would-be knight's attempts at chivalry go consistently and comically wrong. He eventually trudges back home a tired old man, romantic visions a thing of the past. The word *quixotic* lives on, however. It describes any kind of misguided do-gooder, who takes their ideals to an impractical extreme.

The quixotic Don Quixote

**WHY GOODY
TWO-SHOES
DIDN'T GET
BROWNIE
POINTS**

Goody and her two shoes

Not that Don Quixote was the biggest *goody two-shoes* in literature. That honour goes to Goody Two-Shoes herself. The star of an 18th-century nursery tale, Goody is Margery Meanwell, a poor and oh-so-pious orphan girl who starts out life with only one shoe. She has virtue and sweetness in spades, however, and is eventually rewarded for them by a rich gentleman, who hands over a pair of shoes. 'She ran out to Mrs Smith as soon as they were put on, and stroking down her ragged Apron thus, cried out, "Two Shoes, Mame, see two Shoes!". And so she behaved to all the People she met, and by that Means obtained the Name of "Goody Two-Shoes".'

If Miss Meanwell was around these days, she'd probably own a few badges too. Parents in search of some babysitting will often turn to their local scouts, girl guides or brownies. Those organisations don't just feed, clothe and entertain one's rosy-cheeked bundle of joy, they take them far away into the woods.

Brownies also offer merit badges and suchlike—prizes earned by the doing of good deeds, which are each worth a number of points. This most likely explains why **brownie points** have come to mean any kind of reward for self-interested subservience. (Though, of course, there's also another explanation, involving what might happen when you kiss someone's bum.)

**THE FIRST TOADIES AND THEIR TUMS**

Subservient types have often had to do slightly unpleasant things with their mouth. In the 16th century, some even ate toads. In those benighted times, most people couldn't access a hospital, so the sick would instead gather around the latest travelling quack and listen with misplaced hope as he flogged his wares. 'A threepenny cure for cancer? I'll take two thanks!' 'Leeches that ward off leprosy? How much for an entire bag?'

Oftentimes, the travelling doctor would also offer up a cure for poisoning—and what's more, offer to prove it. All eyes would then turn to his hapless assistant, who would take a deep breath and then a mouthful of toad. Happily, the quack would then proceed to 'cure' him of this poison. (Though, since most types of toad aren't actually poisonous, this generally wasn't so hard.)

Nonetheless, they were unpleasant. So a toad-eater or **toady** came to mean the kind of slimy, spineless parasite who'll do anything to get ahead.

**SYCOPHANTS AND YOUR GENITALS**

Ancient Greece was full of toadies: a politician would be accompanied by all sorts of fawning followers as he made his way through the streets. Mostly they were there to sing his praises ('Bravo Dosithios!', 'Hurrah for Lysandros!', etc.) but when an opposition candidate was nearby, these toadies hit a different note. While the politician himself remained aloof and sportsmanlike, his followers would show 'the sign of the fig'.

Eh? Well, as one book explains, the fig sign was 'an ancient copulatory gesture', much like 'giving the finger' today. When they stuck their thumb between two of their fingers, Greeks were 'simulating the penis thrust through a woman's labia. It was called the fig because the inserted thumb is about the size and shape of a fig'.

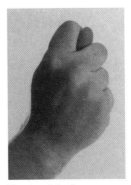

**The sign of the fig**

Mildly interesting if you like a bit of labia-talk. Very interesting if you know a bit of Greek. For 'sykos' in that language means 'fig', and 'fanês' is the verb 'to show'. 'One who shows figs' is, quite literally, a *sycophant*.

### HOW TO MAKE A SLAV YOUR SLAVE

True sycophancy, however, involves more than the occasional hand gesture. If you really want to suck up properly, you need to be somebody's *slave*.

Many Slavs were. Now (fairly) happily settled in the Balkans, these Eastern European peoples had what you might call a difficult neighbour during most of the Middle Ages: the ever-expanding Holy Roman Empire. Living, as they did, right on the empire's border, any Slavic people who weren't killed generally got to be captured, as successive emperors gobbled up their lands.

So common were Slavic captives, after a while, that 'Slav' came to describe pretty much anyone in a position of servitude. English-speakers added an e.

### MAVERICK THE MAVERICK

Samuel Maverick (1803–1870) would not have been a good slave. One of those plainspoken, straight-shootin' Texan types whose descendants were largely to blame for George W Bush, Maverick was something of a *maverick*.

**The maverick Samuel Maverick**

In 1845, the story goes, a man owed him money but was unable to pay off the debt. Maverick therefore accepted 400 cows in place of the money—but, knowing nothing and caring less about the cattle industry, he then allowed them to roam free and unbranded. Any wandering, unmarked cow in the area thus came to be considered 'one of Maverick's'. And the word eventually grew to mean any kind of untamed individual who's more than happy to stray from the herd.

### THE PIKERS OF PIKE COUNTY

Rugged individualism isn't always a good thing, however: some situations call for teamwork. Mavericks in such circumstances might instead be called *pikers*—another term born way out west, specifically in Pike County in God's own Missouri. A great many Pikers made their way from Missouri to California for the 1850s gold rush. But, while there, they didn't make themselves popular. Pikers continually opted out of team-based mining in order to dig alone.

(Although another theory has it that they were excessively frugal with the gold they did find—and so 'piked out' when it came to boozing, whoring and gambling, the typical miner's favourite pastimes.)

**HILLBILLIES, SHAMROCKS AND LEP- RECHAUNS**

While on the subject of Americans who would make bad slaves, perhaps we should also mention the *hillbillies*: snaggle-toothed mountain folk from the Appalachians who use 'cowpoke' as a verb. We know for certain that their ancestors mostly came from Northern Ireland—that being the protestant chunk of Ireland that owes its life to William III's 1690 victory at the Battle of the Boyne. And we also know that supporters of King William were known as 'Billy Boys'.

Is that why their mountain-dwelling descendants eventually became known as 'hillbillies'?

**King 'Hill' Billy**

# FOOD & CLOTHING

## THIRST-QUENCHING WORDS

Coffee, Mocha, Cappuccino, Earl Grey, Milo, Sybaritic, Libation, Bacchanalian, Epicurean, Lush, Grog, Groggy, Admiral, Booze, Scotch, Bourbon, Jack Daniels, Cognac, Armagnac, Bordeaux, Burgundy, Sauternes, Champagne, Chartreuse, Ouzo, Veuve Clicquot, Dom Pérignon, Kir, Bloody Mary, Sherry, Port, Tequila, Daiquiri, Angostura, Curaçao, Kahlua, Margarita, Baileys

## NUTRITIOUS WORDS

Kellogg's Corn Flakes, Bircher muesli, Quaker Oats, Cereal, Apple, Granny Smith apple, Boysenberry, Cherry, Currant, Cantaloupe, Tangerine, Mandarin, Rhubarb, Peach, Caesar salad, Cos lettuce, Waldorf salad, Salad Niçoise, Thousand Island dressing, Pickle, Cayenne pepper, Shallot, Jalapeño chilli, Brussels sprouts, Lima beans, Jerusalem artichoke, Brazil nut, Chestnut, Macadamia nut

## LESS NUTRITIOUS WORDS

Eggs Benedict, Eggs Florentine, Hollandaise sauce, Béarnaise sauce, Mayonnaise, Bolognaise sauce, Neapolitan sauce, Marinara sauce, Puttanesca sauce, Margarita pizza, Sandwich, Club sandwich, Hamburger, Steak tartare, Beef stroganoff, Carpaccio, Porterhouse steak, Buffalo wing, Tabasco, Nacho, Pavlova, Melba toast, Peach Melba, Crepes Suzette, Lamington, Kit Kat, Snickers bar, Mars bar, Milky Way

## STYLISH WORDS

Spruce, Cravat, Windsor knot, Tuxedo, Pants, Jeans, Denim, Damask, Suede, Gauze, Angora, Satin, Silk, Chantilly lace, Chambray, Hessian, Fustian, Tweed, Calico, Cashmere, Jodhpur, Dungaree, Homburg, Fedora, Trilby, Tam-o'-shanter, Milliner, Stetson, Bowler hat, Cologne

## LESS STYLISH WORDS

Nike, Adidas, Wellington, Galosh, Cardigan, Balaclava, Mackintosh, Spencer, Duffel coat, Jersey, Chapel, Knickers, Ok, Bloomers, Bluestocking, Bikini, Leotard, Crew cut, Bigwig, Sideburns

# THIRST-QUENCHING WORDS

**COFFEE, THE PRIDE OF KAFFA**

It may just be possible to live without *coffee*, in the strict, technical sense of the term. But, really, what would be the point?

Blessed opener of eyelids and clearer of heads, this precious wonder-drink may have first given people the strength to go on in Kaffa, a fertile mountain region of Ethiopia that once lay on a trade route to Yemen. The story goes that, one day in the 9th century BC, a goatherd's flock became abnormally frisky after nibbling on a strange new bush. So the goatherd had some himself, perked up considerably and immediately began spreading the word.

Whether or not that's true, we know that coffee travelled from Ethiopia to Yemen in the 15th century and from there spread throughout the Middle East. Much of said spreading was done from the Yemeni port of Al-Mukha. Locals pronounce it Al-**Mocha**.

**THE CAPPUCCINO MONKS**

When coffee finally arrived in Europe, some time around the 16th century, a few Catholics disapproved. A group of them even urged Pope Clement VII to ban the strange new drink—but legend has it that he refused to do so until he had taken a sip himself. One refreshing mouthful later, the brown bean had his blessing. 'This beverage is so delicious,' he reportedly exclaimed, 'it would be a sin to let only misbelievers drink it!'

Clement might have been even more impressed by a *cappuccino*. That drink is, after all, named after some particularly devout Catholics: a holy order of Franciscan friars. Founded in central Italy, the Capuchin monks believed in austerity, penitence and a rural way of life—but more importantly, for our purposes, they also believed in wearing little pointy hats. Often a slightly lighter shade of brown than their monkish robes beneath, these capuches ('little hoods') slightly resemble the milky froth on a cappuccino. And so gave that beverage its name.

**PRIME MINISTER EARL GREY** There wasn't much call for Catholic monks in 1800s England, where Protestantism was the law of the land. A few of the more progressive politicians did at least campaign for Catholic emancipation, however. The best known of them is probably Charles Grey (1764–1845). An MP at 22 and prime minister from 1830 to 1834, he was a man of 'unrivalled talents' and 'unblemished honour'— a courageous opponent of slavery and doughty champion of parliamentary reform. But his main claim to fame is a tea bag. Made an earl after the death of his father, Grey was once presented with a brand-new tea blend by a Chinese diplomat. Specially scented with bergamot, in order to offset the smelly lime-heavy water at the earl's home, the blend became a mainstay of prime ministerial tea parties, and was soon known as, yes, *Earl Grey*.

**MILO THE MACHO MAN** You wouldn't have caught Milo of Croton at some tea party. He was much too busy doing push-ups. A six-time champion at the ancient Olympics, this 6th-century BC Greek wrestler also spent a lot of time eating— washing down 18 kilos of meat and bread every day with around 9 litres of wine. Legend says he 'once carried a 4-year-old bull on his shoulders before slaughtering, roasting, and devouring it in one day'. As to how the bull felt about his piggy-backing buddy turning on him so suddenly, no historical record remains.

In the end, however, Mr Muscles was devoured himself. Legend also says that Milo saw a forked tree while walking through a forest one day, and decided to try and 'rend it asunder'. (Presumably the tree was looking a bit uppity and needed to be taken down a twig or two.) A few yanks later, he got his hand stuck ... and was set upon by a pack of wolves.

And it would seem that we're devouring him still. In 1934, an industrial chemist invented a new chocolate drink for Sydney's Royal Easter Show. He named it **Milo** after the legendary Olympian, perhaps hoping to give

Milo getting ready for action

chocolate-slurping fatties the hope that they could be athletes too.

**NO MATCH FOR MILO: THE SYBARITIC SYBARITES**

There were probably plenty of fat people living in Sybaris, a city Milo's Croton once fought in a war. ('One hundred thousand men of Croton were stationed with three hundred thousand Sybarite troops ranged against them. Milo the athlete led them and through his tremendous physical strength first turned the troops lined up against him.')

Sounds impressive, I know, but the Sybarites weren't exactly hardened soldiers. In Greek legend, a typical citizen of this ultra-rich region once endured a sleepless night because some prankster had placed a rose petal under his mattress. The source of the word *sybaritic*, the Sybarites were lovers, rather than fighters, and luxury was what they loved most.

The ancient world seems to have been full of such degenerate types. And why not, when the gods on offer included Liber, the god of vineyards, a deity who liked to see his congregation getting thoroughly smashed? Sometimes known as 'Bacchus', Liber presided over religious festivals in which the wine flowed so freely that we still say *libation* and *bacchanalian* today.

And for public intellectuals, the ancients had people like Epicurus (341–270 BC), famous advocate of the pleasurable life. But *epicureans* as we define them today would probably horrify that philosopher—a man who ate bread, rather than caviar, and drank water instead of fine wine. In Epicurus's much-misrepresented eyes, pleasure was a state of 'sober reasoning … not continuous drinkings nor the satisfaction of lusts'.

**THE LUSHES OF LONDON**

Not everyone agrees with Epicurus. A bunch of London actors, for example, thought that pleasure was *all about* continuous drinkings and the satisfaction of lusts. So they formed a drinking club in 1750. Calling themselves The City of Lushington, the club's members would drink at the Harp Tavern whenever they weren't working— which, since they were actors, meant they drank all the time. 'Wont to turn night into day', the club had four 'aldermen' named Juniper, Poverty, Lunacy and Suicide and a Lord Mayor who 'jokingly lectured new members on the evils of strong drink'.

We don't really know why they called themselves 'Lushington', a word that, after a few decades, acquired a life of its own. Phrases like 'Alderman Lushington is his master' and 'to deal with Lushington' were once used to imply someone was a drunk. These days we'd just call them a *lush*.

**Admiral Grog**

**ADMIRAL GROG, ENEMY OF FUN**

Admiral Edward Vernon (1684–1757) was certainly not a lush. Nicknamed 'Old Grog' because of his distinctive grogham coat, this famously prickly naval commander liked to keep his ships shipshape. And thus didn't like his men to be drunk. In 1740, therefore, he issued a startling new order. Because of its 'many fatal effects to their morals as well as their health', each sailor's daily rum ration was to be cut and mixed with a quart of water.

Horrified by Old Grog's diluted rum, which just got them mildly tipsy instead of completely shitfaced, the sailors nicknamed it **grog**. The word soon expanded to mean any kind of booze but the original meaning of watered-down alcohol is still reflected in the term **groggy**—meaning, as it does, slightly bleary-eyed.

(All **admirals**, incidentally, can trace their title to one Abu-Bekr (573–634), who succeeded Mohammed in 632. As Islam's new leader, he took the title 'Amir-al-muninin', or 'Commander of the faithful'. Centuries later, Europeans borrowed the title for their naval commanders, not realising that 'Amir-al' actually means 'commander *of*'.)

**MR BOOZ'S BEVERAGE**

We can assume that, since Abu-Bekr was a Muslim, he would have disapproved of **booze**. So he wouldn't have liked EG Booz either. A distiller from Philadelphia, Booz sold a drink called 'EG Booz's Old Cabin Whiskey' that was extremely popular during the 1860s and 70s.

Did it make the word popular too? 'Booze' appears to predate the 1860s (it's probably derived from 'busen', a Dutch word meaning 'to guzzle') but that seems to be the decade in which it became widely used.

**WHY JACK DANIELS NEEDED MORE BOURBON**

Not that Philadelphia was the only place to get whiskey. *Scotch*, obviously enough, comes from Scotland, while the place to get *bourbon* is Bourbon, a grain-rich region of Kentucky that was named after the famous line of French kings.

The whiskey-merchant Jasper (or 'Jack') Daniel could also be found in Kentucky. At least until he kicked a safe one morning, annoyed because he couldn't open it … and proceeded to die from blood poisoning in his toe. Ironically, a splash of *Jack Daniels* would have almost certainly disinfected the wound.

**CHAMPAGNES, WIDOWS AND MONKS**

Jack's final words, it's said, were 'One last drink, please', so it seems a pity he wasn't in France. That country is simply overflowing with alcohol. Towns and regions where you can quench your thirst include *Cognac* and *Armagnac*, *Bordeaux* and *Burgundy*. Not to mention *Sauternes*, *Champagne* and the *Chartreuse* Mountains. Even a well-known Greek aperitif gets its name from a major French city: *Ouzo* comes from 'uso Massalia' ('to be used in Marseilles'), a phrase often stamped on exported crates.

When it comes to naming alcohol, a few French people have done their bit too. Take 'the Grand Dame of Champagne', Barbe-Nicole Ponsardin (1777–1866). She married a banker, wool trader and champagne merchant named François Clicquot. When he died seven years later, Barbe-Nicole, his widow (or 'veuve'), took over the business—and took it from strength to strength. Soon *Veuve Clicquot* champagne was being drunk in all the royal courts of Europe, though no-one seemed to have much use for their wool.

Dom Pérignon (1638–1715) probably wouldn't have had much use for *Dom Pérignon*. Placed in charge of the cellar at a Benedictine Abbey in Champagne, that French monk is generally credited with the invention of champagne, but he actually dedicated his career to removing bubbles. In the 17th and 18th centuries, no-one wanted their white wine to sparkle. Bubbles were just something that occasionally happened after a cold autumn (which would lead to grapes 'refermenting' while in the bottle). Wine-makers hated them because they generated carbon dioxide, and so made the odd bottle blow up.

By contrast, Felix Kir (1876–1968) hated Nazis. A French Catholic priest from Dijon, he was a very active figure in the French Resistance, and helped to free 5000 prisoners of war. After WWII, the local hero was made Major of Dijon and had a favourite local drink named after him. Add a splash of blackcurrant syrup to white wine and you're enjoying a *Kir*.

**BLOODY MARY, NO FAN OF PROTES-TANTS** England's Queen Mary (1516–1558) was a big fan of Catholic priests. She was less fond of Protestants, however, and thought it was important that they knew how she felt. Over 300 such 'heretics' were put to death during Mary's short and violent reign, and many more rotted away in prison.

So was the *Bloody Mary* named after this bloodthirsty ruler? It seems likely but we don't really know.

**JULIUS CHERRY** We do, however, know that another ruler had a drink named after him, albeit it by an indirect path. *Sherry*, the sweet fortified wine, is named after Jerez, the Spanish town where it was first made. But (colonised, as it was, by the Romans) 'Jerez' is actually a later, more Spanish-sounding version of the town's original name: 'Caesaris' (Julius Caesar's city).

Ah, those Spanish. Along with the Portuguese (whose port town of Porto gave us, well, *port*), the Spanish conquered most of South America in the 16th century, and spent the next 300 years hunting for silver and gold. They should have just stuck to drinking. The South American continent is, after all, home to *Tequila*, a town in Mexico, and *Daiquiri*, a beach in Cuba. *Angostura* is a region in Venezuela, *Curaçao* an island off its coast. And *Kahlua* refers to the Acolhua people, who once lived in the Valley of Mexico.

**MARGARET'S MARGARITA**

We don't really know why another refreshing Mexican beverage, the *Margarita*, is so named, but the most popular story points to Margaret Sames. In 1948, this Dallas socialite was holidaying with friends in the Mexican town of Acapulco, at a house with a poolside bar. Bored one day, she decided to create a new drink ('After all, a person can only drink so many beers or so many Bloody Marys, or screwdrivers or whatever'). And after one or two missteps ('I was pushed into the swimming pool quite a few times because some of those first drinks were so bad'), she came up with one that worked.

**BAILEYS AND THE INVISIBLE MAN**

Can we tell a similar story about RA Bailey, the man whose signature adorns every bottle of *Baileys*? No, because he doesn't exist.

First manufactured in the 1970s, the drink's name was actually inspired by the Bailey's Hotel in London. 'There's no Mr or Mrs Bailey,' admits the company's external affairs director. 'We wanted a name that was Irish, but not "show" Irish. The "RA Bailey" was a way of putting a name behind the factory, a way of getting across that the product comes from Ireland … We could produce Baileys more cheaply in New Zealand or Australia, but whenever we've researched the idea consumers say "over my dead body".'

Bailey's Hotel, London

# NUTRITIOUS WORDS

'Health nuts are going to feel stupid someday, lying in hospitals dying of nothing.' So said the comedian Redd Foxx, who had the good sense to die of a heart attack.

Dr John Kellogg (1852–1943) was one such health nut. He was still thriving at 91 thanks to brisk walks, good clean living, and a yoghurt enema every day. Now best remembered as the inventor of **Kellogg's Corn Flakes**, this ever-passionate health campaigner should really be remembered as a psycho. As chief medical officer at a sanatorium, one of Kellogg's less lasting inventions was a high-powered enema machine. It enabled patients to enjoy yoghurt's 'protective germs where they are most needed, and may render most effective service'.

John Harvey Kellogg and his squeaky clean bowels

And that certainly wasn't all they got to enjoy. The many health benefits of dried cereal flakes and squeaky-clean bowels could, Kellogg believed, all be undone by one 'terrible evil'. Masturbation. A bit of quality time with oneself, he argued, could well lead to epilepsy or cancer ('such a victim literally dies by his own hand').

Luckily, Kellogg had a cure. For girls, he found 'the application of pure carbolic acid to the clitoris [to be] an excellent means of allaying abnormal excitement'. And to deter boys, the good doctor proposed circumcision. Or—even better—sewing the foreskin shut. 'The operation should be performed by a surgeon without administering an anaesthetic, as the brief pain attending the operation will have a salutary effect on the mind.' Remind me to have an apple a day.

**LESS SEXUAL BREAKFAST FOODS** Over in Switzerland, it would seem, sanatoriums were a little more sane. The head of a Zurich clinic, Maximilian Bircher-Benner (1867–1939), required his patients to get up early and commune with nature for much of the day, but he considered their genitals to be outside his brief. A good reason, perhaps, to eat **bircher muesli**, the fruit and nut–rich breakfast he based on a 'strange dish' he was once served during a hike through the Alps.

You also can't accuse the person behind **Quaker Oats** of any kind of strange zealotry. For one thing, he wasn't even a Quaker. The company started out in 1850 ... when the German Mills American Cereal Company changed its name. Its owner had recently read an encyclopaedia article about the Religious Society of Friends, which said that they were renowned for their integrity, honesty and purity. He wanted his cereal to be as well.

**THE FOX-BURNING GODDESS OF CEREAL** Though, having said that, there is a sense in which all **cereal** is religious. The word comes from Ceres, the Roman goddess of agriculture. She was 'the deity who had blessed men with the art of cultivating the earth, not only teaching them to plough and sow, but also to reap, harvest and thresh out their grain'.

Ceres was sometimes called 'the bearer of ears of corn', but she was never called 'kind to animals'. Every January, before people sowed their grain, that goddess would be offered an earthenware pot … containing the intestines of a pregnant pig. And every April, during her harvest festival, worshippers would tie fiery torches to the tails of live foxes. And watch them slowly become dead foxes, to the sound of cheers and applause.

**UNA APPLE AL GIORNO**

Ceres didn't always work her magic, however. In the ancient Roman city of Abella, grain was very thin on the ground. The town was extremely blessed when it came to fruit trees, though. It may even have given us the word *apple*, which for many years simply meant 'fruit'.

Or not. That's just a guess. But we can say with certainty where the *Granny Smith apple* got its name. To whit: one Maria Anne Smith (1799–1870) from Sussex, the wife of a farmhand from Kent. The couple and their eight children moved to Australia in 1838, and opened an orchard in rural Ryde. Then one day a bunch of their French crab apples mutated, spawning a new kind of seedling that we all like to munch.

**CHARLES BOYSEN, BERRY FARMER**

The Smiths, alas, never made much from their seedling. Granny Smith's apples were popular around Ryde during her lifetime, but only really took off after her death.

Another horticulturalist, Rudolf Boysen (1895–1950), had even less luck with *his* new fruit, a sort of hybrid of blackberries and raspberries. Broken in spirit after the commercial failure of his *boysenberry*, and then broken in back after a nasty accident, he eventually abandoned his orchard and tried another career elsewhere.

Years later, however, another farmer heard of Boysen's berry experiment and made his way to the deserted farm. Finding a few aged vines in a field full of weeds, he swiped them, grew some berries, and whammo, grew a fortune as well.

**CHERRIES, CURRANTS, CERASUS AND CORINTH**

The Roman general Lucullus (117–56 BC) made several fortunes, and spent most of them hosting lavish feasts. (Larks' tongues dipped in honey? Check. Toasted dormice? Yum.) But even the most exotic delicacies can lose their tang after a while: in around 71 BC, Lucullus needed a new dish to tantalise his tastebuds, and on a military expedition to the Black Sea, he found it. The port city of Cerasus was full of trees with a little red fruit. He returned to Rome with this treat 'of Cerasus', which straightaway became known as the *cherry*.

Cerasus had started out as a Greek colony, much like the state of Corinth. In ancient times, Corinthians had been known to like a good party: their reputation for ungodly frivolousness even led to a stern telling-off in the New Testament. But by the Middle Ages, they'd become a bit more middle-aged, and were instead generally known as good businessmen.

Their main business, as you might have guessed, was grapes. Little black ones dried under the sun. The French called these 'grapes of Corinth', 'raisins de corauntz'. The English got them from France and called them *currants* instead.

**YOU ARE WHERE YOU'RE EATEN: A FEW OTHER WELL-TRAVELLED FRUITS**

*Cantaloupes* would never get a telling-off in the New Testament. Brought to Europe in around 1700, this melon was first grown in one of the pope's summer estates. That estate's name was Castle Cantalupo (English translation: 'the howl of the wolf').

No other fruit howls, unfortunately—but, like the cantaloupe, many came from afar. *Tangerines*, for example, made their way to Europe from Tangier, a busy Moroccan port. *Mandarins*, on the other hand, came from China. Their name probably comes from the mandarins, that country's scholar-bureaucrat caste—many of whom wore bright-orange robes.

*Rhubarbs*, as it happens, also hail from China. But they came to Europe via Russia's Volga River, which, back then, was known as the Rha. And *peach*, in turn, is simply Old English for 'Persian apple'—the fruit coming to England from what we now call Iran.

**CAESAR'S SALAD DAY**

But that's enough fruit, for now. Too many more and we won't need our yoghurt enema. So let's tuck into *Caesar salad* (preferably some made with *Cos lettuce*—a variety first grown on the Greek island of Kos).

Julius Caesar, you may be troubled to learn, did not invent this salad. He was too busy coming, seeing and conquering to care if his fellow citizens enjoyed their greens. The recipe instead belongs to one Caesar Cardini (1896–1956), an Italian-born restaurateur who was based in Tijuana, Mexico. Packed with alcohol and close to the Californian border, Tijuana was a popular destination for Hollywood types during the 1920s, when prohibition was in full swing.

Caesar's restaurant was particularly packed during one public holiday in 1924—but his kitchen was just about bare. With a bunch of drunk, hungry prima donnas set to riot outside, he was forced to improvise a salad … and created an eggy hit. The likes of Clark Gable and Jean Harlow kept returning to Tijuana for more of 'Ceasar's salad', but they could soon get it in the US as well.

You can also get *Waldorf salad* in the US, I'm told. If nowhere else, then definitely at the Waldorf-Astoria, a luxury hotel in downtown Manhattan. *Salad Niçoise* is served in Nice, naturally enough, while *Thousand Island salad dressing* is said to hail from the Thousand Island area of the St Lawrence River, which runs from New York state to Canada.

**MR PICKLE AND SOME PIQUANT FOODS**

But since Thousand Island dressing sometimes has finely chopped pickles, perhaps we can say that it hails from Holland as well. The verb *to pickle* may be derived from a 14th-century

Dutch businessman. William Beukel exported what was then an unheard-of food: fish pickled in brine. But the word more likely comes from the Dutch language, in which 'pekel' means 'piquant'.

Piquant foods, needless to say, can be exported from all over the world. *Cayenne pepper* first came from Cayenne, the capital of French Guiana in South America, while the Greeks got their *shallots* from Ashkelon, an ancient Israeli city. And the Mexican town of Jalapa is to blame for the *jalapeño chilli*, that brightly coloured burner of so many innocent mouths.

**LESS PIQUANT FOODS**

Where we get some rather less piquant foods really ought to be self-explanatory. *Brussels sprouts* come from Belgium, *Lima beans* from Peru. Though, having said that, there's no known connection between Israel and the *Jerusalem artichoke*.

On the nut-naming front, *Brazil nuts* are, yes, from Brazil, while *chestnut* means 'nut from Castana', a city in central Greece. But, no, *Macadamia nuts* are not from Macadamia (if such a place does, indeed, exist). In fact, they were named in tribute to Dr John Macadam (1827–1865), a distinguished Australian scientist with another, entirely unrelated claim to fame. He was an umpire at the first-ever Australian Rules football match.

# LESS NUTRITIOUS WORDS

**BENEDICT THE EGGMAN**

Good health, as many wise observers have noted, merely represents the slowest possible rate at which one can die. Should you ever wish to speed up the process, start your day with some *Eggs Benedict*:

a heart-clogging combination of ham, eggs and butter festooned in a rich, yellow sauce. A gift to cardiologists everywhere, it's said to have been created by one Lemuel Benedict (1867–1943), a New York stockbroker and socialite. One morning in 1894, the story goes, some of this socialising had taken its toll. Benedict staggered into the Waldorf-Astoria Hotel with an almighty hangover, and ordered the fattiest foods that came to his mind. The maître d' was so taken by Benedict's breakfast cure, he put it on the menu straightaway.

When Eggs Benedict is cooked with spinach, it becomes **Eggs Florentine**. But why 'Florentine'? The explanation lies with Catherine de Medici (1519–1589), a member of the powerful Renaissance family who married a French king in 1547. Catherine brought some chefs on the journey from Florence, and they took some Italian vegetables along for the ride. Spinach was one of them, and soon any dish served with these green leaves was dubbed 'à la Florentine' by the French.

**CONDIMENTS TO THE CHEF: THREE REASONS TO LIKE THE FRENCH**

The rich, yellow sauce in both breakfasts is, of course, **Hollandaise**. But no, it doesn't come from Holland. Originally called Sauce Isigny, this butter-rich sauce was invented in or near Isigny-sur-Mer, a tiny town in Normandy, the dairy capital of France. During WWI, however, Normandy was also the trench capital of France. With millions of gun-toting Germans, it was no place to be milking a cow.

So French sauce-makers had to get most of their butter from elsewhere. Specifically, from the Netherlands. Sauce Isigny made with Dutch butter was called 'Sauce Hollandaise'—and, just like butter, the name seemed to stick.

Hollandaise's sister sauce is, of course, **Béarnaise**. Essentially the same sauce, with a bit of this and that thrown in, it was invented at a 19th-century French restaurant called Le Pavilion Henri IV. But while the restaurateur was clearly happy to name his establishment after a king, he thought it wrong to whack his name on a sauce. So he called it *Béarnaise* after Henri IV's birthplace, the French province of Béarn.

But the mother of both sauces is *mayonnaise*. The French generally credit it to the Duc de Richelieu, who defeated the Spanish army at Port Mahón in 1756. He supposedly told his chef to create a special new dish to celebrate the conquest and 'Mahónaise' was what arrived on his plate.

**SAUCY PROSTI-TUTES**

As delicious as mayonnaise may be, it's not much good on pasta. For that you need a sauce like *bolognaise*, from the Italian city of Bologna, or *neapolitan* from the city of Naples.

Another good option, *marinara sauce*, also comes from Italy. It got its name from 'la marinara', the fishermen's wives who would serve it to their husbands after a hard day trawling at sea.

*Puttanesca sauce*, on the other hand, is named after women who work at night. Italian for 'whore's sauce', it's extremely quick and easy to make. Ideal, then, for a prostitute with a few minutes between clients, or a wife hurrying home from her lover.

**QUEEN MARGHERITA PIZZA**

A much more respectable Italian woman was that country's queen consort. The wife (and cousin) of King Umberto, Margherita of Savoy (1851–1926) was a patron of the arts who, politically, was said to lean towards fascism. Gastronomically, she leaned towards French food, like the rest of her class, but all that changed in 1889, after a tasty trip to Naples. As a diplomatic gesture, she ate some of that poor man's food,

**Margherita, Queen of Pizza**

pizza—but she wasn't just being diplomatic when she declared that she liked it. Her favourite, she said, was the one with mozzarella, tomatoes and basil (perhaps not surprisingly, given it matched the white, red and green of the Italian flag). So the locals named it after her.

And who doesn't like *margarita pizza*?

**THE WELL-BREAD EARL OF SANDWICH**

Queen Margherita certainly wasn't the only blueblood to end up on a menu. The 4th Earl of Sandwich (1718–1792) is immortalised in the *sandwich*, a snack he supposedly invented during an all-night card game when he didn't want to faff about with a knife and fork.

But he should really be immortalised for another reason. Once described as 'the most universally disliked man in England',

The Earl of Sandwich, possibly thinking about a sandwich

Sandwich presided over the British navy during the American War of Independence and by all accounts did a bad job. Corrupt, incompetent and 'violently anti-democratic', he 'reduced the British navy to a state of total confusion'. Which was a big reason why the US won. 'Seldom has any man held so many offices and accomplished so little' was one popular suggestion for his epitaph.

And another was 'as mischievous as a monkey and as lecherous as a goat'. As a red-blooded member of the Hellfire Club, Sandwich particularly enjoyed deflowering young virgins. No pastime, he once pervily noted, can ever beat 'the corruption of innocence'.

**A CLUB
AND ITS
SANDWICH**

A very different sort of club can be found at Saratoga Springs, an upmarket town in upstate New York. Women weren't welcome at the Saratoga Club, just rich gents who liked to play cards.

One of those gents, it's thought, also liked sandwiches. Particularly the one he put together at his house one night in 1894, using every ingredient he could find in his kitchen. The next day, he made one for the boys at the club, and they all liked it too. So it went on the menu. And these days it can be found all sorts of menus. Under the name *club sandwich*.

**THE
HAMBURG-
ERS WHO
SAILED THE
WORLD**

*Hamburgers* are on even more menus: nothing beats a bit of ground meat in between two hunks of bread. American diners started serving these pseudo-sandwiches in the late 19th century, but ground meat patties themselves had already been around for a while. Because they could be salted and smoked (and thus made to survive long voyages) they were for centuries very popular in ports.

Hamburg, Europe's biggest port city, sent a great many sailors to New York. To attract their custom, therefore, shops around New York harbour would put up signs advertising that they had beef patties—or, rather, 'meat cooked in the Hamburg style'. Patties duly became known as 'Hamburg steak', so when they got shoved in a bun, the result was a 'hamburger'.

But *was* that meat cooked in 'the Hamburg style'? Not really. European sailors actually got the idea of shredding and spicing tough meat from people much further east. It seems that the Tartars (those violent, nomadic horsemen that roamed Russia in the Middle Ages) kept so busy being violent and nomadic horsemen that they were often left with no time to cook.

Their solution was to not even try. A Tartar warrior would frequently ride all day with some raw meat tucked under the saddle.

By night-time, it'd be (kind of) tender, so he'd slice it up, add some spices and eat. Sadly, this dish is still with us. The French added a raw egg and called it **Steak tartare**.

**OF MEAT AND MEN** Russia, the stomping ground of the Tartars, also made room for some counts. One of these was Count Pavel Stroganoff (1774–1817), a well-known gourmet and member of the Imperial Academy of Arts, who somehow managed to lose all his teeth. Legend says that this prompted his personal chef to invent **Beef stroganoff**, an ever-so-digestible dish.

As a patron of the arts, Stroganoff may have admired Vittore Carpaccio (1465–1525), a painter of the Venetian school who liked to work with light, bright colours. **Carpaccio** (thin slices of raw meat or fish, often smothered in a yellowy sauce) is said to go by that name because of the painter. Its vivid reds and yellows reminded the chef of a Carpaccio picture that was hanging on his restaurant's wall.

The best cut of meat is a **porterhouse**. It seems safe to assume that this cut of steak was named after a porterhouse (that is, a pub that served porter, a sort of ye olde dark brown beer). But the question is, which one? The answer, according to *The Dictionary of Americanisms*, is Martin Morrison's Porterhouse, which operated in New York in the early 1800s.

Not that the porterhouse is New York State's only contribution to the meat industry. Chickens have suffered at its hands as well. 'A blue-collar dish for a blue-collar town', **Buffalo wings** were invented at the Anchor Bar in Buffalo in 1964, as a way of making money out of chicken wings, instead of simply throwing them away. 'Anybody can sell steak,' said bar owner Frank Bellissimo, 'but if you can sell odds and ends of one thing or another, then you're doing something.' (What he's also done, of course, is confuse patrons, who wonder where exactly is the wing on a buffalo.)

**NACHOS, THE QUICK-THINKING MEXICAN**

A slightly more upmarket eatery could once be found in Coahuia, Mexico (not all that far from the sauce-producing region of *Tabasco*). Nicknamed 'Nacho', Ignacio Anaya (died 1975) was maître d' at the Victory Club, a restaurant that often fed soldiers from a nearby US airbase in Texas. One day in 1943, a dozen officers' wives arrived at the eatery—and the chef was nowhere to be found. 'My father said, "Let me go quick and fix something for you,"' recalled Anaya's son a few decades later, and returned with a brand-new snack he called 'Nacho's Especiales'. The name was eventually shortened to *nachos*.

**DIVA DELICACIES: PAVLOVA'S DESSERT AND MELBA'S TOAST**

Anna Pavlova (1881–1931) couldn't have had nachos. As one of those ultra-sinewy ballerina types, that Russian starlet probably had to make do on dry biscuits, with some cold water for dessert. *Pavlova* would have been out of the question too. No-one can quite agree whether this super-sweet meringue dessert was invented in Australia or New Zealand, but it was definitely named after the iconic ballerina, who toured both countries in the 1920s.

Dame Nellie Melba (1861–1931) was definitely invented in Australia: that iconic opera star was born in Melbourne and took her stage name from her home town. Her personality was straight out of the textbook, however. The quintessential diva, Melba refused to share a bow with any other singer, and hung a sign in her dressing room that read 'SILENCE! SILENCE!' She eventually died from blood poisoning incurred during a face lift.

That wasn't the first time the soprano felt close to death, however. Around the turn of the 20th century, she fell ill during a stay at the Savoy. Anxious not to upset her tum tum, the hotel's adoring chef toasted some very thinly sliced bread—and, in tribute, called it *Melba toast*.

**CREPES SUZETTE AND THE PRINCE**

That same chef also named another, more extravagant creation after her, but *Peach Melba* is now rarely served. Far tastier to modern palates is *Crepes Suzette*, a dessert named after someone who may not have been a queen of the stage, but did at least sleep with a prince.

Crepes Suzette were supposedly invented by a Monte Carlo waiter called Henri Carpentier (1880–1961), while he was serving pancakes to the Prince of Wales and his lady friend. 'It was quite by accident as I worked in front of a chafing dish that the cordials caught fire,' Carpentier later wrote. 'I thought I was ruined. The Prince and his friends were waiting. How could I begin all over? I tasted it. It was, I thought, the most delicious melody of sweet flavours I had ever tasted. I still think so. That accident of the flame was precisely what was needed to bring [out] one harmony of taste …'

> He asked me the name of that which he had eaten with so much relish. I told him it was to be called Crepes Princesse. He recognised that the pancake controlled the gender [of the term 'Princesse'] and this was a compliment designed for him; but protested with mock ferocity that there was a lady present. She was alert and rose to her feet and holding her little shirt wide with her hands she made him a curtsey. 'Will you,' said His Majesty, 'change Crepes Princesse to Crepes Suzette?' Thus was born and baptised this confection, one taste of which, I really believe, would reform a cannibal into a civilised gentleman.

**LORD LAMINGTON, KOALA KILLER**

One such civilised gentleman was Lord Lamington (1860–1940). Unless you happened to be a koala. Born Charles Wallace Alexander Napier Cochrane-Baillie, this Eton- and Oxford-educated aristocrat served as Governor of Queensland from

1896 to 1901. There was nothing terribly remarkable about his time in office — except for the day some conservationists invited him to visit a national park and he took the opportunity to shoot a sleeping koala.

**Lord Lamington**

He didn't much like *lamingtons* either, referring to the cakes, for which a recipe first appeared in 1909, as 'those bloody, poofy, woolly biscuits'. But like it or not, it seems certain that in some way or another, those poofy woolly biscuits must owe him their name.

**THE KIT-KAT CLUB AND OTHER CANDY**

*Kit Kats* are less poofy and woolly — but they too have a political namesake. The Kit-Kat Club was a political group in early 18th-century London. Ardent Whigs, they held their meetings at a pie house run by Christopher 'Kit' Catling, a pastry chef famous for his mutton pie. 'Generally mentioned as a set of wits, [but] in reality the patriots that saved Britain', the club's members included such notables as William Congreve, Sir John Vanbruch and Joseph Addison, plus about a dozen different earls and dukes.

When they were not plotting reform over mutton pies, those nobs liked to hob at the races. Had any of them managed to live until the 1920s, they might have seen Snickers, a Tennessee racehorse owned by the Mars family, and trained at their property, the Milky Way Farm. The Mars family, you may not be terribly surprised to read, were confectioners. Over the years, they've come up with such delights as the *Snickers bar,* the *Mars bar* and the *Milky Way*. Geniuses when it came to combining nougat and caramel, but not so creative when it came to names.

# STYLISH WORDS

**GERMANY, LAND OF THE SPRUCE** When the well-to-do want to look *spruce*, they generally shop in Milan. But they should really be going to Prussia. Once an independent kingdom, and nowadays part of Germany, that region has always had plenty to sell. Goods imported from there were traditionally called 'pruisse' (that being the Old French form of 'from Prussia')—a term that in time transformed into 'spruce' (that being a little easier to say). For centuries, Europeans enjoyed 'spruce beer' and 'spruce iron', 'spruce canvas' and 'spruce wood'.

In the 16th century, the especially wealthy also enjoyed 'spruce jerkins'—a rather dapper type of short-sleeved jacket, beautifully tailored with soft, dark leather. These spruce jerkins were so very stylish, in fact, that that word 'spruce' gradually lost its original meaning. No longer denoting 'from Prussia', it became a synonym for well turned-out.

**THE CRAVATS THAT COULD KILL** Cravats—mercenary soldiers from Croatia—also put careful thought into what they wore. In the days before uniforms, soldiers didn't just need to fight well, they needed to dress with care. Look anything like the enemy, and you may just get shot by your friends. One way to save their necks, they realised, was to tie a scarf around them—a then totally unheard-of fashion statement that evolved into what we now call a tie. Sick of those starched lace collars and poncy linen ruffs, France's Louis XIV reportedly spent time with his Croatian regiment and realised that, in *cravats*, they'd found was an easier way.

There are roughly eighty-five different ways to tie a tie—but only one of them actually looks good. This sartorial masterstroke was named after the Duke of Windsor (1894–1972), a famously natty nobleman who liked his tie knots very wide. His valet would use extra-thick material to achieve this effect, but someone else, wanting to emulate it, came up with the bulky **Windsor knot**.

For a short time, it's worth remembering, this ever-chic leader in men's fashion was also the leader of England. The duke was crowned Edward VIII in 1937, then took the crown off later that year. He abdicated because the constitution would not allow him to marry Wallis Simpson, a divorced woman, and he wanted to, oh so much.

**A SCANDAL IN TUXEDO**
The king's abdication rocked high society, of course—but le bon ton were pretty tough. They had long since recovered from a far more momentous scandal, one perpetrated by Griswold Lorillard. The scandal wasn't his name, though I agree that it is controversial. It came about through his taste in suits.

In 1886, this blueblooded tobacco heir was facing the daily trial borne by men of his class. Just like yesterday and the day before that, people were expecting him to dress up for dinner. You couldn't have your pheasant, port and cigars back in the day if you didn't strut about in some seriously long coat-tails and a collar that was all starchy and tight.

Or could you? 'Screw this,' thought Griswold. 'I'm just going to go in my smoking jacket.' To that silky, short black number, he boldly added black pants and a bow tie—and then hopped in his carriage and told his driver where to go. Their destination was a rather hoity-toity men's club in upstate New York. That went by the name of **Tuxedo** Park.

**THE PANTS MAN**
If Griswold had *really* wanted to cause a sensation, however, he'd have entered the place without *pants*. Bare-naked man tackle tends to raise eyebrows, even among people who can overlook a moustache.

But why do we call them 'pants'? Why not 'leg-covers' or 'praddins' or 'splutes'? It's because of Pantalone, a doddery old merchant from Venice who liked to give his genitals lots of room to breathe. Himself possibly named after San Pantaleone (a saint who survived being drowned, burnt, poisoned, stabbed and tortured, only to then have his head chopped off), Pantalone was a stock character in *commedia dell'arte*, a hugely popular Italian pantomime. Every show, and there were literally thousands, would feature Pantalone for at least a scene or two—generally with a scheme to steal money or seduce a woman, which would end up going comedically wrong.

**Pantalone**

Perhaps he should have dressed better. Instead of the knee-breeches and silken hose worn by most would-be wooers in the 17th century, Pantalone wore a pair of strange red leggings. When ordinary people started to put them on too, they called them 'pantaloons' in his honour. Nowadays we just call them 'pants'.

---

**OTHER PANTS MEN**

Not just any pants will do at a place like Tuxedo Park, however. You certainly wouldn't want to wear *jeans*. Until all those 1950s teenagers started rocking them around the clock, *denim* was a tough, sturdy fabric for cowboys and miners, not for genteel folk nibbling brie.

But long before anyone ever wore a Stetson, jeans were for sailors and peasants. *Denim* means 'de Nimes' (a city in France) and *jeans* probably evolved from 'Genoa' (a port in Italy). Whether they toiled in the fields or sailed over the seas, European workers have been wearing the fabric for about 500 years.

Material, it might be worth noting, is very often named after the place that invented it. **Damask**, for example, comes from Damascus and **suede** was invented in Sweden. The canny shopper goes to Gaza for their **gauze** and Ankara for **angora**.

If they take their shopping bag further east, they might find some **satin** in 'Zaytun', the Arabic name of the Chinese city of Tsinkiang. **Silk**, in turn, comes from the Latin word 'Seres', which simply means 'Chinese'.

Staying with the fancy fabrics, we'll find that **Chantilly lace** and **chambray** were both named for French towns—and on a less luxurious note we can thank the German state of Hesse for **hessian**, a kind of coarse sackcloth. **Fustian**, another fabric not usually seen in the best living rooms, was first manufactured in the Cairo suburb of El Fostal. And you can probably guess what they made in Scotland in factories near the River **Tweed**.

We'll end with another coarse cloth, **calico**, which comes from an Indian seaport called Calicut. Though a little further to the north, you can see Kashmir. Whose long-haired mountain goats produce **cashmere**.

**Jodhpurs** are not made out of cashmere, which is bad news for this segue. But, like cashmere, these über daggy riding pants also come from India— specifically, from the town of Jodhpur, where people play a lot of polo.

Not quite as daggy, but getting there, are **dungarees**, yet another souvenir from the subcontinent. Better known in some places as 'overalls', these works of fashion genius were named after Dongri, a suburb in Mumbai that is home to a massive market. A thick, hardy sailcloth named 'Dongari Kapar' used to be sold there—and sailors found it perfect for making overalls.

**HATS WE SHOULD HAVE KEPT ON**

Panama hats, on the other hand, do not come from India. And they don't come from Panama either. Properly called 'Ecuadorian hats', these snazzy straw numbers were never made in that country.

An enormous canal *was* made in Panama, however—and all the Westerners who came there to dig it found that they needed a hat to keep off the sun.

England's 'playful' monarch, Edward VII (1841–1910), did not himself do much digging. When *he* went overseas, it was to picturesque resort towns like Bad Homburg, where wealthy royals kept busy with fine dining and sex. Bad Homburg was home to the German Kaiser's summer residence in the 19th century and became a magnet for Europe's well-to-do.

On one of his 'rest cures', however, Edward found that he needed a break from eating and had about half an hour before he was next booked to have sex. So he went to a shop and bought a stiff felt hat. With a back-to-front dent in the crown, that hat singlehandedly started a trend. Very few people wear a *homburg* these days but, mark my words, they'll be back.

**THEATRI-CAL HATS**

To the untrained eye, a homburg is quite like a *fedora*. (To the trained eye, they're almost identical.) This kind of hat doesn't come from the town of Fedora, however—in part because that town doesn't exist.

Rather, Fedora Romanoff is a character in *Fedora*, an 1882 melodramatic play by Victorien Sardou. Once played by Sarah Bernhardt, she's a Russian princess who endures a series of dramatic tragedies (each one bursting with opportunities to hog the limelight and overact). What people remember most about Bernhardt's performance, however, was that, very unusually for a woman, her character wore a soft felt hat. Gangsters and detectives made fedoras famous in the 1930s, but they started out as female fashion.

But to people in the know, this kind of thing is a little old hat. It turns out that headwear gets named after female characters in plays all the time. The **trilby** owes its name to *Trilby*, a play based on George du Maurier's 1894 novel, which has a main character named Trilby O'Farrell. A slightly dopey artist's model, Trilby comes under the spell of a sinister hypnotist named Svengali. And yes, she has a hat.

**MAD HATS**

Bagpipers wear strange hats too (though this is obviously the least of their crimes). Very rarely seen on the catwalks of Milan, their tartan-patterned, pom-pommed bonnets are named **tam-o'-shanters** after, well, Tam o'Shanter, the hero of a 1790 Robbie Burns poem. If you've read it, you'll recall that 'honest Tam o'Shanter as he frae Ayr ae night did canter'. He 'skelpit on thro' dub and mire, despisin' wind and rain and fire'—only to see 'warlocks and witches in a dance; nae cotillion brent-new frae France'. 'Wither'd beldams, auld and droll, rigwoodie hags wad spean a foal'.

If you'd rather avoid a full page of this, the poem basically involves a man called Tam getting drunk, then riding his horse in the middle of the night. He stumbles upon a bunch of witches and gallops away as fast as he can.

**THE MILLINERS OF MILAN**

But perhaps tam-o'-shanters *should* be seen in Milan. That city is every hatmaker's spiritual home. The word **milliner**, you see, means 'Milan-er'. At one time, it denoted any merchant who sold dainty apparel from that fashion capital. Sixteenth-century Brits wanted bonnets, gloves, ribbons and bows from Milan, and milliners imported them all. But their main product was the city's fine straw hats, which often needed a little trimming or accessorising—a task that milliners themselves took on.

You wouldn't have caught John B Stetson (1830–1906) putting bows and ribbons on *his* hats. No way, he'd rather (you) die. But having said this, it's worth noting that the creator of the cowboy's best friend, the **Stetson**—that broad-brimmed, no-bullshit man-hat whose only accessory is a pair of six-shooters—didn't actually come from the wide open plains o' Texas. No, this devout Baptist actually owned a hat factory in Philadelphia, and never went near a saloon.

The Beaulieu brothers were also hatmakers, but they operated on a much smaller scale. Shunning massive factories and mass production, these London milliners were in the business of designing special hats for special gentlemen who had extra-special needs for their heads.

One such gentleman was William Coke, a red-cheeked squire from Norfolk who liked huntin', shootin' and fishin'. But he didn't like untangling. This was unfortunate because when Coke went riding in a tall top hat, it would get tangled up in branches rather a lot. So in 1849 the Beaulieu brothers designed a low-crowned hat at his request and got some London hatters, Lock & Co, to make it.

Lock & Co called it a 'Coke'—and 150 years later, they still do. Everybody else, however, calls it a Beaulieu. Or, as it's more commonly spelled, a **bowler**.

**THE CITY THAT SMELLS LIKE COLOGNE**

An Italian chemist named Johann Farina had better luck when it came to naming his products. When, in 1709, he named his new perfume *cologne* after the German city he had recently settled in, everybody else was happy to go along.

In a sense, however, Farina was really naming his man-scent after a woman. The city of Cologne started out as 'Colonia Agrippa', or 'the colony of Agrippina'. And Agrippina (15–59), an ancient Roman princess, doesn't exactly come out of history books smelling like roses. For a start, she slept with her brother (the emperor Caligula), then moved on to marry her uncle (the emperor

Claudius). And in order to take this step, she had to poison her first husband. Their son, Nero, may not have appreciated this. In any case, he had her killed.

# LESS STYLISH WORDS

**NIKE, GODDESS OF VICTORY** 'Just do it' says **Nike**, to unhappy workers in its sweatshops. Made for a song in Asia and sold for big bucks all over the world, these super-fancy sport shoes get their name from Nike, the Greek goddess of victory—a woman who spent her time flying around battlefields on a winged chariot, 'rewarding the victors with glory and fame'. The losers got nothing, not even medical assistance, and such callousness continues to this day. Every medal won at the Olympics, whether it be gold, silver or bronze, features a picture of Nike on one side. The losers get nothing at all.

**ADIDAS, A MAN WHO KNEW FEET** Another well-known sport shoe got its name from a god of commerce. Adi Dassler (1900–1978) and his brother both started out as cobblers (and, as it happens, members of the Nazi party). They founded the snappily named Dassler Brothers Shoe Factory, more or less invented spiked running shoes, and watched their business grow and grow.

But the animosity between them was growing too. 'They were very different characters,' says one biographer. 'Adi Dassler was always more thoughtful, a craftsman who enjoyed nothing more than fiddling with his shoes, whereas Rudolf Dassler was more an abrasive, loudmouthed salesman.' When WWII ended, so too did their partnership. Rudolf was accused by American soldiers of being a member of the SS, and 'was convinced his brother had turned him in'. So he left and started his own company: Puma. Adi Dassler took over what was left of the factory. And called it *Adidas*, after himself.

**THE DUKE OF WEL- LINGTONS**

Running doesn't just have a place in sport. It was also a good idea if you saw the Duke of Wellington (1769–1852). If you happened to be one of the enemy, this was because he was intending to kill you. And if you were one of his own soldiers, this is because, in the process, he was prepared to let you die. Nothing Napoleon could do to his men would ever intimidate the Iron Duke. He was very brave in that way.

British soldiers sometimes found it hard to run, however. They were a bit encumbered by their *wellingtons*. Better known by some as the 'gumboot', wellingtons were actually invented by the warmongering duke (or at least by his bootmaker, acting on instructions). Battling Napoleon on the soggy fields of Europe could be a very muddy business, and the hessian footwear of the time tended to slip and slide. Strangely, the farmhands of Europe had mostly been making do on wooden shoes until that time, so the new footwear very quickly caught on.

Those wooden shoes, incidentally, were called *galoshes*. Nowadays denoting a sort of waterproof overshoe, that term for about two thousand years referred to a kind of wooden sandal that was mostly worn by muddy peasants in France.

But hang on a moment: France wasn't called 'France' two thousand years ago.

**The Duke of Wellingtons**

The Franks (the Germanic tribe that gave the country its name) only invaded in around the 4th century. Well, that's all true. And it's instructive to note that the region they invaded was at the time commonly known as 'Gaul'. The Franks were much struck by its residents' galoshes—or *Gaulish* sandals, as they termed them.

**LORD CARDIGAN**

While trudging through mud in winter, it's also a good idea to rug up. English soldiers certainly did so when they fought in the Crimea, a wintry peninsula jutting into the Black Sea. In 1853, Her Majesty declared war on Russia, and she needed her best men to make a stand.

Some of her worst men came along too. But even they felt contempt for Lord Cardigan (1797–1868), 'a foolish, vain and violent-tempered' aristocrat who had used his money and connections to purchase a senior military rank. 'Constitutionally unfit for command', he was especially fond of 'petty-minded bullying', arresting 700 troops for 'disciplinary breaches' during his first year as an officer, and court-martialling over 100. He lived in a luxury yacht throughout the war, while every other man slept in the mud.

Lord Cardigan without his cardigan

But having said that, he did dress well. And on those rare occasions when Cardigan saw his soldiers, he liked them to look good too. The earl spent £10,000 out of his own pocket every year to make his regiment England's dressiest—and one of the things he funded was a sort of button-down, warm woollen vest. Specially designed for the Russian winter, it duly became known as a *cardigan*.

**BALACLAVAS AND THE VALLEY OF DEATH**

Unfortunately, about 250 cardigans later got holes in them, during the Charge of the Light Brigade. Misunderstanding an order one day, the 'bumble-headed' Cardigan ordered 600 horsemen to ride into a heavily fortified 'valley of death'. And then turn around and ride all the way back. The troops protested at the time but, as a poet later put it, theirs was not to reason why, theirs was but to do and die.

That notoriously ill-fated charge was part of a larger battle, which also didn't go so well. But at least people didn't get chilly. Fought in and around the Crimean town of Balaclava, the Battle of Balaclava gave its name to a kind of woolly headgear, which had until then been known as an 'uhlan cap'. So many troops needed *balaclavas* in the bitterly cold battlefield, the old name got frozen out.

**MACKINTOSH THE THIEF**

*Mackintoshes* would have been a good idea too. If you're going to be violently slaughtered, it seems silly to get wet as well.

They should really be called 'Symes', however. James Syme, after all, was the man who actually invented the waterproof cloth that is used to make mackintoshes—though at the time he was more or less a boy. As a student at Edinburgh University in 1818, Syme converted 'a substance from coal tar' into rubber, but didn't immediately realise that it was waterproof. An industrial chemist named Charles Macintosh (1766–1843) did realise it, though, and sneakily patented the process a few months later.

**COAT PEOPLE**

The sort of chap who would say 'mackintosh' rather than 'raincoat' is also likely to produce the word *spencer*. Like wellingtons, this garment was likely named after one of those well-born warmongering types: George Spencer (1758–1834), an earl, and one-time head of the British navy. The good lord preferred sewing to sailing, however:

it's thought that he came up with the idea of a very short and tight-fitting coat after being thrown from his horse one day, and getting his flapping coat-tails caught in a tree.

Another bright idea in the world of coats was bequeathed to all by Belgium. It's to a little town in Antwerp that we owe a big thanks for the *duffel coat.* The good folk of Duffel have been making their very own thick, coarse cloth for centuries, but they really hit the big time when someone thought to get out a needle and thread.

Fishermen from England's cold, wet Jersey Island could all really do with a duffel coat. But they insist on wearing *jerseys* instead.

**WHY CHAPELS WERE ONCE QUITE USEFUL** Though I suppose this is better than wearing nothing. A biography of St Martin (316–397) tells us about one such exhibitionist: a destitute, near-naked beggar slowly wasting away from the cold. Martin, we're told, encountered said beggar one day and proceeded to show everyone the warmth of his heart. That saint took off his cloak and tore it in two, and let the chilly vagrant wrap himself in one half.

Centuries later, St Martin's cloak (or 'capella') had become a sacred relic, and was kept enshrined in a special place. Eventually that special place became known as 'the capella'—and as more and more pilgrims came to worship there, a new word slowly evolved. *Chapel.*

**HERMAN KNICKERS** Herman Knickerbocker (1779–1855) probably should have prayed more. God clearly didn't like him that much. This distinguished American politician and patriarch led a useful and dignified life, but still managed to give *knickers* their name.

How? Well, descended from a Dutch family of brick makers (a 'knicker' is a type of brick), the wealthy Knickerbocker clan arrived in New York in the 17th century and soon took their place among the city's bluebloods. Herman was a credit to his illustrious family, serving as both a judge and a congressman, but then he rather let the side down by befriending an author. Washington Irving was a well-known humorist who occasionally wrote under a pseudonym. And for one wildly successful book, *An Illustrated History of New York*, he decided to call himself 'Diedrich Knickerbocker', being oh-so-impressed by the name of his friend.

So far, so what? But hark what happened next. The book was full of illustrations of people wearing a sort of loose, knee-length style of Dutch breeches. And it was published around the time looser, longer ladies' undergarments were first starting to be worn. British women duly began to dub these new undergarments 'knickerbockers', and as the garment changed, so did the word.

**OLD KINDER-HOOK WAS OK**

Another distinguished Dutch-American was Martin Van Buren (1782–1862)—though he came from upstate New York, rather than Manhattan. Specifically, he came from the small town of Kinderhook. For some reason, this led to him getting the nickname 'Old Kinderhook', which was shortened to 'OK' in 1840 when he ran for the US presidency.

He lost, as it happens, but his nickname was a big winner. Americans didn't really want to vote for **OK** but they were more than happy to say it. Probably standing for 'Orl Korrect', the term seems to have been in occasional use before 1840, but that election is what made it mainstream.

**THE BLUE-STOCKING WHO WORE BLOOMERS**

In 1840, it definitely wasn't ok for a lady to wear pants. But that all changed a few decades later thanks to a women's magazine called *The Lily*.

The editor of said magazine, Amelia Jenkins Bloomer (1818–1894), was one of those early feminists, well known all over the nation for having refused to say 'obey' in her marriage vows. While she didn't invent the original bloomers (a sort of billowing Turkish-style pantaloon), she was the one who made them famous, after *The Lily* published an article about 'sanitary attire'. Traditional female dresses, it argued, could be both inconvenient and a little revealing: whatever convention might dictate, it was a woman's sacred right to wear pants. 'There was no distinction in the fig leaves worn by Adam and Eve.' Church groups, conservatives and assorted wackos vehemently disagreed, and Bloomer took to making campaign speeches across the country. Wearing, yes, **bloomers**.

At the time, Amelia was considered a **bluestocking**. Now a little dated, this was a popular name for women who neglected their looks or, even worse, liked to use their brain. Its origins lie in the Blue Stocking Society, a London book club formed in the 1750s by some otherwise perfectly normal ladies.

The club got its name through Benjamin Stillingfleet, one of the intellectuals of the day. He was a publisher, a botanist and a translator—but not, apparently, much of a businessman. Very, very poor, Stillingfleet was invited to come and address the club—but he simply couldn't afford the black silk stockings that were an essential part of every gentleman's attire. 'Never mind,' said the freethinking ladies, who valued brainpower above a finely clad calf. 'Come in your blue stockings instead.'

**THE NUCLEAR-POWERED BIKINI**

Refreshingly informal for the time. But it probably wouldn't have been ok for him to come in a **bikini**.

Thankfully, these swimsuits weren't actually invented until 1946. Bikinis were the brainchild of a French engineer who had recently taken over his mum's lingerie shop. While making a very close study of women sunbathing on the beaches of St Tropez, he noticed that some of them had great knockers. In passing, however, he also noticed many women tended to roll up their bathing suits in order to get a better tan.

Nobly, he decided to help. So small it could be 'pulled through a wedding ring', the bikini was denounced by the Vatican, banned in Catholic countries and scorned by fashion mags. Perhaps the engineer anticipated this 'explosive' effect? He had, after all, borrowed his brand name from the Bikini Atoll: twenty-three islands in the Pacific that surround a 600 kilometre–deep lagoon. The atoll had been in every newspaper four days before the bikini's launch because the US had begun using it to test nuclear bombs. A controversial policy, you might think. But no denunciation against *that* came from the Vatican.

**THE DARING YOUNG MAN IN THE TIGHT LEOTARD**

While bikinis are especially revealing, there's also no place to hide in a **leotard**. And that's just how Jules Léotard (1842–1870) liked it. As far as that pioneering acrobat was concerned, putting on a good show meant putting everything *on* show — from his bulging biceps to his rippling triceps to the precise contours of his enormous testicles. 'Do you want to be adored by the ladies?' the tackle-happy Frenchman once asked his public. Then 'instead of draping yourself in unflattering clothes … put on a more natural garb, which does not hide your natural assets'.

The inspiration behind the 1867 song, 'The Daring Young Man on the Flying Trapeze', Léotard actually invented the trapeze, as well as the leotard, and was the first man to use one in a circus. He was born to a pair of circus performers and later claimed that the only way they could ever shut him up as a child was by hanging him upside-down.

**THE CREW THAT GOT CUT**

Another early wearer of leotards may well have been Yale University's rowing crew. We do know for a fact that they wore **crew cuts** (short hair being quicker to dry). In the 1890s, says Yale's current rowing coach, a 'captain of the crew wanted a haircut in the style worn by [the German chancellor, Otto von] Bismarck'. 'He went to an Italian barber in New Haven, who refused to do any haircut that had anything to do with Germany, so the barber said, "I'll give you a short haircut, but we'll call it the crew cut."' The crew went on to win six consecutive regattas against Harvard. And then get middle-aged, fat and bald.

**BIGWIGS AND HUGE SIDEBURNS**   Louis XIV (1638–1715) wouldn't have been seen dead in a crew cut. He much preferred a huge frilly wig. France's omnipotent 'Sun King' is generally thought to have pioneered big, fancy fake hair for men — a fashion that became common in the courts of Europe, and is still seen in corridors of power like the courts. Perhaps that makes him the original *bigwig*?

When it came to 19th-century America, however, there were few bigger wigs than Ambrose Burnside (1824–1881). He was a Civil War general and a United States senator, a governor of Rhode Island and a president of the National Rifle Association.

He was also a fashionista. Perhaps inspired to hide his face after his fiancé said 'I *don't*' at the altar, Burnside wore a pair of magnificently bushy side-whiskers, so long they actually met in a moustache. This natty face-feature never quite took off, and nor did his word for them, 'burnsides'. Later generations refined both the word and the fashion, however, which is why groovy types wear *sideburns* today.

The magnificent sideburns of Ambrose Burnside

# RECREATION

## FUN WORDS

*Teddy bear, Barbie, Ken,
Craps, Russian roulette,
Frisbee, Ferris wheel,
Catherine wheel, Hooch,
Assassin, Bogart,
Tobacco, Nicotine,
Addict, Morphine*

## THEATRICAL WORDS

*Thespian, Harlequin,
Zany, Vaudeville,
Titchy, Hollywood,
Paparazzi, Oscar, Tony,
Logie, Nobel Prize,
Pulitzer Prize*

## MUSICAL WORDS

*Music, Calypso,
Flamenco, Saxophone,
Conga, Polka,
Charleston, Foxtrot,
Jitterbug, Limbo,
Macarena, Hokey pokey,
Morris dancing, Mambo*

## SPORTING WORDS

*Olympics, Cynical,
Marathon, Boycott,
Mulligan, Coach,
Canter, Steeplechase,
Dark horse,
Hobson's choice, Oaks,
Derby, Badminton,
Lord's Cricket Ground,
Yorker, Rugby, Barrack,
Mexican wave,
Bronx cheer*

## TRAVEL WORDS

*Chauffeur, Limousine,
Cadillac, Ferrari,
Lamborghini, Peugeot,
Porsche, Ford,
Rolls-Royce,
Mercedes-Benz, Doozy,
Zeppelin, Murphy's law,
Jumbo jet, Gargantuan,
Titanic, Atlas,
Meander*

# FUN WORDS

The US president Teddy Roosevelt (1858–1919) kept over a dozen pets at the White House, including a pony, a pig and a badger. But his favourite animals, on the whole, were the ones he got to shoot in the face. One day in 1902, that enthusiastic hunter was out in the wilds of Mississippi but, alas, found nothing to kill. This was bad news for his hosts (they'd promised the man blood!) so they quick-wittedly wounded a bear and tied it to a tree, then invited big Teddy to take aim.

'No way!' said that sportsman. The bear ended up getting shot anyway, as it was dying from its wounds, but the president's sense of 'fair play' made the national press. A Brooklyn toy store renamed its stuffed bears **Teddy bears** in his honour—and everyone else soon followed suit.

Teddy Roosevelt nobly refusing to shoot a bear

From brutal hunting trips to bitchy fashion shows: at some point most kids dump teddies, and start playing with a **Barbie** instead. Named after Barbara Handler (born 1942), the toymaker's daughter, the eating disorder–thin Barbie is often criticised for being a bad role model, but this is actually the least of her crimes. Incest, let the jury note, is another. Barbara Handler has a brother called **Ken**.

Dice, on the other hand, *can* be an appropriate toy for children (so long as they're not playing for money with men named 'Tony

Two-fingers' or 'Crooked Pete'). ***Craps***, one such way to lose money, may well owe its name to Johnny Crapaud, one such shyster. A professional gambler from France, Crapaud supposedly visited New Orleans in around 1800 and introduced the local casinos to betting with dice.

**THE RUSSIANS WHO PLAYED ROULETTE**

***Russian roulette*** is definitely not a good idea for children (unless they're being really annoying). Played by putting one bullet in a revolver, spinning the cylinder and pulling the trigger, it takes a type of reckless courage that among intelligent people is known as 'stupidity'.

It's worth noting, incidentally, that there's actually nothing especially Russian about the game. Certainly, no history book ever mentions any Russian playing it. The first written reference to 'Russian roulette' actually came in a work of *fiction* — and (involving, as it did, placing *five* bullets in the cylinder) it wasn't so much a game as a form of suicide.

'Feldheim … did you ever hear of Russian Roulette?' a soldier asks the narrator of Georges Surdez's 1937 short story, *Russian Roulette*.

> When I said I had not, he told me all about it. When he was with the Russian army in Romania, around 1917, and things were cracking up, so that their officers felt that they were not only losing prestige, money, family, and country, but were being also dishonoured before their colleagues of the Allied armies, some officer would suddenly pull out his revolver, anywhere, at the table, in a café, at a gathering of friends, remove a cartridge from the cylinder, spin the cylinder, snap it back in place, put it to his head, and pull the trigger. There were five chances to one that the hammer would set off a live cartridge and blow his brains all over the place.

And things were even worse if it didn't. The officer would have to go and live in Russia.

**WHY FRISBEES CAN MAKE YOU FAT**

But what if your child is still determined to spin *something*? In that case, perhaps you give them a *Frisbee*.

But even this wasn't such a healthy option once upon a time, as in order to play you had to first eat a pie. Frisbees get their name from the Frisbie Pie Company of Connecticut, a fatty-snack provider near Yale University that sold its products in a big round tin. One day in 1930-something, a Yale student must have tossed away one such tin and been struck by how far it flew. 'Hey Hank [or Todd or Buck or Chet],' he would have then said. 'Catch this!' And within a year or two, hundreds of Yale students were flinging Frisbie lids around.

**KEEPING IT WHEEL**

Child still unimpressed? Then how about you try another fun spinning thing, a good old-fashioned *Ferris wheel*? Invented for the Chicago Expo in 1893, the Ferris wheel was America's answer to the Eiffel Tower, which had been the centrepiece of France's world expo four years earlier. The railroad and bridge engineer George Washington Gale Ferris (1859–1896) oversaw the construction of this 1200-ton,

Gale Ferris's Wheel

43-metre tall, $385,000 masterwork. And then saw it get sold for $2000. So it could be torn up and used for scrap metal.

Another spinning thing that you no longer see in amusement parks is the *Catherine wheel*: a sort of spinning firework that gets funner and funner and funner until it explodes in your face.

Appropriately enough, this perilous plaything gets its name from a martyr. St Catherine of Alexandria (ca 282–305) was a pious virgin who refused to marry a Roman emperor because she was already 'married to Christ'. Not being one of those people who take rejection well, the emperor ordered his soldiers to nail her to a torture wheel … but at her touch it miraculously shattered.

So he cut off her head instead.

**WHY MARIJUANA IS SOMETIMES CALLED HOOCH**

When your kids get older, they learn another fun thing about fire. You can use it to light a joint.

No-one really knows where marijuana got its name. Some point to Mariguana, a hemp-growing island in the Bahamas; others feel that the story must involve some Hispanic lady ('Maria Juana' = 'Mary Jane'). But we do at least know why it's also called **hooch**. When the US purchased a frozen Russian wasteland in 1867, bottle shops were a little thin on the ground. American soldiers sent to this new state of Alaska had no alcohol to warm their cockles, and their cockles could get pretty damn cold.

But there's no stopping Yankee ingenuity. An enterprising trooper eventually put together his own crude distillery and used it to sell a bit of whiskey on the side. Because he was based in a village belonging to the Hoochinoo Indians, his particular brand of alcohol came to be known as 'hooch'. Eventually (in Australia, at least), the word came to mean another product that could help get your head to spin.

**THE ASSASSINS WHO KICKED BACK WITH A BONG**

Which is not to say that soldiers can't also enjoy dope. Marijuana may have been associated with long-haired peaceniks ever since the '60s, but its image was once very different. The word **assassin** comes from 'hashashin', an Arabic term meaning 'user of hashish'. Some dope smokers back in 11th-century Iran didn't really give peace a chance.

Fact and myth are hard to disentangle when it comes to these 'hashashins', a radical sect of Nizari Ismailis who waged war against the Sunni majority. We know that they captured a series of fortresses in north-western Iran. And it seems certain that they were behind a great many political and religious assassinations, all carried out with surgical precision. But it's less clear whether they actually smoked bongs. Legend insists that the sect gave hash to new recruits—transporting them into a 'garden of paradise' (complete with exquisite food and naked women) for a few days, then offering them more of the same if they killed a few enemies. But this may just be a story invented by those very enemies in an effort to smear their foe.

(If the assassins *were* indeed dope smokers, we must hope that no-one ever **bogarted** one of their joints. Never well received by your comrades, the practice of taking more than your share of puffs from a communal joint was named after an actor who loved a good smoke. The big-lipped Humphrey Bogart [1899–1957] delivered most of his lines with a cigarette dangling out of his mouth. Then died from throat cancer at 58.)

**Humphrey Bogarting**

|  |
| --- |
| ***HOW SMOKING CAN HELP YOUR CAREER*** |

That's right kids, **tobacco** may be fun, but it's just another assassin at the end of the day. Enjoyed by Native Americans for many a millennium, it first entered European lungs in 1498, when Christopher Columbus's crew came by an island in the West Indies and decided to sample one of its crops. The island's name was Tobago.

In his defence, though, Columbus never actually brought any of that tobacco back to Europe. (He was too busy capturing slaves.)

That honour probably belongs to a couple of Dutch sailors, who scooped up a few seeds in 1559 and brought them back across the Atlantic to Lisbon. Their names are now forgotten, but we do know the guy they sold them to: Jean Nicot (1530–1600), the French Ambassador to Portugal. He lovingly cultivated the seeds, grew Europe's first crop, and sent its sweet-smelling leaves to the royal family. Impressed with it—and, more importantly, with him—they named the new plant *nicotine*.

**WHY IT'S NO FUN BEING AN ADDICT**

Nowadays, of course, 'nicotine' just refers to an unfortunate substance within tobacco plants, the one that can make you an *addict*.

Once upon a time, however, it was ancient Rome that could make you an addict. Back then, the word meant 'slave'. If one of Rome's soldiers performed particularly well—by capturing an enemy, say, then burning his house and killing his mum—they could get rewarded with an 'addict': formal ownership of the enemy they just captured. The word only acquired its present meaning at the start of the 20th century, the logic being that addicts are slaves to their drug.

(Addicts often also enjoy *morphine*. Another super-fun substance, if you're able to overlook the way it ruins your life, morphine was first 'isolated' by a German scientist in 1804. Noticing how his discovery could make you a bit sleepy and dreamy, he named it after Morpheus the Greek god of dreams. And then probably had a bit more.)

Morpheus, mid nap

*A Scene from DON GIOVANNI as performed at the Kings Theatre...*

# THEATRICAL WORDS

**THESPIS
THE
THESPIAN**
Being an actor can be very similar to being unemployed, but once upon a time there was no difference at all. Before the 6th century BC, you see, the Greek theatre didn't actually have actors—at least, not in the sense that we understand the term today. Theatre back then didn't involve dialogue—an exchange between different, individual characters, each delivering different, individual lines—but was instead just a series of dances, interspersed with chants from a chorus.

Thespis of Icara changed all that. Around 536 BC, this poet, playwright and stage director is said to have singlehandedly revolutionised the play. For one performance, he arranged for the chorus to chant out particular questions, and then answered them all by himself. Using his voice alone. In doing so, he became the first actor. All *thespians* owe a debt to Thespis (and a much bigger one to the bank).

**SOME ZANY
HARLEQUINS**
Children's parties offer one way to pay that debt. Some lucky actors can get a gig as a clown.

Or, if we want to be more historical about it, as a *harlequin*. One of the starting points of slapstick comedy, with their multi-coloured coats and muddle-headed ways, harlequins have been around since the 16th century, when an Italian created the *commedia dell'arte*. A sort of lowbrow, semi-improvised pantomime, the super-popular *commedia* had three sets of stock characters (masters, servants and lovers) who would bump heads in assorted scenarios. Harlequin was one of the comic servant characters. Think Manuel in *Fawlty Towers*, only with a black mask and colourful pants.

Playing a comic servant required a certain **zaniness**, which should actually come as no surprise. The servant stock characters were collectively known as 'the zanni'—that word being short for 'Giovanni', the most 'common' name of the time.

**VAUDEVILLE IN THE VAU DE VIRE**

Zaniness was a particularly prized quality in *vaudeville* (representing, as it does, a useful substitute for talent). Eventually killed off by the movies, vaudeville shows were America's most popular form of entertainment for half a century, though whether they actually provided any is another matter. Standard vaudeville acts included dancers and comedians, magicians and musicians, and acrobats and athletes. Not to mention lecturing celebrities, performing animals and plays.

All of which would have come as rather a shock to Olivier Basselin. A satirically minded minstrel who lived in Normandy's Valley of the Vire during the 15th century, Basselin 'composed and sang certain sprightly songs which struck the popular fancy'. They were so popular that, within a few decades, any kind of funny song came to be known among Frenchmen as a 'chanson du Vau de Vire'. That is, a 'song of the Valley of the Vire'.

Over the centuries, 'Vau de Vire' contracted into one word but its meaning managed to expand. 'Vaudeville' started to mean any kind of 'funny' entertainment. (Even when it wasn't entertaining or funny.)

### A BIG, AND YET TITCHY, STAR

England's Harry Relph (1867–1928) was a particularly big vaudeville star, in large part because he was small. Standing around 121 centimetres tall, Relph was also a little overweight. In this, and other physical respects, he closely resembled another fatty then in the papers ('Roger Tichborne', the 'long-lost heir' to a title, who turned out to be Arthur Orton, a fraudster). So Relph took the stage name 'Little Titch' to capitalise on the resemblance, and soon had them rolling in the aisles.

Little Titch

Many tributes came the way of this *titchy* music hall comedian, who Jacques Tati called 'a foundation for everything that has been realised in comedy on screen'. He was awarded a Legion of Honour in France, and was even referenced in Monty Python's 'Ministry of Silly Walks'. But his most lasting legacy lies in the dictionary, under the letter 't'.

### HOLLYWOOD, ILLINOIS

These days, most 'comedy on screen' comes from *Hollywood* (particularly when they're trying to make a drama). The home of American cinema for roughly a century, the area was known as the Cahuenga Valley until the 1880s, when it was bought by an enterprising couple from Ohio. They were determined to make and sell housing lots out of this vast expanse of fruit trees—and the first rule of salesmanship has always been to find a good name. So they did just that. On a train trip back home, one of them overheard a woman talking about her stylish summer house on the outskirts of Chicago. Its name was 'Hollywood'.

### MR PAPARAZZI AND HIS PRICEY HOTEL

A downside of Hollywood for actors is that it has so many *paparazzi*: pesky photographers who pop up and take their picture when they're not wearing make-up or striking a pose. Actors like to be seen on a red carpet, not in a car park eating pie.

These snap-happy sleazebags get their name from *La Dolce Vita*. Fellini's 1960 film about an Italian gossip columnist featured a sleazy photographer named Paparazzo, who made a living taking pics of celebs. Fellini got *that* name, in turn, from one Coriolando Paparazzo, a shamelessly money-hungry hotel proprietor who features in a 1901 travel memoir by George Gissing.

**UNCLE OSCARS**

*La Dolce Vita* was nominated for four Academy Awards, and won one for Best Costume Design. But no-one ever designed a costume for the trophy itself. First presented in 1929, the Academy's gold-plated statuette of a naked man originally went without a name. It was just 'my trophy' if you won and 'that shitty trinket' if you lost. In the early 1930s, however, it became an *Oscar*—and nobody's quite sure why.

Some say the name's a nod to Oscar Wilde, who came up with a snazzy quote after winning a poetry prize. ('While many people have won the Newdigate, it is seldom that the Newdigate gets an Oscar.')

But a more popular theory points to one Oscar Pierce, a wealthy Texan wheat grower about whom very little is known. In 1931, the story goes, Margaret Herrick was working for the Academy as a librarian. She was shown the statue and made the remark, 'that reminds me of my Uncle Oscar'.

**TONIES AND LOGIES: THE PEOPLE BEHIND THE PRIZES**

As glorious as winning an Oscar may be, some actors insist that winning a *Tony* is even better. And if they can say so with a straight face, they probably do deserve an acting prize.

But having said that, an award for 'distinctive achievement in American theatre' probably beats an 'Employee of the month' award at your local McDonald's, which is all most of us can ever really aspire to. Tonies get their name from one Antoinette Perry (1888–1946), a successful actor and stage director who founded and chaired the American Theatre

Wing (ATW). She died early of a sudden heart attack, and the ATW instituted the awards in her honour.

If you ever find an actor who can say that a **Logie** beats an Oscar or a Tony, become their manager straightaway. It doesn't even matter if they kept a straight face, it takes talent just to get out the words. Roughly on par with winning a meat tray, 'Logies' are given to the best shows on Australian television. Which is really all that needs to be said.

Appropriately enough, this prize for not really making good television is named after a man who didn't really invent television. People had already created televisual devices by the time John Logie Baird (1888–1946) rolled out his electromechanical TV in 1925 — and that machine was superseded by purely electronic systems within a few short years.

### THE NOBEL PRIZE AND THE MERCHANT OF DEATH

The Logies are far from the world's most inappropriately named prizes, however. Consider the fact that Alfred Nobel (1833–1896) didn't really like peace. Once described as a 'merchant of death', the Swedish-born founder of the **Nobel Peace Prize** was best known in his own lifetime as the inventor of dynamite. His will set aside $9 million to fund the new award, one of the more expensive PR campaigns in history.

Joseph Pulitzer (1847–1911), on the other hand, was a merchant of sleaze. As the owner of New York's grubbiest tabloid, he helped create yellow journalism. But as the owner of a large fortune, he also helped to create Columbia University's School of Journalism — an organisation that hands out the **Pulitzer Prizes** for serious and substantial reportage.

The noble Alfred Nobel

# MUSICAL WORDS

**CALYPSO
THE
KIDNAPPER**

'Without music, life would be a mistake,' said Nietzsche, a man who had clearly never heard Beyoncé. But while any bootylicious airhead can call themselves a musician these days, provided they know how to shake it, we should remember that *music* started out as something much more intellectual, a serious discipline covering all of the arts. Named after the Muses, the nine Greek goddesses of the arts and sciences, 'mousikê' once encompassed play-writing and poetry, history and astronomy, and all forms of literature too.

The best-known Greek literature comes from Homer, a man who, in a sense, also gave us *calypso*. 'Calypso', you see, is a character in *The Odyssey*. She's a naughty nymph who sort of kidnaps Odysseus, promising him immortality in exchange for some sex. 'Calypso music', on the other hand, was actually known as 'kaa iso' among the Trinidadians who invented it (a local term meaning 'continue' or 'go on'). When classically educated European settlers started getting groovy in the 1930s, they changed the word slightly to match a familiar spelling.

## FLAMENCO, THE BELGIAN DANCE

The word *flamenco* also has unlikely origins. Next time you see a raven-haired temptress clicking castanets, or waggling her hips with a sultry pout, don't picture sun-drenched Barcelona, and dismiss all thoughts of a racy tavern in Seville. Instead, think Flanders. A cold, flat mud pit in the south of Belgium, famous for its root vegetables and WWI deaths.

Flanders was part of the Spanish Empire in the 17th century, and Spanish soldiers based there were called 'flamencos'. Quite a few of those soldiers were gypsies and, in return for their services, they received some special dispensations that were denied to other gypsies—a special status which meant they were still called 'flamencos' when they got back to Spain. At some point, the theory goes, either they or one of their descendants must have invented this new style of dancing, which consequently went by the name of 'flamenco'.

## THE JOY OF SAX

Nowadays Flanders is a part of Belgium—a land famous for producing nobody famous. Except, that is, for Antoine (Adolphe) Sax (1814–1894). Born to a well-known instrument-maker, Master Sax was a rather accident-prone child. At different stages, he somehow managed to get 'struck on the head by a brick, swallow a needle, fall down a flight of stairs, topple onto a burning stove and accidentally drink sulphuric acid'—and all before his 18th birthday.

Adolphe Sax

Determined to make the most of a life that could presumably end at any moment, this loveable doofus then became an instrument-maker himself, giving us the sax-horn, the sax-tromba and the sax-tuba. We didn't want them. Fortunately, though, we did want another invention. The *saxophone* was a massive hit—though Adolphe somehow still managed to end up bankrupt.

**THE DARK SIDE OF CONGA DANCING**

Bankruptcy certainly wasn't a problem for Sax's country at the time, however: it had far too many slaves. Named after the mighty river that flowed through it, the Belgian Congo was a major source of money for its colonial masters. Central Africa was jam-packed with rubber trees, as well as Africans who could be made to tap them.

It wasn't as full as it used to be, however. By the late 19th century, a great many Africans from the Congo region had already been kidnapped and made slaves in the Americas. Many of them were taken to Cuba and, when they weren't being beaten and subjugated, it seems that quite a few liked to dance. One such dance involved a line of people marching about. Cubans naturally called it the *conga*.

**REVOL-UTION ON THE DANCE FLOOR**

Of course, all sorts of peoples have suffered at the hands of foreign tyrants over the years. Take the Polish. Sick of continually being invaded by Russia, a country that seems to regard its smaller neighbours as a public park, the Poles staged a rebellion in 1830. It failed dismally, but that didn't stop a few of Russia's other small neighbours from being, all in all, rather impressed.

Some say that the *polka*, a Czech dance that sprang up that same year, was named in tribute to this unsuccessful rebellion. But a more likely source seems to be the Czech word 'pulka'. It means 'half' (i.e. the dance of half-steps).

Ultimately, an even more unsuccessful rebellion occurred in South Carolina in 1861. The south's attempt to take over a fort in Charleston set off the Civil War.

Sixty years later, that city was home to another short-lived revolution. On the dance floor. The **Charleston** quickly spread throughout America's speakeasies and became a symbol of the Roaring Twenties.

The toe-tapping Harry Fox

**HENRY FOXTROT**

But not all guys and dolls did the Charleston; some swingers preferred to *foxtrot*. This rival '20s dance craze is thought to date back to 1914, when a vaudeville performer named Harry Fox (1882–1959) did 'a fast but simple trotting step to ragtime music' during a cabaret show in New York. 'Mr Fox very rollickingly dances with a tendency to put everyone in good humour,' as one critic approvingly noted.

**THE JITTER-BUG AND IMMINENT DEATH**

Doing the *jitterbug* wouldn't put everyone in good humour. Why smile when you're shivering and sweating? Or, indeed, palpitating and twitching and convulsing, and quite possibly staring death in the face? Long before the dance craze of that name came along, 'jitterbug' was another name for delirium tremens: the potentially fatal 'shaking frenzy' that can be brought on by an addiction to alcohol.

Swing dancing is quite a complicated pastime, and when it first appeared in the '20s and '30s, the people who hadn't quite mastered it were mockingly known as 'jitterbugs'. But since pretty much everybody fell into this category (anywhere you looked on a dance floor, you'd see an earnest reveller having some kind of spasm), 'jitterbug' soon became a term that simply meant swing dancing itself.

## LIMBO DANCING BETWEEN HEAVEN AND HELL

But alas, there's not as much call for swing dancing these days. With their scary bogans and bowel-shattering techno, the average 21st-century nightclub has quite a bit in common with hell.

A queue outside a nightclub, if we stick with this metaphor, could therefore be called Limbo. A land just outside the borders of hell (i.e. near, but not actually *in*, the fiery pits of eternal torment), Limbo was a 14th-century solution to the problem of unbaptised babies. Baptism is seen as a prerequisite for getting into heaven—but does a baby who died at birth really deserve to spend eternity in hell? Probably not, all things considered, so priests created a place in between.

Years later, on the island of Trinidad, some bright spark created the *limbo dance*. While its name might simply be a short form of 'limber',

Life in Limbo

people dancing it can indeed be thought to be in limbo—suspended, as they are, between the 'heaven' of successfully moving past the horizontal pole and the 'hell' of accidentally hitting it.

## WHY MARRIED MEN SHOULDN'T DO THE MACARENA

There should be a special place in hell for people who do the *Macarena*. Described as 'the greatest one-hit wonder of all time' by one music channel, and as 'fucking annoying' by everyone else, this Spanish dance song ultimately owes its name to Mary Magdalene, the penitent prostitute of the New Testament.

In some parts of Spain, however, people aren't so sure that she was penitent. There, to call a woman a 'Magdalena' is to suggest that she's 'sassy or sensuous'.

And the song began because a woman was just that. In 1992, the Spanish band Los del Rios were performing at a private party. The host had arranged for a local flamenco teacher to strut her stuff while they played, and the band's lead singer was so impressed with her moves, he made up a song on the spot. 'Dale a tu cuerpo alegría, Magdalena, que tu cuerpo es pa darle alegría y cosa buena' ('Give your body some joy, Magdalena, 'cause your body is for giving joy and good things to'). The less controversial name 'Macarena' was simply substituted later on.

**RELIGION ON THE DANCE FLOOR**

Mary Magdalene might have liked to do the *hokey pokey*. In an ever-so-roundabout way, you see, that kooky dance could *be* Jesus Christ.

To explain: most people agree that the nonsensical term 'hokey pokey' is a contraction of 'hocus pocus', the age-old magician's incantation—but what the hell *that* means, nobody knows. The best theory seems to be that it's a reworking of 'hoc est corpus' ('this is my body'), the Latin phrase Catholic priests utter when they're giving their congregation little wafers of bread. It sounds vaguely similar to 'hocus pocus' and is likewise meant to have magical properties. Transubstantiation supposedly takes place when the priest says it, turning the bread into the body of Christ.

*Morris dancing* has rather less Christian credentials. Now considered firmly English, this 15th-century folk dance actually began with the Moors. Working their way west via Africa, the Moors were a bunch of Arabic Muslims who came to Spain in about 711 and apparently liked what they saw. The last of their descendants were forced to flee in 1492, but they left behind the 'morisco', a communal dance full of rhythmic steps.

Cuba's iconic *mambo* is even less Christian, if etymologists are to be believed. The name comes from a Creole word meaning 'voodoo priestess'.

# SPORTING WORDS

**GETTING NAKED IN GREECE: THE OLYMPICS**

'It may be that all games are silly,' Robert Lynd once reflected, 'but then again, so are humans.' Such silliness has, of course, been occurring since at least 776 BC, when Greek men first started to gather together in a grassy valley beside the River Alpheus, then get naked and cavort. Strictly forbidden to women, the valley of Olympia also functioned as a religious sanctuary, with several temples and statues and shrines.

About 2500 years later, French archaeologists stumbled across some of what remained of these temples, and began methodically excavating the rest. Their discoveries so excited one of their fellow countrymen, Baron Pierre de Coubertin (1863–1937), that he sought to recreate the games themselves. Which is why we all have the *Olympics*.

**WHY CYNICS SHOULD GO TO THE GYM**

Of course, not all the ancient Greeks were drawn to sport. Many preferred to exercise their minds. One such ponderer, Antisthenes (ca 445–365 BC), did most of his pondering on the subject of happiness (what is it, how do you get it, and so on). The answer, he basically concluded, lay in being totally self-sufficient. It's only by placing no value whatsoever in external things like wealth or fame or power (or honour or education or love or kindness) that happiness can be truly achieved.

Do you think that sounds rather *cynical*? Full marks to you, if so. Antisthenes and his followers did most of their teaching outside a gym in Athens, a haven of silly sportsmen called the 'Cynosarge'. So people called them the 'Cynics'.

**THE BATTLE OF MARATHON**
Pheidippides (ca 530–490 BC) was not a cynic. When this Greek messenger was given a message, he would put his heart and soul into delivering it. He ended up giving his body as well. In 490 BC, a small Greek force managed to trap an invading Persian army in Marathon (a narrow valley 42 kilometres from Athens) and defeat it with the loss of just 192 men. Or 193 men, as it turned out. Dispatched to share the good news, Pheidippides ran all the way back to the Athenian parliament, weakly gasped 'We have won!' … and died on the spot.

Baron de Coubertain wanted a glorious last-day showpiece for the first modern Olympics, and was inspired by this story to create a 42-kilometre race. He called it the *marathon*—probably because 'the Pheidippides' didn't exactly trip off the tongue.

**THE BOYCOTT OF CAPTAIN BOYCOTT**
No Americans ran the marathon in the 1980 Moscow Olympics, however—or, indeed, entered any other event. And no Russians went to Los Angeles four years later. The Olympics just wouldn't be the Olympics without a good old-fashioned *boycott*.

And a boycott just wouldn't be a 'boycott' without Captain Charles Boycott (1832–1897). After a few decades of bloodstained soldiering, this British army officer was looking for a quiet life—and, for a time, thought he'd found one in Ireland. Employed as the land agent for an absentee landlord, Boycott's job was basically to squeeze rent money out of poverty-stricken farmers and kick out whichever ones couldn't pay.

For some reason this made him unpopular. Boycott's enthusiastic evictions led to his becoming a test case for the Irish National Land League—a reform group founded after

**Charles Boycott**

the Great Potato Famine to try and reduce rents for the working man. Mindful of legalities, its president had come up with a non-violent protest method: shunning. 'You must shun him on the roadside … you must shun him in the streets … you must shun him in the shop … By isolating him as if he were a leper of old, you must show your detestation of the crime he has committed.' The captain's tenants declined to harvest his crops and his servants refused to serve him. Shopkeepers wouldn't sell him anything and the mailman didn't deliver his post. In other words, they organised a boycott. He got the hint and quit.

**GOLF WITH THOMAS MULLIGAN**

Personally, I feel that golfers should boycott the *mulligan*. Taking a sneaky second tee shot because you muffed up your first is simply not acceptable under the rules of the game. In a more just world, it would be against the law.

The first man to go to jail would have been an Irish aristocrat named Thomas Mulligan (1793–1879). Presumably a terrible golfer (and clearly not much chop with a pen), he once argued that

> inasmuch as strokes taken after play is concluded on the 18th hole do not count towards the total entered on one's tally card, it seems to me eminently reasonable that any shots struck before play is

properly commenced with a satisfactory drive on the first tee should be of no more consequence to one's score than those swings which one has made by way of practice in the course of hitting balls upon the driving ground.

In other words, 'Yes, ok, I'm a crap golfer, but check out how well I can cheat'.

**WHY THE BEST COACHES COME FROM HUNGARY**

What Mulligan really needed was a ***coach***: someone to make him adjust his grip and waggle his hips, bend his knee and keep both eyes on the ball.

But you can't take a horse to a golf course. The word 'coach' comes from 'kocsi szekér', a Hungarian term meaning 'a horse cart from Kocs'. A tiny village not far from Budapest, Kocs became famous all over Europe in the 15th century for producing what were then state-of-the-art vehicles. But soon other manufacturers adopted its 'compact, elegant and sturdy' design, and eventually any kind of four-wheeled wagon became generally known as a 'coach'.

So where do sports coaches come in? Well, in the 18th century, 'a coach' also came to mean a tutor, perhaps because these people tended to 'carry' their students. Another theory is that private tutors would often use long, boring coach journeys to read to their charges and quiz them, a process which became known as 'coaching'. Either way, it wasn't too long before people in charge of sports teams found themselves 'coaching' too.

**CHASING STEEPLES AND CANTERING TO CANTERBURY**

Not everyone in the Middle Ages could afford a wagon, however—let alone a luxury item from Kocs. Most pilgrims had to get around on an uncomfortable saddle, so it's little wonder that they travelled fast. Far and away the most popular pilgrimage in medieval England was from London to Canterbury Cathedral, where the much-revered St Thomas A'Beckett was buried. So many horses did the 'Canterbury gallop' that their fastish trot became known as a **canter**.

Horses have run towards other churches too. The first **steeplechase** was literally run from one such building to another, as a result of a bet between two Irishmen. In 1752, it's said, Cornelius O'Callaghan and Edmund Blake raced their thoroughbreds 6 kilometres through County Cork, from St John's Church in Buttevant to St Mary's Church in Doneraile. (Since the latter steeple kind of sticks out on the landscape, it would have made a good finishing line for such a long race.) We don't know which man won, but it's safe to assume that, whoever it was, he gloated enough to make the race take off.

**Canterbury Cathedral**

**A DARK HORSE NAMED DUSKY PETE**

Of course, people can lose a lot of money betting on these sorts of things. If there's anything worse than plonking all your money on an expertly trained, superbly fit dead certainty, only to see it slow down and take a nap mid-race, it must have happened during the war.

At a Tennessee horse carnival in the late 19th century, many punters shared in this pain. The story goes that a shady horse-breeder named Sam Flynn had come along to pull his usual trick: entering an unknown 'workhorse' for a 'joke' at the last minute, getting long odds and acting surprised when it won.

Flynn's horse for this carnival was called Dusky Pete—and at least one man wasn't taken in. 'Gentlemen,' he warned, 'there's a dark horse in this race that will make some of you sick before supper.' His warning was ignored but his turn of phrase wasn't. A *dark horse* came to describe any unknown outsider who somehow manages to overcome the odds.

**THOMAS HOBSON'S CHOICE**

Some bets are safe, however. For example, you always knew what you were going to get with Thomas Hobson (1544–1631). Just like Henry Ford 300 years after him ('You can have any colour you like, so long as it's black'), this employee of Cambridge University didn't believe in giving his customers too wide a choice.

Placed in charge of the college stables some time during 16th century, Hobson quickly realised that 'scholars ride hard'. He became sick of domineering, aristocratic youngbloods demanding they be given his fastest horse, and then galloping it to the brink of exhaustion. So he introduced a policy of rotation, placing the freshest horse near the stable door, and the most recently ridden furthest away. *Hobson's choice*—any horse you like, so long as it's this one—became notorious among a generation of haughty bluebloods who weren't used to being denied anything at all.

**LORD DERBY AND THE OAKS**

The 12th Earl of Derby (1752–1834) attended Cambridge about a century after Hobson. Which was fortunate, because he liked to ride fast. Not by all accounts the most devoted of husbands (when his wife died, he married an actress a few days later), the earl was at least a devoted horse breeder.

Simply dripping with sporting blood, Derby founded two widely mimicked races in his time: **The Oaks**, named after his manor house, and **The Derby**, named after himself. We almost never had a 'derby' though. One of the earl's friends was equally involved in setting up this trendsetting race for 3-year-olds, so the two men tossed a coin to see who would lend it their name. It could have easily been called 'the Bunbury'.

**BADMINTON, GLOUCES-TERSHIRE**

The Oaks is nice enough, as ancestral manors go, but you'll find a much snazzier one in Gloucestershire. Home to the dukes of Beaufort since the 17th century, Badminton House boasts 26 square kilometres of pristine lawn, every one of them suitable for sport.

So someone invented one. In 1870, a guest at one of the 8th Duke's garden parties introduced guests to a brand-new game. He or she was presumably just back from India, where racquet-and-shuttlecock sports have been played for years, but no-one was concerned with such trivialities, so they all called it the **Badminton** game.

**THOMAS LORD'S CRICKET GROUND**

**Lord's Cricket Ground** wasn't so named because of some lord, however. If you had a mental image of dukes and earls duelling with leather and willow, you must banish it from your mind.

Rather, the ground was named for an 18th-century labourer from Yorkshire, who went to London to become a mediocre bowler. Thomas Lord (1755–1832) subsequently found work as a sports administrator, and it was in that capacity that he was approached by some gentlemen cricketers who wanted a more private venue for their hobby, and were prepared to cover against any losses he might make. Lord thus founded Lord's, and found himself making a steady profit.

But who wants a steady profit when you can make a huge one? An interesting historic sidenote for those who revere his name is that Lord actually did his best to sell the hallowed turf to developers in 1814, so they could build a few hundred houses. An MCC consortium bought him out at the last moment.

('Lord's', of course, isn't the only cricket term to come from Yorkshire. Who could overlook the **Yorker**, those straight, hard, fast full tosses that bluff northern bowlers hurl in an effort to mash up your toes?)

**RUGBY, THE SCHOOL OF HARD KNOCKS**

*Rugby* players, on the other hand, try to mash up your entire body. Behaviour that in any other context would lead to a conviction for assault, coupled with some stern remarks from the bench, leads in *that* sport to cries of 'Well played!'

The venerable Rugby School, just east of Coventry, must take the blame for this legalised thuggery. Founded way back in 1567, its most famous moment supposedly came during a soccer game in 1823, when 'with a fine disregard for the rules', a student named William Webb Ellis 'took the ball in his arms and ran with it, thus originating the distinctive feature of the rugby game'.

**MEXICAN WAVES IN AMERICA AND BRONX CHEERS IN SPAIN**

War, of course, is even more painful than rugby — but it does have its consolations. In Australia during the 1880s, one of them was organised sport. Soldiers at the Victoria Barracks got to booze on noisily while watching the football at a nearby waste ground — which may well be why Australians *barrack* for their sports teams today.

One of the more irritating forms of barracking is the **Mexican wave**. But don't go blaming it on Mexicans. According to *The*

*New York Times*, the 'wave' was first unveiled at a University of Washington gridiron game in 1981. It didn't come to international attention until the 1986 World Cup in Mexico, however, when TV viewers all over the world watched soccer fans go wild.

On the other hand, there's no reason to blame Americans for the equally annoying **Bronx cheer**. It almost certainly didn't originate in the Bronx (one of New York City's five boroughs). A much more likely theory is that it came from 'branca', a Spanish word meaning 'a rude shout'.

# TRAVEL WORDS

**WHY CHAUFFEURS BELONG IN JAIL**

Travel can be pretty exhausting, so who wouldn't want a **chauffeur**? In the late 18th century, the answer was everyone. 'Chauffeurs' had nothing to do with cars back then and everything to do with crime. They were a brutal group of house-breakers who got their name from the French word for 'heat'. Led by one 'Jack the Scorcher', the gang's modus operandi involved breaking into a house through a window then lighting a cosy fire. And if after they beat you up, tied you up and then beat up you some more, you *still* refused to say where your money was hidden, scorching was what they'd do to your feet.

The 1700s weren't just an innovative time for French burglars, however: French mechanics had a few ideas too. The first self-propelled vehicles started to appear a few decades after the

Chauffeurs. Steam-powered, they required people to stoke—that is, *heat*—the engine, as well as drive it, so these employees became known as chauffeurs too.

**THE SHEP-HERDS OF LIMOUSINE**

These days, chauffeurs are generally only seen in snooty cars—big, black *limousines* and the like. But they weren't always so classy. For centuries before cars came along, a 'limousine' was just a sort of hooded coat—a tatty garment worn by lowly shepherds in the French province of Limousin.

But then the first large luxury car was invented in 1902. It boasted a compartment for up to five passengers, well away from the smelly driver outside. When it rained, he had to huddle under a sort of curved roof that projected out from the compartment. People thought that it looked a bit like a shepherd's hood, so they called these new luxury cars 'limousines'.

**BAD PILOTS, BEAVER-SKINNERS AND SEVERAL LUXURY CARS**

You wouldn't have caught Antoine Laumet de la Mothe (1658–1730) hanging out with any shepherds. Familiarity with such working-class types might have blown his cover.

Born to a small-time lawyer near the French town of Cadillac, Antoine slipped off to America in 1693. In the new country, he told anyone who'd listen that he was an aristocrat—but certainly not one of those dissolute, idle ones. The 'Sieur de Cadillac' won fame as a fur trapper and enthusiastic supplier of alcohol to Indians. He also helped found Detroit. In the early 20th century, two of its residents paid homage to him, naming their new line of cars the *Cadillac*.

By and large, however, cars tend to be named after their makers: tedious, mechanically minded business types with names like Enzo *Ferrari* (1898–1988), Ferruccio *Lamborghini* (1916–1993), Armand *Peugeot* (1849–1915) and Ferdinand *Porsche* (1875–1951).

Apart from that supercharged capitalist Henry **Ford** (1863–1947), the only one who's really worth mentioning is Charles Stewart Rolls (1877–1910). Not because he founded **Rolls-Royce** with a mechanic named Henry Royce (1863–1933), but because of his interest in another new transport technology, the plane. The success of his car company allowed this Eton-educated aristocrat to buy one. And in 1910, he became the first Englishman to die in one, when the tail of his Wright Flyer broke off.

**MERCEDES JELLINEK, HOME WRECKER**

Mercedes Jellinek (1889–1929) was even younger when she achieved her claim to fame—though essentially all she'd managed to do was be born. This daughter of an Austrian car-maker was a rosy-cheeked 12-year-old in 1901, when the world was first offered a **Mercedes**.

Things continued to go well after that: Herr Jellinek joined forces with Carl Benz's car company, and Mercedes married a baron. But with the advent of WWI, the charming young couple was ruined. Rendered destitute, Mercedes even spent some of 1918 begging on the streets of Vienna. But don't worry, good business sense ran in her veins: she abandoned her husband and two kids shortly afterwards, and ran off with another baron.

Mercedes Jelinek

**THE CAR THAT WAS A DOOZY**

You can say many nice things about a Mercedes car—they're sleek, they make you look young— but you can't say that they're a **doozy**. This is because the Deusenberg car is a doozy, thank you very much. Founded by two German-born brothers in 1913, and bankrupt a few decades later, the state-of-the-art Deusenberg car company once produced the world's most upmarket cars.

The problem was that there weren't enough upmarket people. Combining, as they did, the speed of a Bugatti with the precision of a Rolls-Royce and the spacious elegance of a small Renaissance palace, Doozies were so very chic that no-one could actually afford them. Clark Gable and the Duke of Windsor drove them, but two glamorous celebrity customers doth not a business make.

### COUNT ZEPPELIN'S BIG IDEA

Count Zeppelin

Count Ferdinand von Zeppelin (1838–1917) certainly couldn't have afforded one, but that was no problem, since he preferred to fly. That German army officer caught the flying bug during the US Civil War, where he was a military observer attached to President Lincoln's 'Balloon Corps'.

Inspired, he became convinced that balloons could do more than just float up; with the right technology, they could also be steered. And in 1900 he proved it, inventing the engine-powered, hard-shelled *Zeppelin*. This new flying machine (which much later gave its name to an emerging rock band, who someone said was likely to 'go down like a lead Zeppelin') was embraced by the German air force during WWI. The Huns manufactured eighty-eight Zeppelins for bombing raids at vast expense … only to realise that they'd essentially made a bunch of big balloons that just needed one bullet to 'pop'.

### EDWARD MURPHY'S LAW

Some Zeppelins didn't even need a bullet. The count's flying machine stopped being used after the Hindenburg disaster of 1937, which saw thirty-six people go up in flames.

That tragedy, a pessimist would say, provides a good example of **Murphy's law**. And there's a good chance Murphy would agree. He was an aviator himself. Between 1948 and 1949, the US Air Force carried out a series of high-speed rocket-sled experiments to test human tolerance for g-forces during

**Edward Murphy**

rapid deceleration (or something like that). Edward Murphy (1918–1990) was the aerospace engineer who designed the pilot's specialised harness. And he was an angry man when someone strapped it on wrong.

Part of Murphy's tirade—a phrase to the effect of 'If that guy has any way of making a mistake, he will make it'—became notorious among the team, and was jokingly referred to as 'Murphy's law'. An air force spokesman subsequently used the phrase in a press conference, and the joke became widespread.

**JUMBO JETS AND THE LORD OF THE BEASTS**

Murphy's law is no joke when you're on the receiving end of it, however. Jumbo the elephant (1861–1885) certainly wasn't laughing the day he stumbled onto some railway tracks and got killed by a speeding train.

In the 1860s and '70s, Jumbo had been a moderately popular tourist attraction at London Zoo. Named after an African word for 'chief', he weighed in at a largish 6 tonnes and stood a little over 3.5 metres tall. Big but not ludicrously so, as far as elephants go.

**Jumbo the magnificent**

After being bought by a hyperbole-prone American circus owner, however, Jumbo became JUMBO. That's Jumbo 'the towering monarch of his mighty race'. Jumbo 'the gentle and historic lord of the beasts'. Jumbo 'the universal synonym for stupendous things'. In short, the ads said he was big. And they were so successful at conveying this that soon, any big thing began to be called 'jumbo', which is why we have **jumbo jets**.

**WAS THE 'TITANIC' REALLY TITANIC?**

Gargantua could also be called jumbo—though a more appropriate word would be **gargantuan**. This synonym for 'big' (not to mention 'large' and 'immense' and 'enormous') dates back to *The Life of Gargantua and of Pantagruel*, a series of 16th-century French novels about two somewhat vulgar giants. Gargantua is an oversized king whose main interests are eating and drinking.

The good ship **Titanic**'s main interest was floating, but you can't always get what you want. This famously huge passenger liner, which managed to sink on its maiden voyage, was named after a bunch of famously huge gods, the Titans of Greek mythology.

Only they weren't actually *that* huge. These powerful deities may have ruled the earth during the Golden Age (before being overthrown by a bunch of younger 'Olympian' gods, like Zeus) but their bodies weren't too much bigger than ours. The modern-day word **titanic** came about because we generally confuse them with the Gigantes, a group of, yes, giants, with whom the Titans' story is intricately tied.

**ATLAS AND YOUR ATLAS**

One Titan you may have heard of was called Atlas. He didn't accept his demotion well after the war and so took part in a conspiracy to overthrow Zeus. But, Zeus being Zeus (all-powerful, all-seeing, all-knowing, etc.), the conspiracy naturally failed—and it turned out that he wasn't all-merciful.

As his punishment, Atlas was condemned to carry the weight of the world on his shoulders for every moment of every day of his life. Which, given that he's immortal, seems like a pretty long time.

**Atlas holding the world**

Anyway, the image of Atlas buckling under the weight of a giant globe has always been pretty popular with artists. In the 16th century, a Flemish cartographer decided to bung one of their pictures on his new book of maps. Many other cartographers followed suit, which is why we call such books an ***atlas***.

**THE
MEANDERING
MAIANDROS
RIVER**

If you don't have an atlas (or, better yet, a GPS) it can be hard to travel properly. Yes, life is about the journey, not the destination, etc., but no-one wants to just *meander*.

No-one, except Turkish fishermen. 'Meander' comes from that country's Maiandros River—a long and winding waterway that has been a byword for circuitousness since classical times.

# SCIENCE & NATURE

## UNHYGIENIC WORDS

*Syphilis,
Venereal disease,
Venerable, Venerate,
Condom, Panacea,
Hygiene, Jacuzzi, Spa,
Maelstrom, Petri dish,
Crap, Salmonella,
Listerine*

---

## SCIENTIFIC WORDS

*Hertz, Joule, Watt, Ohm,
Amp, Volt, Galvanise,
Decibel, Bunsen burner,
Fahrenheit,
Celsius, Algorithm,
Pythagoras's theorem,
Pasteurisation, Banksia,
Gardenia, Dahlia,
Magnolia, Camellia,
Fuchsia, Boronia,
Lobelia, Flora, Iris,
Iridescence, Frangipani,
Bougainvillea,
Hyacinth, Diesel engine,
Tarmac, Luddite, Robot*

## COLOURFUL WORDS

*Bronze, Copper, Magnet,
Rhinestone, Sapphire,
Jet black, Alabaster,
Turquoise, Azure,
Blue ribbon, Blueblood,
Magenta, Yellow peril,
Yellow belly*

---

## ANIMAL WORDS

*Fauna, Python,
Arachnid, Tarantula,
John Dory fish, Guppy,
Sardine, Sardonic,
Hippopotamus, Tiger,
Tabby, Tomcat,
Raining cats and dogs,
St Bernard, Chihuahua,
Labrador, Akita,
Dalmatian, Alsatian,
Scotty, Maltese dog,
Airedale, Pomeranian,
Saluki, Rottweiler,
Sealyham, Doberman,
Jack Russell,
Canary, Rosella,
Turkey, Pheasant,
Bantam chicken,
Cock and bull story,
Gorilla, Lemur,
Behemoth, Leviathan*

## ANATOMICAL WORDS

*Guy, King Dick,
Hermaphrodite,
Fallopian tube,
Fanny, Sweet FA,
The full monty,
Cell, Adam's apple,
Achilles tendon,
Achilles heel, Hector,
Stentorian, Mentor,
Odyssey, Siren,
Siamese twins*

# UNHYGIENIC WORDS

'Cleanliness,' as PJ O'Rourke once pointed out, 'becomes more important when godliness is unlikely.' When sexed-up Spanish sailors 'discovered' the New World, they didn't just bring back fruit: some brand-new bacteria was also onboard. Transmitted by sexual contact, the spirochaete *Treponema pallidum* can really ruin your day. Early symptoms involve hair loss, scaly rashes and genital sores; later ones include liver failure and blindness. The final symptom is generally death.

But instead of some randy Spaniard, we all blame this disease on a shepherd. The common name for *Treponema pallidum* comes from a poem written in 1530 about a hapless shepherd. His flock starts dying due to a drought one day, so in exasperation he curses the Sun God. And the Sun God curses him right back, giving the shepherd a terrible new illness because he'd taken the divine name in vain. 'He first wore bubos dreadful to the sight. First felt strange pains and sleeplessly passed the night. From him the malady received its name. The neighbouring shepherds caught the spreading flame.'

The shepherd's name, we should probably add, was **Syphilis**.

But was the Sun God really to blame? Syphilis, after all, is just another type of *venereal disease* — a term that comes from Venus, the Roman goddess of love.

Perhaps it's a little unfair that this saucy deity should be forever linked to pustules and genital discharge; all she did was encourage procreation. But them's the breaks in language. Venus at least has the consolation of knowing that, so wholeheartedly did the ancient Romans revere her, she also inspired *venerable* and *venerate*.

**DR CONDOM, AT YOUR SERVICE** To avoid venereal disease, you need a venerable invention. *Condoms* have been around since at least 1200 BC, when Minos, the king of Crete, supposedly popped his little buddy in a goat bladder. Linen, silk, tortoiseshell and sheep guts were all used with varying degrees of success until around 1855, when Charles Goodyear (of car-tyre fame) had the bright idea of using rubber.

What's interesting, though, is that it wasn't until the 17th century that they were actually *called* condoms—and nobody really knows why. Various fairly dubious explanations have been put forward, including Condom, 'a fortress of considerable strength' in Germany, and a small town of that name in France. But the most popular story points to one Dr Conton, a (probably mythical) physician in the court of England's Charles II (1630–1685). It's said that the doc used lamb intestines to help his majesty shag in safety. If this is true, he had mixed success. Charles's genitals may have stayed disease-free, but they produced at least a dozen illegitimate kids.

**THE POWER OF HYGIENE** Big wigs were a big fashion during Charles's reign—not least because they allow people to shave off their hair, and so not have to deal with lice. Allowing hot water to open your pores was considered deeply dangerous in the 17th century (imagine all the diseases that might creep in!) so the average aristocrat bathed maybe once a year.

Good news for wigmakers, bad news for Hygeia. The Roman god of medicine (and sister of *Panacea*, goddess of healing), this goddess had the power to ward off pestilence. Something else has that power these days. We call it *hygiene*.

**BABY KENNETH AND THE JACUZZI** If you want to please Hygeia, have a bath. But if you find ever find yourself in the 1970s, and want to have group sex with some fellow groovers, go get a *Jacuzzi* instead.

The story of the whirlpool bathtub began around 1915, when seven mechanically minded brothers migrated from Italy to the US, and began to manufacture aeroplanes. Business boomed for the 'Jacuzzi Brothers' plane company … until one of the boys got killed in a crash and their mum ordered them to make something else. Using their knowledge of hydraulic aircraft pumps, the brothers turned their attention to deep-well agricultural pumps—and sold them with considerable success.

Enter generation two. In 1942, baby Kenneth Jacuzzi was born with rheumatoid arthritis. Stricken with constant pain, Kenneth's only relief came with hydrotherapy treatment at the local hospital, but he wasn't able to get it every day. So a Jacuzzi brother started wondering whether there was some way the company's pumps might help. Funnily enough, the answer was 'yes'.

**A SPA IN SPA**

Of course, hot tubs *did* exist before the Jacuzzi. They just tended to be rather lukewarm. The Belgian resort town of Spa, for example, boasts one of nature's great Jacuzzis: a mineral spring that Europe's sick and elderly flocked to once they'd realised that a good scrub doesn't lead to bad health.

One such tourist was so impressed by Spa that he tracked down a mineral spring on his return to England and set up an enclosed well of his own. That resort he built, Harrogate, was frequently referred to as 'the English Spa'. And, eventually, as simply a *spa*.

(Nature isn't always so kind, however. In the Arctic Ocean off the coast of Norway lies an altogether more savage whirlpool, which for centuries sank many a ship. Its name is **Maelstrom**.)

**JULIUS PETRI'S DISH**

But back to bacteria. What makes washing so useful is the fact that we're covered in microbes: on every millimetre of human skin there lie a million creepy-crawlies. You could spend your whole life in a shower, scrubbing away with bleach, and on a microscopic level you'd still look like something the dog vomited, mixed up with some fungus and dust mites.

If you don't believe me, check out a **Petri dish**. Julius Richard Petri (1852–1921) did all the time. Before this German bacteriologist came along, scientists tended to culture their bacteria in a kind of liquid broth. He came up with the idea of whacking it in a shallow, cylindrical covered dish. Then, hopefully, he went and washed his hands.

**THOMAS CRAPPER, TOILET-MAKER**

A toilet, of course, can also serve as a Petri dish, should one forget to flush. For the fact that more bathrooms aren't home to streptococci, E. coli and campylobacter, we can sit down and applaud one Thomas Crapper (1836–1910), an enterprising plumber from Yorkshire who helped to refine the flushing toilet.

Thomas Crapper

But did he also help refine the English language, by giving us an alternative to 'bog' and 'shit'? Maybe or maybe not is the slightly crappy answer. The word **crap** has been around since about the 15th century (it comes from a Dutch word for 'scraps') but was mostly used in the sense of general waste.

These days, of course, it means a very specific kind of waste — and this may be where Crapper comes in. Every one of the flushing toilets produced by his company had his name written on it in big, bold letters. (The same also applies to the company's manhole covers, incidentally: a few can still be seen in Westminster Abbey.) The theory goes that American troops stationed in Britain during WWI found this *hilarious* and a new word quickly emerged.

## DANIEL SALMONELLA AND DR LISTERINE

If you're ever finding it hard to have a crap, just tuck into some *salmonella*. Sometimes found in undercooked chicken and pork, this bacterial genus actually has nothing to do with salmon (undercook that and you just get sashimi). The name instead comes from one Daniel Elmer Salmon (1850–1914), a distinguished American vet who was employed by the Bureau of Animal Husbandry in 1883 to develop a nation-wide system of meat inspection. Salmonella was one of the bacteria he banned to make America a safer and less smelly place.

*Listerine* also does its bit to reduce smelliness. Drink, gargle and spit twice a day, and you can kiss with an easy mind. That mouthwash company actually invented the phrase 'Always a bridesmaid, never the bride' for a 1930s ad campaign, convincing single ladies everywhere that sweet-smelling breath was how to hunt down a man.

The minty fresh Joseph Lister

Another successful marketing ploy was Listerine's very name. Dr Joseph Lister (1827–1912) was a world-famous surgeon—the first one in history to wear gloves, clean his instruments with carbolic acid and use antiseptics on every wound. A British icon in the 19th century, his bold new idea (hygiene!) revolutionised hospital practices and has since saved millions of lives.

He never set out to play Cupid, however. Lister neither invented nor endorsed Listerine and strongly objected to the company using his name.

# SCIENTIFIC WORDS

**DR HERTZ
AND DR
JOULE**

For Thomas Huxley, the great tragedy of science was 'the slaying of a beautiful hypothesis by an ugly fact'. For many teenagers, conversely, the great tragedy of science is that schools insist on teaching it every week. If there's anything more boring that an hour-long lecture about how a *hertz* is a unit of frequency equal to 'the number of cycles per second of a periodic phenomenon', it's an hour-long lecture about how a *joule* is a unit of energy 'equal to the energy expended (or work done) in applying a force of one newton through a distance of one metre'.

No offence, Heinrich Hertz (1857–1894). Or, indeed, James Prescott Joule (1818–1889). Both good men to have in a laboratory. But possibly less useful at a dinner party.

**FOUR
OTHER
BRIGHT
SPARKS**

Electricity, on the other hand, is always welcome at a dinner party. Try setting mood lighting without it (or, indeed, cooking the food). So next time you're serving up your signature dish, and dazzling one and all with some ready quips, spare a thought for *watts*, *ohms*, *amps* and *volts* — all units of something-or-other-to-do-with-electricity that do so much to light up our lives.

In doing so, you'll also be remembering the four boffins after whom they were named: Scottish engineer James Watt (1736–1819), who came up with the steam engine; German physicist George Ohm (1789–1854), who discovered something complicated about electric currents; French academic André Amperè (1775–1836), who founded the study of electrodynamics; and Italian physicist Count Alessandro Volta (1745–1827), who invented the first electrical battery.

**HOW TO GALVANISE A FROG**

Electrifying stuff. All these scientists were shining intellects: men of vision, breadth and depth. But on the downside, they didn't think much about frogs' testicles.

Thankfully, Luigi Galvani (1737–1798) did. A colleague of Allessandro Volta, this professor of anatomy was dissecting a frog's legs one day in the hope of proving that testicles lie somewhere inside. (They don't.) But while this experiment didn't show Galvani to be such a bright spark, it did accidentally *create* a bright spark when his metal scalpel touched a brass conductor. And here's the thing: that electric current caused the frog's legs to twitch.

Galvani was deeply excited by this, theorising that electricity was some kind of bodily fluid. Volta, on the other hand, realised that electricity must be some kind of external force, and created the first-ever electric battery in order to prove it. Galvani, in other words, spurred him into action. Or, in one far better word, **galvanised** him.

**ALEXANDER GRAHAM DECIBEL**

If you want to see an adolescent's legs twitch and shake, turn some music on really loud. A few *decibels* will simply not do when someone like Lady Gaga starts to shriek.

Being unable to hear Gaga, of course, is a major consolation for the deaf—but she wasn't around in the 19th century. Alexander Graham Bell (1847–1922) was thus pained by his mother's deafness, and devoted his life to the study of acoustics, in the hope of being able to help. Bels and decibels get their name from Bell, the man who filed a patent for the world's first telephone on 7 March 1876.

(Or *was* it the world's first telephone? Another inventor filed a very similar patent on 14 February 1876 … and spent the rest of his life in court. And yet another inventor, Antonio Meucci, had actually come up with a telephonic device of his own about five years earlier. 'When Bell's patent was registered in 1876, Meucci sued. He'd sent his original sketches and working models to the lab at Western Union. By an extraordinary coincidence, Bell worked in the very same lab, and the models had mysteriously disappeared.')

**ROBERT BUNSEN'S BURNER**

The name 'Peter Desega' has also disappeared from scientific posterity, even though you'll find one of his gas burners in every lab. A technical assistant to Robert Bunsen (1811–1899), Heidelberg University's famous professor of chemistry, Desega invented the *Bunsen burner* at the request of his boss, who needed a hot (but not very bright) flame for his research.

**HERR FAHRENHEIT AND HERR CELSIUS**

To find out how hot, you'd need a thermometer — but what kind of one should you use? In America, you can get a model based on the formula of one Gabriel Fahrenheit (1686–1736), which suggests that water freezes at 32° and boils at 212°. Pretty much everyone adopted the *Fahrenheit* scale after this German physicist first proposed it in 1714.

And then pretty much everyone ditched it. In 1742, a Swedish astronomer called Anders Celsius (1701–1744) suggested a rather simpler scale: *Celsius*, whereby water becomes freezing at 0° and ready for a tea bag at 100°. As metric systems became more common in the 20th century, most countries began to see this made sense.

The slightly odd-looking Anders Celsius

**THE MATHEMAT-ICIAN OF BAGHDAD**

To convert Fahrenheit into Celsius, authorities inform me, you 'subtract 32 from 212 and take five-ninths of the remainder'. If reading that sentence made your jaw sag a bit, and caused a dull, thudding ache in the head, you're clearly no Muhammad al-Khwarizmi (ca 780–850). A mathematician, astronomer and scholar from Baghdad, al-Khwarizmi was the sort of egghead who could instantly tell you that $(x + a)^n = \sum_{k=0}^{n} \binom{n}{k} x^k a^{n-k}$, then casually add that

$$A = \sin \alpha \pm \sin \beta = 2 \sin \tfrac{1}{2}\left(\alpha \pm \beta\right) \cos \tfrac{1}{2}\left(\alpha \mp \beta\right)$$

Renamed 'Algorithmi' by his Latin translators, al-Khwarizmi's books revolutionised Western maths in the 12th century, when they were first published in Europe. For one thing, they popularised Hindu-Arabic numerals (1, 2, 3, etc.)—a much more practical system than all those Roman VIIs and Cs and Xs. And for another, they brought us algebra (the word comes from 'al-jabr', an Arabic term meaning 'broken parts'—like your calculator after you've smashed it trying to figure out how to split a bill). 'Algorithmi' also worked wonders in trigonometry and, just in case you haven't guessed, he came up with some *algorithms* too.

|   |   |
|---|---|
| **PYTHAG-ORAS'S THEOREM (IN THEORY)** | Geometry, however, did not come from Algorithmi. It had already been part of Western maths for the best part of two thousand years. |

One of its earliest practitioners was Pythagoras (570–495 BC). Possibly the first man to call himself a 'philosopher' (a Greek word meaning 'lover of wisdom'), he is now best known for boring maths students: **Pythagoras's theorem** states that the square of the hypotenuse of a right-angled triangle is equal to the square of the other two sides.

But Pythagoras was actually much better known in his own lifetime as the founder of a cult. Based in Southern Italy, his 'Pythagoreans' believed in the transmigration of souls and the harmony of the spheres. They 'loved wisdom' like their leader, and almost certainly studied heaps of maths. In fact, the theorem was probably the brainchild of some anonymous Pythagorean, rather than the Great Leader himself.

## DR PASTEURISATION AND SOME SERIOUS DISEASES

The Pythagoreans were also an animal-friendly community, and avoided eating meat and eggs. It's not known what they thought about dairy products but given they lived long before Louis Pasteur, most lovers of wisdom would have stayed away. Before this French chemist invented *pasteurisation* (sterilising milk by heating it and then cooling it very rapidly), most milk was basically liquid bacteria. A good way to cure constipation, so long as you didn't mind risking death.

**Dr Louis Pasteur**

## FLOWER MEN

Not all scientific researchers are so bacteria-obsessed, however. Some prefer the simple joy of smelling a flower, and then naming it after themselves. Botanists who have given their names to a plant include Sir Joseph Banks (1743–1820) — the *Banksia* — and Dr Alexander Garden (1730–1791) — the *gardenia*. *Dahlias* are named for Anders Dahl (1751–1789), *magnolias* for Pierre Magnol (1638–1715).

I could ramble on and on. In fact, I'll do just that. *Camellias* were named after Georg Kamel (1661–1706) and *fuchsias* after Leonhart Fuchs (1501–1566). Francesco Borone (1769–1794) gave his name to the *boronia*, and *lobelia* comes from Matthias de l'Obel (1538–1616).

Having said that, not all plants are named for botanists. The word *flora* itself comes from Flora, a minor Roman goddess who presided over plants; while *iris* (and *iridescence*) comes from Iris, the personification of the rainbow in mythology.

*Frangipani*, on the other hand, was the name of a real-life Roman. Born sometime in the 16th century, Marquis Muzio

Frangipani made a popular perfume. It smelled rather like a flower that was later discovered in the New World.

Louis Antoine de Bougainville (1729–1811) was one of the men doing all this discovering. The first Frenchman to navigate the planet, he brought back a woody climbing shrub from Brazil and modestly called it *bougainvillea*.

In and amongst their bright flowers, bougainvilleas often have nasty little thorns. But if you're really keen to experience some pain, have a Greek god throw a discus at your head. This is what happened to Hyacinth, the beautiful boy lover of the god Apollo, and, sad to say, he instantly died. But legend tells us that a brand-new flower, the *hyacinth*, then sprang from his blood, which no doubt consoled his mum.

### THE STRANGE DEATH OF MR DIESEL

Plenty of people die from car accidents too, sadly, and Rudolf Diesel (1858–1913) is partly to blame. In 1898, that German engineer was inspired by a bumpy eight-day train trip to invent the *diesel engine*. He became a millionaire within a few months.

**Rudolph Diesel**

He himself died after a boat accident, as it happens—and to this day, we're not quite sure how. All we do know is that, one evening on a boat trip to London, Herr Diesel bade a normal-sounding goodnight to his fellow passengers … and was never seen alive again. Ten Diesel-less days later, his body was found floating in the English Channel.

### MR MAC'S TARMAC

Sadly, John Loudon MacAdam (1756–1836) lived to a ripe old age. This wealthy amateur engineer dreamed of a world where all roads led to more roads, and he did his best to make it come true.

His story began in 1783. Returning to his native Scotland after several years in the US, MacAdam got into a major huff about the sad state of the roads. So he set about building new ones at his own expense, covering up all the dirt with *tarmac*, a combination of tar and small pebbles that he in large part invented himself.

Eventually appointed general surveyor for all highways in England, MacAdam made that green and pleasant land as grey as he possibly could. Ta, Mac!

**LUDDITES HAVE RIGHTS TOO**

He had plenty of help in this quest, however. A bleak, smoggy greyness spread all over England during the 19th century, as more and more factories appeared. The industrial revolution was bad news for nature lovers—and Joe and Mary Worker had a problem too. The new factories made many old skills obsolete. Workers everywhere were losing their jobs or seeing their wages get slashed to the bone.

Naturally, some of them objected. Legend had it one such worker was Ned Ludd, a humble weaver from Leicester. He supposedly smashed two mechanical knitting machines in a symbolic fit of despair. Real or not, textile workers everywhere later borrowed his name, joking to one another that 'Ned Ludd did it' whenever a machine broke down.

Between 1811 and 1817, however, things got beyond a joke. Exploited, angry and starving, thousands of workers began to break into factories and smash up whatever they could. Naturally, they called themselves the *Luddites*—a word that soon came to mean any kind of hostility to new

An angry mob of Luddites

technology, whatever form it happens to take.

**THE
FIRST
ROBOTS**

It seems safe to assume that they wouldn't have liked *robots*. A reworking of a Czech term meaning 'forced labour', the word comes from *Rossum's Universal Robots*, a 1921 science-fiction play by Karel Čapek. Soulless, synthetic humans (as opposed to wire-and-metal machines), Čapek's robots are mass-produced by a futuristic society for people to use for drudge work. Until, that is, they rebel and wipe all humanity out.

# COLOURFUL WORDS

**THE CITY
OF BRONZE
AND THE
ISLAND OF
COPPER**

Euripides once told us to 'Leave no stone unturned' and it very much appears that we haven't. The history of mankind is a history of stumbling across something, putting it to use, then getting someone else to dig up the rest.

It all began with the **Bronze** Age. Sometime around 3000 BC, a Stone Age man was messing about by the campfire, with a little bit of copper and tin. By mixing them together like so, he suddenly discovered, you could produce a very sturdy new metal. For the next few millennia, everyone cooked with bronze pots and built with bronze nails, farmed with bronze ploughs and killed with bronze swords. Stones, it suddenly seemed, were passé.

But why did they call it 'bronze'? The answer probably lies in Brundusinum, an ancient Italian port city by the Adriatic. A major player in Bronze Age commerce, it manufactured bronze products on a massive scale and exported them east and west.

All this made Cyprus a pretty important place too. Bronze's main ingredient, *copper*, actually got its name from that island (then called 'Kupros'), such was its abundance of the stuff. 'Much of the copper known to the Mediterranean world came from Cyprus, where clumps of almost pure metal lay loose on the ground.'

**THE COLOUR OF MONEY**

The Iron Age, then, must have come as an economic blow. Stronger than bronze, and able to stay sharp for longer, this new substance even had its own party trick. Put it anywhere near a certain hard, black stone found near the ancient city of Magnesia and it could somehow move of its own accord. 'Magic,' said Iron Age man. *Magnetic*, says you.

For some people, on the other hand, it's jewels that have a magnetic pull. Though, unfortunately for bargain-hunting boyfriends, someone has decided that this category of rocks does not include *rhinestones* (a sort of colourless crystal found around Germany's Rhine River, which tend to be very competitively priced).

*Sapphires* are less competitively priced. While until now these gems have only been found on earth, they actually get their name from another planet. 'Sapphire' is the English version of a Sanskrit term that means something like 'precious to Saturn'.

**COLOURFUL TOWNS**

It's their colours that make gems so precious—and it's from gems that some colours got their names. And those gems, in turn, get their names from places: no-one had ever seen *jet black* until somebody unearthed the first jet stone in Geet, a Turkish mining town. And *alabaster* white was first seen in Alabastron, an ancient Egyptian city that was built with a calcite-white gypsum that we now call alabaster.

The blue-green colour *turquoise* is in turn named after a blue-green gem called turquoise—which was, yes, found in Turkestan. And one of that country's mines, Lajward, also gave its name to a bluish colour. The word *azure* comes from the purplish-blue gemstone lazurite, a name which in turn derives from the Latin phrase 'lapis lazuli', meaning 'stone of Lajward'.

**THE BLUE RIBBON ON KING EDWARD'S KNEE**

People clearly love blue stones, and the same attitude seems to apply to ribbons. The first **blue ribbon** set may have been the Most Noble Order of the Garter, an exclusive club for England's most distinguished (or, at least, well-connected) knights. To this day, they all wear a blue ribbon beneath their most noble left knee.

It's said that the order's founder, Edward III (1312–1377), came up with this fashion statement after an incident at a medieval ball. The Countess of Salisbury was dancing with or near the king, when her blue garter slipped off, exposing some leg. But Edward was chivalrous to a fault (when he wasn't burning witches), so he didn't smirk or snigger—and he immediately silenced all who did. Picking up the garter and tying it to his left leg, the king declared, 'Shamed be the person who thinks evil of it'—a phrase that later became the motto of the order.

**BLUE-BLOODS AND WHITE ARMS**

To become a Knight of the Garter, it helps to be a **blueblood**. Current members include Prince Charles and Prince William (though John Major somehow got a gig too).

'But hang on,' you say, all keen-eyed and incisive. 'Blood isn't blue, it's *red*.' That's true enough, compadré, when it drips out of your body, but what about when it's still in your veins? In people with light, white skin, veins can indeed appear blue—and for medieval Spanish noblemen, this was deeply important.

Like many countries, Spain is a glorious cultural melting pot that every now and then overboils. It was colonised by the Goths (a bunch of white-skinned Germanic Christians) in the 5th century and then the Moors (a bunch of dark-skinned African Muslims) wandered in a few centuries after that. The two groups didn't get along. By the 9th century or so, some of the more nobly born descendants of the Goths had had enough, and decided that it was time to reclaim 'their' land. They launched a sort of guerrilla war against the Moorish 'invaders', managing to force those infidels out of the country in a mere 500 years.

Yes, quite a triumph. In any case, it was very important to these nobles that their birth be, indeed, 'noble'—which to them meant untainted by Moorish blood. So it was common for them to display the veins on their sword arm to strangers, as a way of saying 'Look at me, aren't I white!'

**RED AND DEAD: MAGENTA BLOOD**

If anyone needed further proof that noble blood isn't actually blue they could have found it at the Battle of Magenta, a town 24 kilometres west of Milan. Fought in 1859, around the time a synthetic red dye called fuchsine was discovered, this stoush between France and Austria didn't really have a winner but plenty of people lost. About 14,000 corpses ended up dying on the blood-soaked battlefield, a relatively enormous number given how few soldiers had actually fought.

Anyway, whether because of the blood that was shed (or—another theory—because the French soldiers wore red pants), the new dye got a new name: *magenta*.

**YELLOW BELLIES AND THE YELLOW PERIL**

Alas, such hostility between cultures has always coloured human societies. In the late 19th and early 20th centuries, to take a more recent example, Westerners lived in fear of 'the Oriental hordes'. And a widely used term to express that fear was, of course, the *Yellow Peril*. Only long before then it was actually used to express an entirely different kind of fear. Of people with yellow fever.

'Persons residing in marshy situations' also tend to have 'yellow, sickly complexions' according to A *General Dictionary of Provincialisms*. The author suggests that this is why people born in the fens of Lincolnshire have been nicknamed **yellow bellies** since at least 1787. The American version of the term, meaning 'cowards', actually only dates back to the 1850s.

# ANIMAL WORDS

**FAUNA AND COW SEX**

Would you like to spend your life eating sows' entrails and sleeping on a bed made of sacrificed lambs? No? Then you wouldn't have much in common with Fauna, the ancient Roman goddess of animals, after whom the planet's **fauna** is named.

She probably wouldn't have needed your company, however. Constantly surrounded by goat-men called 'fauns', she kept busy (in some way I thought best not to research) by encouraging Italy's cattle to breed.

**PYTHON'S DAY OF DOOM**

Fauna was also interested in snakes. Pictures typically show a snake wrapped around her wrist (that phallus-shaped reptile being associated with fertility) and snakes were kept in her temple in Rome.

Never **pythons**, though. In ancient times, that was the name of a dragon. A slender, snake-like beast that had been spawned from rotting slime, Python was 'a fierce monster' who was 'wont to do great mischief to men upon earth'. 'Whosoever met [her],' wrote Homer, was saying hello to their 'day of doom'.

But don't despair, dear reader; Python got her just desserts. One day, the god Apollo,

> who deals death from afar, shot a strong arrow at her. Then she, rent with bitter pangs, lay drawing great gasps for breath and rolling about ... An awful noise swelled up as she writhed continually this way and that amid the wood: and so she left her life, breathing it forth in blood. Then Apollo boasted over her: 'Now rot here upon the soil that feeds man! You at least shall live no more'.

## ARACHNID, THAT POOR, SWEET GIRL

That's right Apollo, you tell her. Whenever those Greek gods punished someone, they liked to temper justice with spite.

Another example of this approach to discipline was provided by Athena. The goddess of the weaving arts, she was a little affronted when a mere mortal named Arachne suggested that she, and not Athena, was the best weaver in the world. And even more affrontingly, the humble seamstress then went on to prove it, by weaving a truly magnificent tapestry.

So Athena destroyed it. And then smashed her loom. And then slashed her face. And then watched smilingly as the seamstress hanged herself, all cowed and 'crushed with shame'. As a final touch, just in case she hadn't quite got her point across, Athena then turned Arachne's noose into a spider web, and Arachne herself into an *arachnid*. 'So you shall live to swing now and forever, even to the last hanging creature of your kind.'

So don't be scared of spiders, feel sorry for them. Unless, of course, they're a *tarantula*. Very rarely invited to children's birthday parties, these super-creepy critters are named after the Italian town of Taranto, which at one time had them in hordes.

**ST JOHN
DORY
AND THE
REVEREND
GUPPY**

You won't see hordes of tarantulas in heaven, however; St Peter will see to that. Sometimes called 'the janitore' ('the doorkeeper'), Jesus's fave disciple famously stands guard at the gates of Paradise, and makes sure none of the riffraff gets through.

But perhaps you're worried that *you* might be riffraff? Time to lead a better life, if so. Alternatively, you can just befriend a **John Dory**. Some suggest that this species of fish actually gets its name from 'the janitore' — St Peter was, after all, a fisherman.

*Guppies* also have a religious namesake. Native to the Caribbean, but now mostly found in fish tanks, this colourful little fish got its name from the Reverend Robert Guppy (1836–1916), a British-born clergyman who was doing God's work in Trinidad, and some marine biology on the side.

**SARDINES
AND
CERTAIN
DEATH**

*Sardines* are less attractive, as little fish go, but they'll be happy to know that they're a lot more edible. People have been scoffing them down in Sardinia for at least two thousand years.

Also on ancient menus in that Mediterranean island was a native plant called the 'sardonian'. People ate it if they wanted to die. In their final moments on earth, it's said, whoever ate it would go through a series of body spasms and terrible facial convulsions: when death finally came, 'their final contorted expression [would resemble a] bitter, scornful grin'. The Greeks called these spasms 'Sardinian laughter' — and it's from that phrase that we get the word *sardonic*.

**A TALE OF
TWO RIVERS**

But back to fish. Like the *hippopotamus*, one might say.

One would be wrong, obviously, but it's worth noting that the word 'Hippos-potamios' literally means 'river horse'.

Those lumbering land mammals spend their days wallowing in rivers and lakes. Their closest relatives are actually whales.

So which river might they be named after? Well, who knows, but it's worth noting that the same language structure is present in 'Mesopotamia', the ancient Greek name for what's now Iraq. It means 'the area between the Tigris and Euphrates rivers'.

*Tigers*, as it happens, may also be named after the Tigris River. Or maybe not. 'Tigris' means 'speed' in Old Persian. The river

and the animal probably each earned the name independently because both, in their own way, run fast. Or did someone on the banks of the Tigris River once see a strange stripy cat?

**CAT CHAT**

We know a bit more about the name of another stripy cat—that humble tenant of alleyways, the *tabby*. The word ultimately derives from Attab, a Umayyad prince from the 7th century who lived in on the outskirts of Baghdad. The area was named Attabiya in his honour, and centuries later it became famous for its fabrics. The local speciality was a sort of striped silk that became known as 'tabby cloth'. Eventually 'tabby' came to mean anything that is liberally covered in stripes.

Tom the Cat may have been a tabby. He certainly wasn't pedigree. The promiscuous, gutter-dwelling hero of *The Life and Adventures of a Cat* (an anonymous story published in 1760), Tom gave rise to the term *tomcat* for a male cat, which had previously been 'rams' or 'boars'. He could also be responsible for the phrase *tomcatting*, which means men who like to sleep around.

With upwards of fourteen wives, the Germanic god Odin was himself a bit of a tomcat, but he made time for real cats too. His heavenly abode contained two pets, a dog that could turn into wind, and a cat that could turn into rain—and they didn't really get along. Particularly wild weather, people thought, represented a particularly nasty scrap. This may well be why we sometimes say that it's *raining cats and dogs*.

**ST BERNARD THE CASHED-UP MONK**

If you get wild weather up on a mountaintop, you might need a *St Bernard*. These enormous alpine dogs have been rescuing travellers for close to a thousand years.

But let's go back a thousand years, to St Bernard (923–1008) himself. Bernard de Montjoux was a wealthy French nobleman who found God fairly late in life and duly became a monk. Now, back then churches required new monks to divest themselves of all their worldly goods, preferably by giving them to the Church. But Bernard decided to do it a little more creatively. To make their holy way to Rome, he was aware, French pilgrims often had to trek through the treacherous Swiss Alps. And then stop trekking, because they'd frozen to death. So Bernard cannily used his money to build a holy hospice for travellers, in what subsequently became known as 'St Bernard's pass'. Monks at the hospice recruited local herding dogs to help them in their endeavours—and the breed duly became known as the St Bernard.

**PLACES THAT HAVE GONE TO THE DOGS**

Most dogs, conversely, are named after the first place in which they were bred. *Chihuahua* is a state in Mexico, *Labrador* a peninsula in Canada, and *Akita* a place in Japan. *Dalmatians* come from Dalmatia (a part of Croatia), *Alsatians* from Alsace in France. *Scotties*, of course, hail from Scotland, just as *Maltese dogs* come from Malta and *Airedales* from Yorkshire's Aire Valley.

Rather less straightforwardly, *Pomeranians* come from Pomerania, a region long since swallowed up by Germany and France. Saluq, the Arabic city that gave us the *Saluki*, also vanished a quite a while ago. And Rottweil, a town in Germany once known for its **Rottweilers**, may as well have vanished, for all that anyone's heard of it these days.

But the prize for true geographic obscurity goes to **Sealyhams**. They derive their name from the home of one John Edwardes, an enthusiastic dog breeder: Sealyham House in Haverfordwest, Wales.

**HERR DOBERMAN THE DOG MAN**

Louis Dobermann (1834–1894) was another enthusiastic dog breeder, though his main interest was self-defence. A tax collector, nightwatchman and dog catcher, this native of Thuringia (in west Germany) was a man of many dangerous jobs. In around 1890, however, it occurred to him that he could use his dog-catching to make all three jobs less perilous. By mixing a bit of Great Dane with a splash of German Shepherd, then adding a drop of Rottweiler and God-knows-what-else, he created what he called a 'harsh dog'—a hound of hell now known as a **Doberman**.

**JACK RUSSELL, 'THE SPORTING PARSON'**

**Jack Russells** are also a harsh dog, should you happen to be a fox. Specially designed to dig 'vermin' out of their holes, and then tear them into tiny bits, the breed dates back to a spotty white terrier called Trump, who was owned by a milkman in Oxford. One day in 1819, when they were busy doing their rounds, Trump and the milkman were spotted by a student of divinity, who, when he

Jack Russell, the 'Sporting Parson'

wasn't busy praying and studying, more or less lived for the hunt. Jack Russell (1795–1883) immediately bought Trump, thinking that here was the perfect hunting dog. Thousands of dead foxes have proved him right.

Smart foxes avoid the Canary Islands. They are absolutely packed with dogs. The Romans called this tiny island chain near Morocco 'Canarii', a Latin phrase meaning 'The Isle of Dogs', because its inhabitants mummified (and presumably worshipped) their canines.

We don't know what they thought about their finches—but later visitors were rather impressed. The archipelago's native yellow songbirds are now found in cages all over the world. People call them *canaries*.

An even more colourful bird is the *rosella* (though its singing isn't quite up to scratch). English-speakers first spotted this brightly coloured parrot in Parramatta, the first colonial settlement in Australia. A place that, back then, they called 'Rose Hill'.

Early American colonists in the 17th century also spotted plenty of brand-new birds, but they didn't always realise it at the time. *Turkeys*, for example, got that name because the Pilgrims thought they were from Turkey—a familiar species of guinea fowl that was occasionally exported to Europe from the east.

*Pheasants*, on the other hand, really did come from the east—specifically, from Georgia's Phasis River. 'Phasianos', the Greek root word, literally means 'Phasian bird'.

Less surprisingly, ***Bantam chicken*** literally means 'chicken from Bantam', a major Indonesian seaport in the 17th century.

If you think that sounds like a ***cock and bull story***, sorry but you're wrong. For one of those, you need to go to Buckinghamshire. Legend says that this phrase originated in the market town of Stony Stratford, a major stopping-off point for 18th-century Londoners who were travelling to and from the north. During these stopovers, they had the option of staying at one of two coaching inns—The Cock or, yes, The Bull—and the theory goes that, while people were in those inns, they'd all swap tall tales of their travels.

Clearly that could itself be a cock and bull story—as could be the one told by Hanno the Navigator. In 500 BC or thereabouts, this Carthaginian explorer set out from what's now Tunisia and sailed down the African coast as far as Sierra Leone. There he and his men encountered 'a savage people, the greater part of whom were women, whose bodies were hairy and whom our interpreters called Gorillae … We took three of the females, but they made such violent struggles, biting and tearing their captors, that we killed them'.

Who or what were they? No-one really knows. But when an American missionary became the first person to scientifically describe Africa's ape population in 1847, he decided to draw on some history. To the largest, most human-like primates, he gave the name *gorillas*.

**LEMURS AND OTHER MYTHICAL BEASTS**

Hanno certainly wasn't the only African adventurer to come up with a wacky tale. Take a group of Portuguese explorers about 2100 years after him. Having ventured deep into the dark, tangled forests of Madagascar, these men went to bed for the night. But they didn't manage to get much sleep. Awoken by sinister, spine-chilling howls, they saw large, shining eyes staring back at them, flickering creepily in the light of the campfire.

In the morning, everyone's spines warmed up again. It turned out that those bloodcurdling ghosts were just a bunch of big-eyed monkeys. As a joke, the men named this new monkey species *lemurs*, after some evil spirits in Roman mythology who spend their time avenging the dead.

Mythology is full of creatures that you wouldn't want to meet in a dark alley. Take **Behemoth** and **Leviathan**, two enormous beasts in the Bible that have now become synonyms for big. The Book of Job tells us that Behemoth's limbs are 'as strong as copper' and goes into detail about 'the sinews of his thighs'. Leviathan, on the other hand, is a sea monster, and Job does 'not fail to speak of his limbs, his strength and his graceful form … Any hope of subduing him is false; the mere sight of him is overpowering'.

# ANATOMICAL WORDS

**THE GRIM FATE OF THE WORLD'S FIRST GUY**

Back hair, unsightly genitals, social pressure to know something about cars … being male can be hard work. But being a Guy would be even worse. Guido 'Guy' Fawkes (1570–1606) was a Catholic soldier of fortune who was 'highly skilled in matters of war'. Since one of those skills was making bombs, he was recruited by group of Catholic conspirators who were plotting to blow up England's protestant King James. On the morning of 5 November 1605, therefore, Guy could be found hiding underneath the Houses of Parliament, next to thirty-six barrels of gunpowder.

On the evening of 5 November 1605, Guy could be found in jail. Someone had tipped off the authorities, so it really *was* 'long live the king'. Guy, on the other hand, was executed—and every year, Brits still 'remember, remember the fifth of November' by burning his effigy on a bonfire.

Such effigies are, naturally, called a *guy*. A word that has since come to mean anyone who takes the outward form of a man, even if they know nothing about cars.

**Some Englishmen burning a guy**

**WHEN KING DICK SAT ON THE THRONE**

Guy Fawkes's problem, once he got arrested, was that King James was a bit of a *King Dick*. Is there anything more arrogant than hanging, drawing and quartering someone? Let's not mince words, it's just plain rude.

Technically speaking, however, James wasn't King Dick. That was actually somebody else. In 1642, England began a civil war, which ended with the monarchy being overthrown. Instead of a king, the country suddenly had a 'Lord Protector': Oliver Cromwell, a militaristic Puritan.

Oliver couldn't live forever, though, so when he finally carked it, the question became 'Who should rule?' His deeply unqualified son Richard Cromwell (1626–1712) thought that the answer was … Richard Cromwell, and in the absence of any clear alternative, the parliament let him have a bit of a go. But after nine months of this 'coxcomb and poltroon' (who a visiting prince described as 'the basest fellow alive'), a king started to look pretty good, so 'King Dick' had to sod off to France.

**A BOY AND HIS BOOBS**

The hapless Richard was also sometimes called 'Queen Dick'. Which, given he wasn't a *hermaphrodite*, was perhaps a little unfair.

Hermaphroditus, on the other hand, *was* a hermaphrodite, though that's not how he started out. The son of Venus and Mercury, this ancient god was all boy in his early days. All remarkably-handsome-boy, in fact. But this very handsomeness was to prove his undoing. One day, legend says, Hermaphroditus was swimming in a lake when a randy wood nymph saw him naked and thought 'Phwooooooar, I'll have some of that!' Overcome by lust, she leapt into the water and wrapped herself around his manly chest, crying to the gods that they must never part. The gods nobly granted her wish and merged them into 'a single creature of both sexes'.

**ONE MAN AND HIS FALLOPIAN TUBES**

Bad news for Hermaphroditus, but good news for lovers of art. This reluctant she-man can still be found in thousands of paintings and statues—generally still sporting some man tackle, but with two girly lumps on his chest.

It's never very clear what kind of gender division is going on *inside* his/her body, though. Does (s)he have any *fallopian tubes*, for example? Gabriello Fallopio (1523–1562) might have been able to tell us. It's after him, after all, that they're named. One of the most celebrated academics of the Italian Renaissance, Fallopio headed up the anatomy department at Padua University and managed to map most of the human body during the course of a distinguished career. It's because of that professor that we talk of 'palates' and 'placentas' and 'cochleas'. And if he hadn't found and named the 'clitoris', men might be unaware of it still.

**FANNY TALK**

Fallopio also coined 'vagina'. The word *fanny*, however, came about much later—and most likely through literature, not science. This time-honoured term for lady-land first appeared in the mid-18th century, around the time *Memoirs of a Woman of Pleasure* came out. This wildly popular novel was about a prostitute called Fanny Hill—an innocent, poverty-stricken 15-year-old who travels to London from the countryside and finds herself in a brothel by about page ten. She quickly loses her innocence to a fellow prostitute 'whose lascivious touches lighted up a new fire' and then her virginity to Mr H, a rich man with an enormous schlong.

> Disengag'd from the shirt, I saw, with wonder and surprise, what? Not the play-thing of a boy, not the weapon of a man, but a maypole of so enormous a standard, that had proportions been observ'd, it must have belong'd to a young giant. Its prodigious size … the broad and blueish-cast incarnate of the head, and blue serpentines of its veins, altogether compos'd the most striking assemblage of figure and colours in nature. In short, it stood an object of terror and delight.

**WHY YOU SHOULD GIVE AN 'F' ABOUT SWEET FA**

Yes … delightful. In any case, Fanny Hill is not the only Fanny who lives in our language. We also mention another one when we use the phrase *sweet FA*.

Yes, I know you're thinking: 'Wrong, sir! This man knows "Sweet fuck all!"'—but just stop there, take a breath, and read on. You need to know about Fanny Adams (1859–1867), a sweet 7-year-old from Hampshire who met someone who wasn't sweet at all. On 24 August 1867, several parts of Fanny's horribly butchered body were found scattered across a field. They were still finding parts in September.

Thankfully, the murderer was soon found too. (One of his diary entries was a bit of a giveaway: '24th August, Saturday: killed a young girl. It was fine and hot.') But Fanny still couldn't rest in peace. In 1869, a particularly dog food–like brand of tinned mutton was introduced into the British navy and it became a bit of a sick joke amongst the seamen to call the unappetising meat 'sweet Fanny Adams'.

'Fuck all' was another common phrase at the time, but it didn't always seem appropriate to use. So at some point someone must have noticed the identical initials, and started saying 'Sweet FA'.

**THE NAKED TRUTH ABOUT THE FULL MONTY**

It's usually pretty easy to guess whether someone has a fanny, but unless they go *the full monty*, you can't be entirely sure. We're also pretty unsure about where that term for nudity comes from, but the best guess is Sir Montague Burton (1885–1952).

Born in Lithuania, Mosche Osinsky came to England as a teenager, changed his name and started selling suits. A decade later, he was still selling suits but on a somewhat larger scale. Supported by the biggest clothing factory in the world, Burton's 400 tailor shops made a quarter of all British military uniforms during WWI, and clothed millions of civilians as well.

Some of those customers, it's said, spent their money on 'the fully mont': a full three-piece suit, with waistcoat, that was specially tailored to fit their measurements. Providing those measurements meant stripping off to some degree, so perhaps that's how the phrase came to mean naked.

**THE MONKS INSIDE YOU**

If you ever see me naked, please try not to giggle — and, really, this shouldn't be hard. All you're really seeing, at the end of the day, are some *cells*: those tiny little biological thingummies with atoms and other whatsits that I never quite got the hang of at school.

Something they never mentioned in science class, however, is that the word 'cell' comes from religion. The first man to see one was Robert Hooke (1635–1703), an English scientist with a

homemade microscope. Peering at some very thin slices of cork one day, he noticed a pattern of tiny shapes … and was immediately reminded of a medieval monastery. Tiny, bare-walled and packed tightly together, monks' bedrooms were generally known as their 'cells'.

Hooke's microscope

---

### ADAM'S APPLE (OR OLIVE OR FIG)

Monks, being monks, mostly believe the story of Adam and Eve. To recap, God creates Man (being Adam) and then Woman out of said man's rib. Both creations then frolic about in the Garden of Eden for a bit, wearing fig leaves over their privates. There was only one actual rule in this magical paradise—don't eat the forbidden fruit—and so, of course, they do that too.

But what exactly was that forbidden fruit? Historically, there's been a lot of disagreement. Jews generally say a fig, some Muslims maintain an olive. As far as Christians are concerned, though, it was an apple; one that got stuck in Adam's throat, and is still wedged in his descendants today. The *Adam's apple* symbolises the Fall of Man. To cover up Man's original sin, you just have to buy a scarf.

Adam, his apple, and Eve

**ACHILLES'
HEEL AND
SOME
UNBLEM-
ISHED
THIGHS**

Achilles should have covered up his calf muscles. As the ancient Greek epic *The Iliad* tells us, this handsome homosexual he-man was shot in the heel during the Trojan War. The arrow, alas, was poisoned and so our hero died.

And the Greek-tragic thing, double alas, was that he would have been just fine if he was shot elsewhere. When he was a baby, Achilles' mum had dipped him in to a magical river, which, being magical, served to make him invulnerable. But the bit she was holding on to remained undipped, and so very vulnerable. His **Achilles tendon** was his **Achilles heel**.

*The Iliad* actually put all sorts of words in the dictionary. Before he dies, for example, Achilles kills Hector, a warrior who had slain his boyfriend (a comely youth with 'unblemished thighs'). While Hector is actually presented as a hero — a noble leader, not a **hectoring** bully — his name came became synonymous with 'loudmouth' in the 17th century, when a gang of London street-thugs started calling themselves 'The Hectors'.

If only Stentor could have had a word with them. With his **stentorian** 'voice of bronze … as loud as 50 men together', that ear-splitting soldier from *The Iliad* knew how to keep men in line.

But what wayward youths really need is a **mentor**. *The Iliad* has the original. When Odysseus leaves Ithaca to go and fight in Troy, he asks a favour of his wise friend Mentor: please keep an eye on my son.

After the war, Odysseus has to get back to Ithaca. His long and eventful journey home is the subject of *The Odyssey*, *The Iliad*'s sequel — and, of course, the source of the word **odyssey** itself.

Unfortunately, Odysseus's journey takes him past a dangerous island, one from which many a good man had been lured to his doom. Not because of rocks or rifts or some other nautical feature, but because it was home to the **sirens**. Half-woman, half-bird and all evil, these monsters could so entrance men with their haunting melodies that they'd forget to eat or drink or sail. The cunning Odysseus, however, just stuffed wax into his sailors' ears and sailed on. You'd think someone else would have thought of that.

**THE SEX LIFE OF SIAMESE TWINS**

Chang and Eng Bunker's (1811–1874) lives would have been quite the odyssey. Born in Siam (modern-day Thailand) in 1811, and brought to America by a travelling 'freak show', these men were the original *Siamese twins*.

The Bunkers eventually left the show, having earned enough money to buy farms in North Carolina. They then married two sisters, and had … twenty-two children between them, none of whom were conjoined.

**Chang and Eng Bunker, the original Siamese twins**

# GEOGRAPHY

## ASTRONOMICAL WORDS

*Jupiter, Saturn,
Mars, Martial, Venus,
Mercury, Mercurial,
Uranus, Uranium,
Neptune, Pluto, Ogre,
Aquarius, Pisces, Aries,
Gemini, Taurus, Cancer,
Leo, Sagittarius*

---

## EUROPEAN WORDS

*Europe, Britain,
Scotland, England,
Anglo-Saxon, Wales,
France, Russia,
Bulgaria, Belgium,
Romania, Rome, Lisbon,
Portugal, Athens,
Parthenon, Ireland,
Vatican City*

## AMERICAN WORDS

*America, Louisiana,
Virginia, Georgia,
North Carolina,
South Carolina,
Maryland, New York,
Brooklyn, Harlem,
Bronx, California,
Los Angeles,
San Francisco,
San Antonio, Texas,
Austin, Houston,
Cleveland, Denver,
Delaware, Pittsburgh,
New Orleans,
Albuquerque,
Charleston, Charlotte,
Orlando, Pennsylvania,
Cincinnati, Arkansas,
Illinois, Missouri,
Oklahoma, Utah,
Seattle*

## AUSTRALIAN WORDS

*Australia, Tasmania,
Hobart, Auckland,
New South Wales,
Sydney, Brisbane,
Queensland, Victoria,
Melbourne, Adelaide,
Alice Springs, Darwin,
Fremantle, Perth*

---

## LANDMARK WORDS

*Sistine Chapel,
Colosseum, Big Ben,
Eiffel Tower, Taj Mahal,
Mount Everest,
Ayers Rock,
Mount Rushmore,
Easter Island,
Rock of Gibraltar,
Amazon River, Volcano*

# ASTRONOMICAL WORDS

### JUPITER, PLANET OF THE GRAPES

'As I looked out into the night sky, across all those infinite stars, it made me realise how insignificant they are,' a philosophical Peter Cook once remarked—but the ancient Romans took a different view. The planets, at least, were a big deal for the conquerors of the ancient world. In fact, so big that they named them after their gods.

Naturally, the biggest planet got the name of the biggest god. *Jupiter* owes its name to, well, Jupiter: divine overlord of thunder and lightning (and, less awe-inspiringly, seeds and grapes). Also known as 'Jove', Jupiter was the supreme god of the Roman pantheon and chief protector of the city itself. Roman consuls would take their oath of office in his name, then castrate an ox as a token of thanks.

The ever-horny Jupiter

### SATURN THE BABY EATER

Saturn would have benefited from castration. He was the king of the gods before Jupiter, and it was a position that he wanted to keep. Every time his wife gave birth to a baby, Saturn would eat it so it didn't threaten his reign. For some reason, his wife didn't like this, and she decided that things would be different for child #7. So she wrapped up a rock in a baby blanket and tricked Saturn into swallowing that instead.

The child that survived was Jupiter—and he eventually became a pretty big man. Backed by some many-headed monsters, he overthrew papa-dearest and assumed his rightful position as the king of the gods. Saturn himself was banished to the underworld. But you can still look up and see **Saturn**, his namesake in the night sky.

**THE MAN OF MARS AND THE WOMAN OF VENUS**

Turn your head a bit and you might also see **Mars**. It's that one with the reddish tint.

When people these days see red, they might think about roses, or perhaps cherry tomatoes atop a crispy bruschetta. The Romans, on the other hand, were Roman; seeing red made them think about blood. Also the source of the word **martial** (as in 'martial arts'), Mars was the god of war: a fully armed, battle-hungry psychopath, who required regular sacrifices of bulls and sheep.

Not too many people lost their lives because of Venus, but quite a few gave her their hearts. As the Roman goddess of love and beauty, she was supposed to be pretty lovely and beautiful herself. So the Romans gave her name to **Venus**, the brightest (and thus most beautiful) planet in the sky.

**THE MERCURIAL PLANET OF MERCURY**

**Mercury**, in murky contrast, can be much harder to see. Being the closest planet to the sun, it lives life in the fast lane, zipping all around outer space as it orbits at breakneck speed.

The Roman god Mercury had similar habits. The god of trade and travellers, who occasionally served as a messenger for his colleagues, he was a lightning-quick professional speedster, with winged sandals and a big winged hat.

Mercury's fast-moving unpredictability also explains his place in other words: ***mercurial*** (meaning volatile) and ***mercury***, the super-slippery element.

**Mercury, messenger of the gods**

**URANUS
AND YOUR
ANUS**

Mankind didn't move very quickly when it came to naming the remaining planets, however, as they couldn't be seen with the naked eye. It wasn't until 1781 (when telescope-makers started, well, making telescopes) that another one was discovered. And its silly discoverer wanted to call it Georgium Sideus ('George's planet'), after England's mad King George.

'No way,' said everyone else. Determined to continue the tradition of naming planets after Roman gods, scientists reached for their history books, and began a search of the mythical *mot juste*. Eventually, as a favour to schoolchildren everywhere, they chose Uranus, the Roman god of the sky.

But despite the almost endless potential for new gags (e.g. 'Did you know that there's a ring of debris around ***Uranus***?'), the real story of Uranus is actually no laughing matter. It appears that, after his wife bore him eighteen children, she wanted a bit of 'me' time. So she got one of the kiddies to cut off his balls.

Ok, that's a little bit funny. But **uranium**, lifeblood of the bomb, is definitely no laughing matter. It was first isolated in 1789, just eight years after the new planet was discovered, and was duly named in its honour.

**NEPTUNE AND THE OGRE**

In 1846, a boffin found planet number seven—and did his darndest to have it named after himself. Sadly for him, however, scientists stuck to tradition. They eventually decided to call the bluish new discovery **Neptune**, after the Roman god of the deep blue sea.

Still sadder news lay in store for another boffin, who discovered planet number eight. Scientists now think of it as a sort of largish asteroid, and not really a planet at all. But no-one was to know that in 1930, so a competition was held to find the most appropriate god. The winner, as it happens, was an 11-year-old girl from Oxford, who was rewarded with a prize of £5. She suggested that, since it was the outermost planet in the solar system, an appropriate name would **Pluto**, the divine ruler of the underworld, who was able to make himself invisible at will. Also called 'Orcus' (a name that may have led to the word **ogre**), Pluto was a pitiless tyrant. If a mortal accidentally stumbled into his kingdom of the dead, they could never, ever hope to return.

**AQUARIUS THE BOY TOY**

Grim. But preferable, all things considered, to talking to someone who believes in star signs. It's unclear who is to blame for these pitiless tyrants of the modern world, but we do know that, while the planets owe their names to Roman gods, all the constellations get their names from the Greeks.

*Aquarius*, for example, was a handsome young Trojan prince—
a 'most beautiful of mortals', who caught the ever-horny eye of Zeus.
That deity purchased the prince from his father and took him to
heaven to be his official 'cupbearer'. (And unofficial sex toy.)

Also known as Ganymede (a word which can be translated as
'gladdening genitals'), Aquarius clearly did both jobs well. He was
such a star, in fact, that he was rewarded with a place among the
stars: Zeus turned him into a constellation.

**PISCES THE COWARDLY FISH**

*Pisces*, the next constellation on the calendar, also
had good sexual credentials. Vaguely fish-like in
appearance, it gets its name from an incident in
Greek mythology involving Aphrodite (she of the
'aphrodisiac') and Eros (her 'erotic' son). These two saucy gods were
once forced to disguise themselves as fish, in order to get away from
a monster.

**ARIES, AN UNLUCKY RAM**

The story of *Aries* is more heroic. The Greek
word for 'ram', this constellation is named after a
golden ram that was sent by a goddess to save her
son from a big bunch of sword-wielding Greeks. It
nobly swooped down from the clouds and scooped him up to safety,
carrying the boy to a distant land that promptly made him a prince.

A nice story. With a nasty ending. The newly installed prince
then showed his gratitude to the gods—and something less than
gratitude to his rescuer—by sacrificing the ram to Zeus.

**THE GEMINI, TWO BROTHERS IN ARMS**

The ram's golden fleece was placed in a holy
garden, where it was later sought by all manner of
adventurers. The most famous were Jason and the
Argonauts. Two of those Argonauts, as it happens,
were Pollux and Castor: twin brothers who were
alike in all things, except one was mortal and one was not.

When Castor, the mortal one, was dying, Zeus gave his brother a choice: Pollux could share half his immortality with Castor and thus be bound to him forever more. He accepted. Which is why the constellation of two bright stars is called *Gemini*, a Latin word meaning 'twins'.

**TAURUS THE HORNY BULL**

Zeus didn't always believe in giving people a choice, however. A god who liked to keep busy in the bedroom, he was sometimes forced to abduct his lovers when for whatever reason they couldn't be bought.

This was what happened with Europa, a Phoenician princess who caught his eye. Disguising himself as a friendly bull (or *Taurus*), Zeus lay down one day and enticed her to hop on. He then swam her away for some good times, forcing the hapless princess to either hang on or drown.

**CANCER, THE OBEDIENT CRAB**

Understandably, Zeus's wife Hera was never very happy about these little affairs, particularly when they resulted in offspring, like Hercules. But it seems unfair to blame the child. And even worse to try and kill him with the aid of a giant serpent.

She didn't seem very remorseful, however. While Hercules was busy fighting the serpent, Hera sent down a giant crab (or 'cancer') in order to seal the deal. The idea was that the cancer would distract him, but—being Hercules—he just crushed it and fought on.

Nevertheless, Hera was pleased by the crab's sacrifice. She sent it into the sky and made the constellation of *Cancer*.

**LEO, THE UNLUCKY LION**

Hercules seems to have spent a lot of his time fighting large animals. The nastiest of them may have been the 'Leon Nemios', a huge lion from the hills of Nemea that had long terrorised all the locals.

Our hulking hero didn't know the meaning of fear, however. (He probably didn't know the meaning of a lot of words.) So he strolled into the lion's cave and strangled it to death, then tore off its hide to make a lion-skin cape. The rest of the carcass Hercules threw into the heavens, where it now resides as a constellation called **Leo**.

# EUROPEAN WORDS

**EUROPA THE ANIMAL LOVER**

Herd the myth about the bull? (Sorry, terribull pun.) Anyway, it seems that that insatiable hornbag, Zeus, was gazing down from the heavens one day when he noticed Europa, a saucy princess from Syria. So he naturally turned himself into a gentle and 'hugely attractive' white bull and approached her while she was gathering flowers. Charmed, the fair maiden 'caressed his flanks' and hopped on his back for a hug. She was then less charmed when he then plunged into the sea and swam her away for a shag.

Not a nice story but some people in a small, northern part of Greece must have liked it, because they made **Europe** the name of their land. By about 500 BC, however, ancient Greek cartographers started using it to mean *all* the land north of Greece—and then the land to the west as well.

**THE BLUE MEN OF BRITAIN**

Europa certainly wasn't the last person to take a trip through Europe. Anyone who gets their all-white knickers in a twist about migration should be made to study history at gunpoint. The word **Britain**, for example, comes from Greece ('pretani', meaning 'painted people', after the tribesmen who wore blue face paint in battle). And the people of Britain come from everywhere.

The Scots, from example, aren't from **Scotland**. The Scoti were an Irish tribe who took a boat-trip some time during the 5th century, bringing their kilts and haggis along for the ride.

**England**, similarly, gets its name from a big bunch of Germans. Angeln, a small peninsula in what's now Schleswig-Holstein, was once the home of the Angles, a big group of blond-haired barbarians who decided that they'd all benefit from a bit more room. So together with some tribes from nearby Saxony, they headed to what became known as 'Ang-land'—and created a new people known as **Anglo-Saxons**.

Their arrival was bad news for the people who were already in Britain, so many of them fled west, where there was a natural barrier of mountains. Among the Anglo-Saxon invaders, that territory became known as 'Wĕalas'—'foreigners' land'. Nowadays we call it **Wales**.

**MORE MIGRANTS: FRANCE, RUSSIA, BULGARIA AND BELGIUM**

Things were much the same on the continent. Another Germanic tribe to stretch its legs was the Franks, a people from east of the Rhine. So-named for the 'frankon', a kind of spear that they used to stab people, the Franks kicked the Gallia tribe out of Gaul in the 4th century and turned it into a new country. Nowadays we know it as **France**.

In Finland, Sweden is known as 'Ruotsi'. This ancient name dates back to the Rus people, a group of Vikings from the Swedish coast. But, being Vikings, they didn't stay there for long. The Rus sailed east in search of plunder … and arrived in a place that we now call **Russia**.

The Bulgars, on the other hand, came west. **Bulgaria** is apparently named after this 'Turkic people with some Iranian elements', who began life in Central Asia.

We're also pretty hazy where it comes to the Belgae. They were a fierce tribe first described in Julius Caesar's war dispatches, which he sent from an area roughly corresponding to **Belgium**. The Belgae lived far away from 'civilisation', and Caesar thought that they were much better fighters because of it. 'Merchants less frequently resort to them, and import those things which tend to effeminate the mind.' But he also thought that 'the greater part of the Belgae were sprung from the Germanic peoples … having crossed the Rhine at an early period, they settled there on account of the fertility of the country'.

**ROMANIA, ROMULUS AND ROME**

The Romans also visited **Romania**, conquering what was then known as the Dacian kingdom in around 106 AD. While they only ruled the area for 165 years, they 'colonised with settlers from all parts of the Empire who intermarried with the local population and Romanised it'. To this day, Romania is the only Eastern European country to speak a Romance language (i.e. one derived from Latin).

**Rome** itself, of course, is supposed to be named after Romulus: one of two twins left to die on a hill, only to be saved by a slightly odd she-wolf. She can't have brought them up very well, however, as both grew into violent men. The short version of the story involves Romulus killing his brother and founding a city, then abducting lots of women from other tribes to populate it.

The long version involves lots of corduroy-wearing, party-pooping historians, pointing out that it's all a myth.

**LEGENDARY CITIES: LISBON AND ATHENS**

**Lisbon** is also home to a legend. You can read it for yourself in *The Odyssey*. As Homer tells us, Odysseus took quite a while getting home from the Trojan War, in part because of sea monsters and sirens, but mainly because he couldn't read a map. As he was sailing from Turkey to Greece past … Portugal, Odysseus saw a bolt of lightning strike an unknown land one day, and then burst into a magical flame. Zeus, the god of thunder, told him to build a city on that land, and so of course he did. The city of U*li*saypo. Which, who knows, may have just been Lisbon.

**Portugal**, more prosaically, is named after one of its cities. Porto. So-called because, well, it's a port.

When Odysseus finally arrives home, he meets up with Athena and gets given some friendly advice. The Greek goddess of wisdom and warfare, Athena was always doing this kind of thing: one of her nicknames was 'protectress of heroes'.

She also protected herself. Ever staunch in defence of her 'purity', her full title was

Athena

'Athena Parthenos' ('Virgin Athena'). Which explains why, in her patron city of **Athens**, there's a big temple called the **Parthenon**.

**CATHOLIC COUNTRIES, PAGAN GODS**

The ever-so-Catholic **Ireland** is also named after a pagan goddess, strangely enough. Along with her sisters Fódla and Banba, Éiru was one of a triumvirate of goddesses who agreed to help out with the invasion of Ireland by the Milesian people, so long as they named it after her.

It's not known what another pagan god thinks about **Vatican City**, the most Catholic country of them all. Rome's Vatican Hill, where this tiny city-state is based, got its name long before Christianity came along—and got it from a Roman god.

According to St Augustine (354–430), Vaticanus was the god of childbirth and presided over the beginnings of speech. He was 'the one who opens the mouth of the newborn in crying'. An altar to Vaticanus was built on what became known as Vatican Hill, possibly because people who were high up could be better heard by Heaven.

# AMERICAN WORDS

**A TALE OF TWO AMERICAS**

Even before the United States existed, the world had too many **Americans**. Amerigo Vespucci (1454–1512) and Richard Amerike (1445–1503) both helped to map the New World after Christopher Columbus 'discovered' it in 1492. But to this day we don't know which (if either) of them actually gave the land its name.

Most people say Amerigo Vespucci. Named after St Emeric (i.e. 'St Henry') of Hungary, he was a merchant and navigator from Renaissance Florence who took four trips across the Atlantic. (We think. Some people say Amerigo merely helped to outfit ships for bona fide explorers, and then swiped their stories after they came back.) Either way, he wrote at great length about the New World, and was possibly the first man to identify that it *was* in fact a new world. (To his dying day, Columbus maintained he'd landed in India. Which is why we have 'Red Indians' and the 'West Indies'.)

Amerigo Vespucci

Richard Amerike came from Wales — and then travelled to Bristol, where he became a wealthy merchant. In 1497, he used some of that wealth to sponsor an English exploration across the Atlantic, which mapped much of North America. And 'as the chief patron of the voyage, he would have expected discoveries to be named after him'.

So were they? Well, the oldest surviving reference to 'America' can be found in a small map buried in a 1507 book, the *Cosmographiae Introductio*. Its French author appears to believe that the name comes from Vespucci. However, other, slightly later, documents suggest that the English had been using the word 'America' since 1497. The French author may have simply made that assumption because he hadn't heard about the merchant from Bristol.

**THE UNITED STATES OF TOADYING**

Another argument in favour of Richard Amerike can be found in the conventions of the time. Usually when a new place was named after someone, it would reference their surname, not their first name. If people had really wanted to pay homage to Amerigo Vespucci, Barack Obama would be the president of 'Vespuccia'.

The one exception to this rule is royalty. British and French explorers kept returning to America in the years that followed, and kept naming new discoveries after whatever monarch was in power at the time. *Louisiana* is named after Louis XIV of France, *Virginia* after England's 'Virgin Queen' Elizabeth I and *Georgia* after England's George II. *North Carolina* and *South Carolina* owe their names to England's Charles I ('Carolus' is Latin for 'Charles'), while *Maryland* remembers Henrietta Maria, his wife.

**THE DUKE OF NEW YORK**

Future monarchs sometimes got a mention too. *New York* isn't actually named after York, the ancient town in England's north, but after James Stuart (1633–1701), the Duke of York, who later became James II. In 1664, when he was still a humble duke, James sent four frigates to the Dutch colony of New Amsterdam, and demanded that its governor clear out. The English, he felt, were the ones who'd actually discovered North America, so the Dutch could take their clogs and piss off.

This they did, rather begrudgingly, but New York's Dutch beginnings can still be seen all over that city, from **Brooklyn** to **Harlem** to the **Bronx**. Breukelen and Haarlem are towns in the Netherlands, while Jonas Bronck (died 1643) owned a big farm just north of Manhattan.

### CALIFORNIA, WARRIOR QUEEN

Sunny *California* is also named after royalty, in a manner of speaking. This region first came to European notice in 1533, when Spanish conquistadors sent a scouting party from Mexico. Slightly thrown by the Gulf of California, they thought they'd found a large island, and so named the new find after a fictional island from a popular book of the time.

In 1510, the trashy author Garci de Montalvo had published his trashiest offering yet, a romance novel about a sexy black warrior queen whose name was Calif. 'Strong of limb, large in person and full in the bloom of womanhood', Calif was the ruler of California, a island paradise filled with sexy black warrior women ... and not a single man. Good stuff. But the problem was that she's also a pagan. Falling in love with a handsome Christian king changes all that, however, and Calif soon embraces the one true faith. 'It is clear that the law which you follow must be the truth, while that which we follow is lying and falsehood.'

As it happens, it's a good thing Calif converted, considering how Christian are the cities in her state. **Los Angeles**, of course, means 'the city of angels', while **San Francisco** is Spanish for 'St Francis', and **San Antonio** means 'St Anthony'.

### THE FATHER OF TEXAS AND ONE OF ITS UNCLES

As far as some Americans were concerned, Stephen Austin (1793–1836) was a bit of a saint too. In 1821, this businessman did a deal with the Mexican government, which allowed Americans to settle within Texas's borders. The 'Father of Texas' never got to be the president of Texas, however. That honour went to Sam Houston (1793–1863), a soldier who managed to defeat a Mexican army in a little under eighteen minutes, and make *Texas* an independent state. The cities of *Austin* and *Houston* stand as memorials to both men.

**MOSES CLEAVE-LAND, VISIONARY**

Austin certainly wasn't the only nation-building visionary to gaze upon a distant horizon and think, 'Now, if I could just rip off a few locals, that place could make me some cash'. A lawyer named Moses Cleaveland (1754–1806) made sure he brought plenty of beads and whiskey with him in 1796, when he led a party of fifty settlers through the wilds of Ohio. The company he worked for had bought a big chunk of this untamed wilderness, and it was his job to convince the punters that it was a good place to live. To that end, he picked a spot for a new city. Then got the hell back to civilisation.

Four years later, 'it had grown into a village of one resident: a guy named Lorenzo Carter who built a log cabin by the river and complained about the flies'. But Moses was not discouraged. 'Some day,' he declared, '*Cleveland*, Ohio will grow to be as big as Wyndham, Connecticut!'

**CITY FOLK**

Other founders were a little more modest, naming new regions after friends or, more frequently, patrons. *Denver* was named after James Denver (1817–1892), a governor of the Kansas territory; Dallas after George Mifflin Dallas (1792–1864), who served as vice-president under Polk. *Delaware* commemorates Baron De Lar Warr (1577–1618), Virginia's first colonial governor, *Pittsburgh* honours William Pitt (1708–1778), a distinguished British PM. *New Orleans* and *Albuquerque* are both named after French dukes, while *Charleston* is named after an English king (Charles II) and *Charlotte* after an English queen (Charlotte, wife of George III).

**MR PENN-
SYLVANIA
AND HIS
BOWELS**

Other regions are named after soldiers. *Orlando* comes from Orlando Reeves, a possibly mythical soldier who was supposedly killed there in 1836, during a skirmish with local Indians. *Pennsylvania* gets its name from Sir William Penn (1621–1670), an English admiral who was described by his next-door neighbour as 'a mean fellowe' full of 'falseness and impertinences' ... who kept a very smelly 'shitten pot'.

For its part, Ancient Rome stank of corruption—but Lucius Quinctius Cincinnatus (519–430 BC) was a breath of fresh air. *Cincinnati* is named after this ancient statesman whom the Senate was forced to make a dictator when Rome was threatened by nearby tribes. Cincinnatus saw the tribes off, a heroic feat, and then did something even better. He resigned from office, thus reinstating the republic. An icon of democracy and civic virtue, which some Americans evidently thought they should emulate.

**REVERTING
TO THEIR
NATIVE
STATES**

Chief Seattle

White settlers also saw off plenty of tribes (though that sort of thing becomes a lot easier when you have machine guns). Many of those tribes do live on as state names, however. *Arkansas*, *Illinois*, *Missouri*, *Oklahoma* and *Utah* are all English names for local Native American tribes.

Not all white settlers just bulldozed their way in, however. Some of them more or less worked in partnership with the local people (or at least the ones that were still alive). Such was the case in Duwamps, a timber town in America's north-west. Settlers established such a relatively friendlyish relationship with Chief Seattle, the leader of the Duwamish, that they gave the little town a new name: *Seattle*.

# AUSTRALIAN WORDS

**THE AUSTRIA OF THE SOUTH?** Was *Australia* named after Austria? Maybe. Sort of. Some say. To explain, the word 'Australia' is generally thought to come from 'Australis', an ancient Greek term meaning 'the south'. But how did we get from 'Terra Australis'—the British government's original name—to 'Australia', the one used today? The explorer Matthew Flinders generally gets the credit here. He wrote a book asserting that 'Austra*lia*' was 'more agreeable to the ear' and most readers seemed to agree.

But did he actually come up with that name? In 1606, a Spanish explorer sailed from South America in search of the great south land—and decided that he'd found it when he landed in Vanuatu. Spain was ruled by an Austrian family at the time, so he called the new land 'A*ustria*lia', a hybrid word combining 'Austria' and 'Australis', and declared that it applied to 'all this region of the south, as far as the pole'. Back in Spain, some say, the new word didn't really trip off the tongue, so many people simply dropped the first 'i'.

**TASMANIA AND THE HANGMAN** Of course, it wasn't just Brits and Spaniards that went in search of the great south land. The Dutch arrived there before either of them (and did their best to have it called 'New Holland'). They weren't entirely sure what manner of landmass they were dealing with, however, and so dispatched Abel Tasman (1603–1659) to find out. He then stumbled across another, stand-alone island and called it 'Van Diemen's Land', after Anthony van Diemen, governor-general of the Dutch East Indies.

That was pretty much Tasman's career highlight. The Dutch weren't happy on his return, complaining that a 'more persistent explorer' would have more fully explored the strange land, or at least found a few opportunities for trade. And a few years later he lost his job, because he'd hanged a sailor without a trial. But posterity decided to smile on him anyway. Van Diemen's Land was later renamed *Tasmania*.

*Hobart*, Tassie's capital, gets its name from Lord Robert Hobart (1760–1816), a British Tory MP who never went near it. But he did have a short stint as Secretary of State for the Colonies, during which the new town happened to be founded. (An exhaustive search for interesting facts about his life has uncovered that he married the daughter of Baron *Auckland*—think New Zealand—and then died from a fall off his horse).

## SYDNEY AND ST DENNIS

While he never went near Australia, however, Lord Hobart had at least been to Wales. Can the same be said for Captain Cook (1728–1779)? No-one quite knows why that navigator decided to name this new British possession *New South Wales*. Was it a 'new' version of 'South Wales' or a 'new, southern' version of Wales? And why Wales, anyway? It's a mystery wrapped in a riddle.

**Lord Sydney**

The explanation for *Sydney*, on the other hand, is all too tediously clear. When Britain's Pitt government decided to use NSW as a penal colony, the man in charge of organising it was the 1st Viscount Sydney, Thomas Townshend (1733–1800). A man who 'owed his political career to a very independent fortune' ('for his abilities, though respectable, scarcely rose above mediocrity'), Townshend appointed the governor of the new colony, and was repaid by having it named after him.

But where did Townshend himself get the name 'Sydney'? No-one quite knows, but it seems likely that his ancestors came from St-Denis, a French town that's pronounced 'Sint Denny'. It got its name from a Bishop of Paris who had his head hacked off by some pagans. It's said that St Denis then picked up his head and walked with it for 6 miles, preaching a sermon every step of the way.

**MAJOR BRISBANE, AND THE RIFFRAFF**

Major-General Sir Thomas Makdougall Brisbane (1773–1860) would have been horrified by this information. He'd spent his whole military career fighting the French and didn't want any coming back from the dead.

Appointed Governor of NSW in 1821, Brisbane was a veteran of the Napoleonic Wars and a good chum of the Duke of Wellington. But as Wellington himself later conceded, 'there are many brave men not fit to be governors of colonies'. Brisbane was regarded by contemporaries as 'a man of the best intentions, but disinclined to business and deficient in energy'.

He did manage to achieve something, though. By 1824, Sydney's more respectable citizens were getting restless about all the riffraff (those convicts who, after being transported to Australia, had somehow managed to get arrested again). Under pressure to send the 'worst convicts' elsewhere, Brisbane dispatched an expedition north. The party encountered a new waterway, which they named the Brisbane River. It now straddles a city called ***Brisbane***.

**LORD MELBOURNE, ORPHAN-WHIPPER**

A few years after that, Brisbane ceased to be a part of NSW and became the biggest fish in a pond of its own: the capital of a new colony called *Queensland*.

They couldn't call it **Victoria** because that name was already taken. The 18-year-old Queen Victoria (1819–1901) took the throne in 1837, around the time local businessman set up a new colony on Port Phillip Bay. Victoria's main city was in turn named **Melbourne** after the Queen's prime minister, Lord Melbourne (1779–1848), a famously amiable aristocrat who considered it 'a damned bore' when he was asked to form a government.

**Lord Melbourne**

But Melbourne was never boring in the bedroom. Fond of 'spanking sessions with aristocratic ladies', and known to whip 'orphan girls taken into his household as objects of charity', Melbourne was a romantic radical in his youth who hung out with Byron and Shelley. He first came to public notice, indeed, when his wife had a long and tumultuous affair with Byron. She was the one who said that the poet was 'mad, bad and dangerous to know'.

**QUEEN ADELAIDE THE DOOMED**

Another aristocrat also knew what it was like to be cheated on. An obscure German princess, Adelheid of Saxe-Meiningen (1792–1849) didn't expect fidelity when she married Queen Victoria's predecessor, William IV. Which is good, because she didn't get it.

William already had ten illegitimate children by an actress, but he needed a legitimate one to be his heir. After negotiations with other candidates fell through, he had to settle on Adelheid, a highly religious girl he'd never met, even though she was twenty-seven years his junior. 'She is doomed, poor innocent creature, to become my wife,' William wryly said of his prospective spouse, who later changed her name to the more English-sounding 'Adelaide'.

She was also doomed, poor innocent creature, to be associated with *Adelaide*, a city people move to in order to lessen their fear of death.

**ALICE TODD'S SPRINGS**

In *Alice Springs*, people actually look forward to it. Located in the exact middle of nowhere, in the centre of Australia's central desert, that town is a little light-on for entertainment, unless you happen to like flies and dust.

Though in fairness, it also has telegraph poles. Named after Alice Todd (1836–1898), the wife of South Australia's postmaster general, Alice Springs was a crucial part of the Overland Telegraph Line, a 3200 kilometre–long cable that connected Adelaide to Darwin and thus to news from the outside world. We don't know much about Alice herself beyond the fact she was from Cambridge. She got married when she was 17, and popped out the first of six children the very next year.

**DARWIN: GOOD SCIENTIST, BAD PORT**

These days, of course, we know a lot about Charles Darwin (1809–1882). But, in 1839, when a sailor named John Stokes gave his name to the city of *Darwin*, that groundbreaking biologist wasn't a celebrity at all. The Father of Evolution didn't actually publish his theory until 1859. Until then, he was just an obscure bird-fancier who'd spent a few years travelling around the world.

But that one long voyage, as it happens, had been on *The Beagle*—the very same ship that Stokes was on a few years later, when he saw a potential place for a port. Not thinking much of the find, he named it Port Darwin in tribute to his friend, never imagining that it would become a major city. The name was simply 'an appropriate opportunity of convincing an old shipmate and friend that he still lived in our memory'.

**CHARLES FREMANTLE, CHILD MOLESTER** Western Australia had lived on in European memory since 1616, when the Dutch explorer Dirk Hartog first landed there, but no-one's memories were especially fond. It wasn't until 1829 that the British dispatched Captain Charles Fremantle (1800–1869) to formally claim it as a colony, by sticking a Union Jack in what's now *Fremantle*. (His other claim to fame, according to Graeme Henderson, was getting away with the rape of a 15-year-old girl. His family apparently paid off witnesses and leaned on the judiciary to avoid a charge.)

A little later that year, sixty-nine colonists set up camp under the leadership of Lieutenant Governor James Stirling. He formally named their surrounds *Perth* 'according to the wishes of Sir George Murray', the then-Secretary of State for the Colonies, who had been born in the small Scottish town of that name.

# LANDMARK WORDS

**SEX AND THE SISTINE CHAPEL** It's a minor miracle that Michelangelo got to paint the *Sistine Chapel*—the pope who commissioned him generally liked to hire relatives. But while he was famous for turning nephews into cardinals (as well as for the chapel that now bears his name), Sixtus IV (1414–1484) didn't just make appointments on the basis of nepotism. He also promoted people because they put out. Labelled a 'sodomite' by a Venetian ambassador, Sixtus made one man the bishop of Parma because of his 'gifts of the spirit and body'.

Sixtus was also in favour of heterosexual sex: he fathered a child with his eldest sister. Once accused of drafting plans to fill nunneries with the 'choicest prostitutes' (ones 'lean with fasting but full of lust'), he was also the first pope to license Rome's brothels, a move that earned the Church 30,000 ducats a year.

**THE CROSS-DRESSING COLOSSEUM**

Nero (37–68) was less close to his family. Some historians think that he poisoned a couple of relatives to become emperor—and we know for certain that he executed his mum and his first wife, and kicked his pregnant second wife to death. 'Malodorous and marked with spots', Nero has also been accused of raping vestal virgins and castrating one of his slave lovers to turn him into a 'girl'.

But you can't accuse him of being humble. One of this emperor's more lasting legacies was the 'Colossus of Nero', a 30-metre-tall bronze statue of himself that outlasted the Roman Empire by 600 years. At some point during that time, it began to share its name with a decrepit, long-abandoned sports stadium that stood right next door. Roman gladiators fought at the Flavian Amphitheatre. The name *Colosseum* came later on.

**BIG BEN CAUNT**

A more modern-day gladiator was Benjamin Caunt (1815–1861). Weighing up to 108 kg, this bare-knuckled, big-bellied boxer was for a brief time champion of England. Caunt was very much in the public consciousness in 1857, as he had just come out retirement to fight a sixty-round draw. Could it be a coincidence that a gigantic new bell in a clock tower then nearing completion was given his nickname, *Big Ben*?

Ben Caunt

Yes, say some people. They instead point to England's then-Commissioner of Works, Sir Benjamin Hall (1802–1867), 'a large and ponderous man known affectionately in the House as "Big Ben", who oversaw the construction of the tower'. The story goes that he was boring parliament with a long speech about the tower's 10-ton bell one day, when an MP jokingly interjected that they should call it 'Big Ben'.

*Hansard* records no such interjection, however, so there's a crack in the story. And in 1859, there also turned out to be a crack in the bell, so it had to be recast. Hall wasn't known as 'Competent Ben', after all.

**GUSTAVE EIFFEL'S TOWER**

France's national symbol, on the other hand, has never cracked. Gustave Eiffel (1832–1923) was just too good. Already famous for building the steel framework of the Statue of Liberty, the brilliant engineer's *Eiffel Tower* could have easily been called the Bonickhausen Tower. Eiffel was born Gustave Bonickhausen, then changed his name to sound a little more French. (Though as it happens, 'Eiffel' is a French version of 'Eifel', the region of Germany that his ancestors were from.)

**Gustav Eiffel**

Designed as the front entrance to the 1889 Paris Universal Exhibition, the tower was intended to be torn down after twenty years, a lifespan that Paris's intellectuals thought was about twenty years too long. The much-maligned 'black blot' was only saved because its height proved useful for radio transmissions. It wasn't actually considered attractive until recent times.

**TAJ MAHAL, TEMPLE OF LOVE**

The *Taj Mahal* was also nearly torn down. In 1830, the British governor of India, Lord William Bentinck, made plans to ship its white marble to England. He only abandoned the idea when he couldn't find enough buyers.

Perhaps this was the power of love? India's most famous palace was built for, and named after, Mumtaz Mahal (1593–1631), the third of Mughal emperor Shah Jahan's five wives. But she was ranked number one in his heart. 'The intimacy, deep affection, attention and favour which His Majesty had for the Cradle of Excellence [Mahal] exceeded by a thousand times what he felt for any other' woman, wrote one court chronicler. 'In appearance and character' Mahal stood alone 'among all the women of the time'.

Touching stuff. But one day, alas, she lay down alone, and never got up again. The emperor is said to have 'abandoned himself to mourning' after Mahal's untimely death from a miscarriage, disappearing from court for a week. For two years, he didn't listen to music, wear jewellery or use perfume. His hair turned grey, his back became bent, and his eyes came to need spectacles as a result of constant weeping.

Then his thoughts took a more practical turn. Within eighteen years, thousands of master craftsmen had built the Taj Mahal, a white-domed marble mausoleum where the Cradle of Excellence shall forever rest.

**THE MISPRO-NOUNCED MOUNT EVEREST**

Unless, of course, some other genius decides it should be dismantled. Colonial India was full of great thinkers. Take the bunch of British cartographers who conducted the 'Great Trigonometric Survey' of India over the first half of the 19th century. Smart guys, undoubtedly. Using all sorts of fancy tools and trigonometry, they established that Peak XV, in the Himalayas, was in all likelihood the highest mountain in the world. But somehow they didn't manage to establish that it had a name.

Actually, it did, as you might just conceivably expect of something 8839 metres tall. It was 'Deohungha' in Darjeeling and 'Sagarmatha' in Nepal. 'Zhumulangma' in China and 'Chomolungma' in Tibet. But as the mountain appeared to be 'without any local name that we can discover', India's surveyor-general named it **Mount Everest** after his predecessor, a cartographer who'd never laid eyes on it.

**SIR HENRY AYERS' ROCK**

An interesting side note about this 'illustrious master of accurate geographic research' is that his name was pronounced George *Eve*-rest. But if you want an interesting sidenote about Sir Henry Ayers (1821–1897), I wish you the best of luck. Apparently he could get pretty passionate about tariffs, and had much to say about inland customs duties, but that's about as racy as things seemed to get.

A major shareholder in a South Australian copper mine, Ayers managed to become chief secretary of that colony five times in just ten years. While his first few governments lasted just a few weeks each, by 1867, he seemed to have got the hang of things and governed for sixteen glorious months.

What made those months memorable, in modern eyes, is that on 19 July 1867 (a few days before Ayers lost his job again), an expedition his government had sent inland reported back a remarkable find. In the middle of the desert was 'a huge mass of rock of honeycombed granite from 6 to 7 miles in girth at the base, and about 1100 feet in height'.

Much like certain cartographers before them, the expedition ignored the local name ('Uluru') and chose instead to give a nod to their boss. Had they stumbled across it just a few days later, *Ayers Rock* would have probably been called 'Hart Rock', after the new chief secretary, John Hart.

**CHARLES RUSHMORE'S MOUNTAIN**

In all fairness, though, there are worse ways to name a slab of rock. Sir Henry Ayers and George Everest don't particularly merit immortality, but they're more deserving than Charles Rushmore (1857–1931). A wholly unremarkable man in a wholly unremarkable job, Rushmore was a New York lawyer who one day went to South Dakota to work on an unremarkable case. While there, he noticed a grand granite mountain and asked his guide what its name was.

'Never had any but it has now,' the guide jokingly replied. 'We'll call the thing Rushmore.'

Forty years later, this fairly big hill became a very big deal. The government of South Dakota launched an audacious bid for more tourist dollars by blasting the faces of four presidents into the rock. The original plan had been to carve the sculpture into some granite pillars known as the Needles, but that was changed at the last minute because they didn't get quite enough sunlight. Washington, Jefferson, Lincoln and Roosevelt are now all immortalised by *Mount Rushmore*—along with a lawyer who got lucky.

**EOSTRE'S ISLAND** We don't know who's commemorated by the *Easter Island* statues, but it doesn't seem like they were so good looking. Encountered by Dutch sailors on Easter Sunday in 1722, these 800-odd human figures each have heads twice the size of their bodies (and, one would imagine, some very sore necks).

Another way to get a pain in the neck is trying to work out where the word 'Easter' comes from. Most likely it derives from 'Eostre', a pagan goddess in whose honour a grand feast was once held every spring. Chances are she had something to do with fertility (eggs, it's worth noting, are a source of life, and bunnies, well, breed like rabbits). It's thought the Church just took over this old pagan fertility festival and said, 'Hey guys, this is now about God'.

**THE ROCK OF JABAL TARIQ** As a Muslim, Tariq ibn Ziyad (died 720) didn't celebrate Easter—but he did seem to be a fan of fertility. When this Umayyad general sailed with his 7000 men to Spain's southernmost point, he immediately burned all their boats. 'Oh my warriors, whither would you flee?' he inquired rather dampeningly. 'Behind you is the sea, before you the enemy.'

But, perhaps conscious that he was being a bit of a downer, Tariq then told his men that, if they invaded Spain, they'd find 'a large number of ravishing beautiful maidens, their graceful forms draped in sumptuous gowns'. So invade the soldiers damn well did.

Tariq's speech was delivered from a huge monolithic chunk of limestone. It had long been known as one of the 'Pillars of Hercules'—the westernmost point of the Mediterranean, and thus the outer limit of the ancient world. After his speech it became known as 'Jabal Tariq', the 'mountain of Tariq'. In English, that's the **Rock of Gibraltar**.

### INFANTICIDE AND THE AMAZON RIVER

The Greek hero Hercules was a bit of a tough guy—one of those annoying alpha males you see strutting about in lion skins, flexing his muscles and waving a club. But even he got scared when he was asked to fight the Amazons. Hell hath no fury like a big horde of *them*.

This mythological race of women warriors (who are generally placed in modern-day Georgia) supposedly reproduced by mating with their male captives … then getting rid of the child if it was a boy. Young girls, on the other hand, were taught how to fight, kill and wound—and some were also ritually wounded themselves. According to one 5th-century source, 'a-mazos' means 'without a breast'. Some girls would have their right breast chopped off to help them fire a bow better.

So what's that got to do with the **Amazon River**? Well, that name started when Spanish conquistadors arrived in South America and began conquista-ing everything they could see. In 1541, fifty of them sailed down what was variously known as Grande Río ('Great River'), Mar Dulce ('Freshwater Sea') or Río de la Canela ('Cinnamon River')—and managed to get roughed up by a bunch of chicks. These women warriors were 'a marvellous thing to behold', the Spaniards later reported. Just like the Amazons of legend and myth, they were 'very white and tall … very robust … and went about naked with their privy parts covered … doing as much fighting as ten Indian men'.

**Some Amazons (with both breasts intact)**

**VOLCANO, BLACK-SMITH TO THE GODS**

Rome, incidentally, may also be named after breasts. Putting the legend of Romulus and Remus to one side, the actual founders of Rome were a tribe called the Etruscans, in whose language the word 'ruma' meant 'teat'. For a long time, Rome was just composed of two fertile, nurturing hills, the Aventine and the Palentine. Did someone think they resembled boobs?

Anyway, they certainly didn't resemble *volcanoes*, which was a lucky thing for the future of Rome. These real-estate killers get their name from Vulcan, the Roman god of fire. A sort of celestial blacksmith, he was said to operate a giant underground forge, from which he made things like Neptune's trident and Jupiter's thunderbolts, as well as the divine armour of Achilles.

But accidents happen in every workplace. Vulcan's involve lots of lava.

# INDEX

Academia 94
Achilles heel 224
Adam's apple 223
addict 165
Adelaide 246
Adidas 149
admiral 124
Adonis 57
Airedale 214
Akita 214
alabaster 207
Albuquerque 241
algorithm 202
Alice Springs 247
Alsatian 214
Amazon River 254
America 238
amps 199
Anglo-Saxon 235
angora 145
Angostura 127
aphrodisiac 50
apple 130
April 42
Aquarius 232
arachnid 211
Aries 232
Arkansas 242
Armageddon 76
Armagnac 125
Aryan 104
as rich as Croesus 36
assassin 163
Athens 237
atlas 191

attic 21
Auckland 244
August 43
Austin 241
Australia 243
Ayers Rock 252
azure 207
babble 11
bacchanalian 123
back of beyond 6
Badminton 183
Baileys 127
balaclava 152
banana republic 35
Banksia 203
Bantam chicken 216
barbarian 63
Barbie 160
barmy 107
baroque 20
barrack 184
batty 107
bayonet 69
Béarnaise sauce 135
bedlam 107
Beef stroganoff 138
beggar 39
Behemoth 217
Belgium 236
berserk 109
beyond the pale 3
Bible 14
Big Ben 249
Big Bertha 69
bigot 101

bigwig 157
bikini 155
Bill, the 29
bircher muesli 129
biro 18
blackguard 88
blanket 24
Blind Freddy 6
Bloody Mary 126
bloomers 155
blue ribbon 208
blueblood 208
bluestocking 155
blurb 16
Bob's your uncle 33
bobby 29
boffin 95
Bogarted 164
Bogus 89
bohemian 65
bolognaise 135
boofhead 97
booze 124
Bordeaux 125
boronia 203
bougainvillea 204
bourbon 125
bowler hat 148
boycott 178
boysenberry 130
brainiac 95
brains trust 96
Brazil nut 133
Brisbane 245
Britain 234

Bronx 240
Bronx cheer 185
bronze 206
Brooklyn 240
brownie point 114
Brussels sprout 133
Buckley's chance 2
Buffalo wing 138
bugger 55
Bulgaria 235
bungalow 21
bunkum 32
Bunsen burner 201
Burgundy 125
byzantine 20
Cadillac 186
Caesar salad 132
Caesarian section 43
calico 145
California 240
calypso 171
Camellia 203
canary 216
Cancer 233
cannibal 67
cant 14
cantaloupe 131
canter 181
capital 34
cappuccino 121
Carbine rifle 69
cardigans 151
Carpaccio 138
cashmere 145
Catherine wheel 162
Caucasian 67
Cayenne pepper 133
cell 222
Celsius 201
cereal 129
chambray 145
Champagne 125

Chantilly lace 145
chapel 153
charlatan 86
Charleston (the city) 241
Charleston, the 174
Chartreuse 125
chauffeur 185
chauvinist 102
cheap 40
cherry 131
chesterfield 23
chestnut 133
Chihuahua 214
china 25
Cincinnati 242
Cleveland 241
club sandwich 137
coach 180
cock and bull story 216
coffee 120
Cognac 125
cologne 148
Colonel Blimp 5
Colosseum 249
Colt revolver 69
condom 195
conga 173
copper 206
cor blimey 102
Cos lettuce 132
crap 197
Craps 161
cravat 142
Crepes Suzette 140
cretin 98
crew cut 156
cross the Rubicon 4
Curaçao 127
currant 131
cynical 178
Dahlia 203
Daiquiri 127

Dalmatian 214
Damask 145
dark horse 182
Darwin 247
deadline 76
decibel 200
Delaware 241
denim 144
Denver 241
Derby 183
Derringer 69
devil to pay 7
devil's advocate 7
diehard 73
diesel engine 204
digger 71
Doberman 215
doctrinaire 101
doily 25
dollally 106
dollar 37
Dom Pérignon 125
donnybrook 80
doozy 187
Dorothy Dixer 31
Doubting Thomas 8
Down syndrome 67
Downing Street 34
Draconian 26
drongo 97
duffel coat 153
dunce 98
dungarees 145
Earl Grey 121
Easter Island 253
Eggs Benedict 133
Eggs Florentine 134
Eiffel Tower 250
El Dorado 37
England 235
epicurean 123
erotic 50

Europe 234
Even Stevens 8
Fabian Society 74
Fahrenheit 201
fallopian tube 220
fanny 220
fascism 103
fauna 210
February 43
fedora 146
Ferrari 186
Ferris wheel 162
fink 30
Flamenco 172
flashy 90
flora 203
Ford 187
forensics 27
foxtrot 174
France 235
Frangipani 203
frankness 17
Fremantle 248
Friday 45
frieze 21
Frisbee 162
fuchsia 203
fudge, to 86
full monty 222
furphy 90
Fustian 145
galoshes 150
galvanise 200
gardenia 203
gargantuan 190
Gatling gun 69
gauze 145
Gemini 233
Georgia 239
gerrymandering 32
ghetto 81
gibberish 12

Good Samaritan 8
goody two-shoes 113
gorgon 57
gorilla 217
gosh 102
gothic 64
Granny Smith 130
Great Scott 4
grog 124
groggy 124
guillotine 25
guinea 37
Guppy 212
guy 219
gypsy 66
hack 16
hallmark 36
hamburger 137
Hansard 31
Happy as Larry 10
Harlem 240
harlequin 166
harlot 58
hatchet man 72
hector 224
hermaphrodite 220
hertz 199
hessian 145
hillbilly 117
hippopotamus 212
Hobart 244
Hobson's choice 182
hokey pokey 176
Hollandaise sauce 134
Hollywood 168
homburg 146
hooch 163
hoodlum 79
hooker 58
hooligan 79
hoover 24
Houston 241

Hun 71
hussy 59
hyacinth 204
hygiene 195
hypnotism 110
ignoramus 100
Illinois 242
In like Flynn 3
Iran 104
Ireland 237
iridescence 203
iris 203
Jack Daniels 125
Jack Russell 215
Jacuzzi 195
jalapeño chilli 133
janitor 44
January 44
jeans 144
jerry-built 21
jersey 153
Jerusalem artichoke 133
jet black 207
jezebel 59
Jingoism 102
jitterbug 174
Jodhpurs 145
John Dory fish 212
joule 199
jovial 91
juggernaut 106
Julian calendar 43
July 43
jumbo jets 190
June 42
Jupiter 228
Kahlua 127
Keeping up with the
    Joneses 6
Kellogg's Corn Flakes 128
Ken 160
King Dick 219

Kir 126
Kit Kat 141
knickers 153
Labrador 214
Labyrinth 19
laconic 93
Lamborghini 186
lamington 141
Latin lovers 48
lemur 217
Leo 234
leotard 156
lesbian 55
lethal 74
lethargy 74
Leviathan 217
libation 123
Life of Riley 10
Lima beans 133
limbo 175
limousine 186
Lisbon 236
Listerine 198
lobbyist 30
lobelia 203
Logie 170
Lord's Cricket Ground 183
Los Angeles 240
Lothario 48
Louisiana 239
lounge 23
Luddite 205
Luger 69
lumber 40
lunatic 106
lush 123
lynch mob 27
macabre 77
Macadamia nut 133
Macarena 175
mackintosh 152
maelstrom 196

magenta 209
magnet 207
magnolia 203
malapropism 13
Maltese dog 214
mambo 177
mandarin 131
Manila folder 15
marathon 178
March 42
margarita cocktail 127
margarita pizza 135
marinara sauce 135
Mars 229
Mars bar 141
martial 229
martinet 102
Maryland 239
masochism 54
maudlin 94
Mauser 69
mausoleum 75
maverick 115
May 42
mayonnaise 135
meander 191
Melba toast 139
Melbourne 246
mentor 224
Mercedes-Benz 187
mercurial 230
Mercury 229
mesmerise 111
Mexican wave 184
Midas touch 38
Milky Way 141
milliner 147
Milo 122
Miranda rights 28
Missouri 242
mocha 120
Molotov cocktail 70

Monday 45
money 36
mongoloid 67
month 42
morgue 75
moron 99
morphine 165
Morris dancing 176
Morse code 17
Mount Everest 251
Mount Rushmore 253
mulligan 179
mumbo jumbo 12
Murphy's law 189
muse 96
museum 96
music 171
nachos 139
namby-pamby 112
name was mud 2
Narcissism 56
Neanderthal 68
neapolitan 135
nemesis 27
Neptune 231
New Orleans 241
New South Wales 244
New York 239
Nicotine 165
Nike 149
nincompoop 98
Nobel Prize 170
North Carolina 239
nosey parker 61
Oaks 183
odyssey 224
Oedipus complex 57
ogre 231
ohm 199
OK 154
Oklahoma 242
Olympics 177

Onanism 56
Orlando 242
Oscar 169
ottoman 23
Ouzo 125
palace 18
pamphlet 15
Panacea 195
pandemonium 108
Pandering 112
panic 109
pants 143
paparazzi 168
parchment 14
pariah 87
Parthenon 237
pasteurisation 203
Pavlova 139
peach 132
Peach Melba 140
Peeping Tom 61
Pennsylvania 242
Perth 248
Petri dish 197
Peugeot 186
Pheasant 216
philistine 65
pickle 132
piker 116
pioneer 72
Pisces 232
pistol 69
Pittsburgh 241
platonic love 52
pleased as punch 9
Plug-ugly 79
Pluto 231
Poindexter 96
polka 173
Pomeranian 214
Porsche 186
port 126

porterhouse steak 138
Portugal 237
Pressgang 83
priapism 52
psychology 110
Pulitzer Prize 170
Put up your dukes 9
Puttanesca sauce 135
pyrrhic victory 74
Pythagoras's
      theorem 202
python 210
Quaker Oats 129
Queensland 245
quisling 104
quixotic 113
raining cats and dogs 214
Real McCoy 9
Red Indians 66
redneck 105
rhinestones 207
rhubarb 132
roam 49
robot 206
Rock of Gibraltar 254
Rolls-Royce 187
romance 49
Romance languages 49
Romania 236
Rome 236
Rosella 216
Rottweiler 215
Rugby 184
Russia 235
Russian roulette 161
Sad Sack 5
sadism 54
Salad Niçoise 132
salmonella 198
Saluki 214
San Antonio 240
San Francisco 240

sandwich 136
Sapphic 55
sapphire 207
sardine 212
sardonic 212
satin 145
Saturday 45
Saturn 229
Sauternes 125
saxophone 173
Scotch 125
Scotland 235
Scotties 214
Sealyham 215
Seattle 242
serendipity 92
shallot 133
shambles 40
shanghaied 83
Sherry 126
shopping mall 41
shrapnel 70
shyster 89
Siamese twins 225
sideburns 157
silhouette 38
Silk 145
Silly Billy 99
siren 224
Sistine Chapel 248
skid row 80
slave 115
sleazy 62
Smart Alec 89
sodomy 54
solecism 13
South Carolina 239
spa 196
Spartan 93
Speak of the devil 7
Spencer 152
Spoonerism 13

Spruce 142
St Bernard 214
St Valentine's Day 50
Steak tartare 138
steeplechase 181
Stentorian 224
Stetson 148
stoic 92
stonewall 73
suede 145
Sunday 45
Svengali 111
sweet FA 221
sybaritic 123
sycophant 115
Sydney 244
Syphilis 194
Tabasco 139
tabby 213
Taj Mahal 250
Tam-o'-shanter 147
Tangerine 131
tantalise 51
tarantula 211
tariff 39
tarmac 205
Tasmania 244
Taurus 233
tawdry 62
Teddy bear 160
Tequila 126
Texas 241

thespian 166
thin blue line 28
Thousand Island
    dressing 132
thug 82
Thursday 45
tiger 213
Titanic 190
titchy 168
toady 114
tobacco 164
tomcat 213
Tommies 70
Tommy gun 69
Tony 169
Tory 34
trilby 147
true blue 105
Tuesday 45
turkey 216
turncoat 88
turquoise 207
Tuxedo 143
tweed 145
uranium 231
Uranus 230
Utah 242
Uzi 69
vandalism 64
Vatican City 237
vaudeville 167
venerable 194

venerate 194
venereal disease 194
Venetian blind 24
Venus 229
Veuve Clicquot 125
Victoria 246
villain 87
Virginia 239
volcano 255
volt 199
vulgar 62
Waldorf salad 132
Wales 235
watch 44
watt 199
Wedgewood 25
Wednesday 45
wellingtons 150
welsher 88
wench 59
What the dickens! 7
Whig 34
whipping boy 112
Windsor knot 143
Xanadu 19
yellow journalism 15
yellow peril 209
Yorker 184
young Turk 35
Zany 167
zealot 103
Zeppelin 188

# ACKNOWLEDGEMENTS

Many thanks to Chris Mildren for some thigh-slapping gags, and to Mum, Dad, Caitlin Evans, Tim Petterson and Tom Bamforth for all their constructive criticism. And, after looking back on the first draft recently, I'm even more grateful for their destructive criticism!

Thanks also, as always, to the fine folk at Hardie Grant—in particular Rose Michael, Allison Hiew, Brooke Clark, Josh Durham—and to Patrick Cannon of Cannon Typesetting for going above and beyond the call of duty. And then going there again.